Berlitz®

RIVER CRUISING IN EUROPE

BY DOUGLAS WARD

THE WORLD'S FOREMOST AUTHORITY ON CRUISING

Table of Contents

Barge cruising

Rivership listings

Maps

From the Author

Would you like to tour Europe in comfort, delivered from A to B with no need to change hotels every night, with your meals cooked for you and with fabulous scenery to enjoy as you go along? Take a river cruise. River cruising in Europe is all about visiting destinations and it is very different from cruising aboard large ocean-going cruise ships, where passengers can number in the thousands, and embarking, disembarking and security queues can be an exercise in frustration. On a river cruise, the maximum number of passengers is around 200, so any visits are done in much smaller groups, or even individually, and all on a very personal scale.

Rivers were here eons before roads were created and have always been vital to human settlement and survival. Among the many of Europe's great cities that grew up on the banks of the river are London (Thames), Paris (Seine), Cologne (Rhein), Frankfurt (Main), Prague (Elbe/Vltava), Budapest (Danube) and Vienna (Danube).

Rivers have long been used as lifelines by which nations conduct commerce and organise the transportation of goods. They are used for drainage, irrigation, water supply and the production of hydroelectric power. But they are also sources of adventure and romance.

Today, around one million people each year (and growing) choose to cruise on riverships (note they are always referred to as 'rivership', rather than 'boat' or plain 'ship'). These vary from the equivalent of a waterbus to what some, amusingly, like to think of as *eau couture*. The hassles of ordinary travel are almost eliminated in one pleasant package, with someone else doing all the driving. Don't worry about getting seasick, either – it's usually all smooth sailing. The finance is straightforward, too – because you pay in advance, you know what you will spend on your holiday, without any hidden surprises. It's all quite low-key – there are no casinos, bingo or knobbly knees contests or other potentially irritating parlour games on board (unlike on an ocean cruise), and any events that are organised tend to be geared towards quite a cultural crowd. And, when your rivership docks, you simply walk off the vessel. You never have to take a tender to go ashore, because most riverships dock close to the centre of a city or town.

A European river cruise is like an upscale bus tour, only far superior and more comfortable, be-

cause, unlike bus tours, where passengers stay in a different hotel each night, you only have to unpack once. In almost all cases, you will have a river view from your cabin, too, plus you will dine in familiar surroundings for most meals, with familiar food on the menu.

It's always worth bearing in mind, of course, that rivers are natural entities, and Mother Nature can be unpredictable. Variable conditions mean that nothing – such as the depth, the current or flow of water – is fixed. River cruise operators and passengers alike must, therefore, be flexible in their approach to this type of holiday. But assuming all goes roughly according to plan, a river cruise can be relaxing, educational, inspirational, sociable and a lot of fun. The biggest difficulty is deciding exactly which river cruise to go on – they do, of course, vary in terms of quality, food and service – which is where this guide comes in.

I have been travelling the world's oceans, rivers and inland waterways for more than 45 years and have endeavoured to appraise some 280 riverships operating in the heart of Europe at the time of printing. I have concentrated on the established river cruise companies, whose cruises can be purchased through specialist travel agents and tour operators, and on seven key rivers in Europe (the Danube, Rhein, Elbe, Rhône, Seine, Po and Douro), with a rundown of the destination highlights visited along those waterways. Finally, there is my breakdown of over 280 European riverships, with brief summaries for each, plus our Berlitz rating based on amenities, service and the general product delivered.

Douglas Ward

Why take a river cruise?

Here, I argue the case for booking a river cruise and answer some questions that beginners to river cruising might ask before taking the metaphoric plunge.

The ideal river cruise should be welcoming, scenic, peaceful, comfortable, effortless, small-scale, inclusive, unhurried, organised and memorable. River cruising provides an antidote to the pressures of life in a fast-paced world, in comfortable, unfussy surroundings, with decent food and enjoyable (often, international) company. Riverships provide a harmonious blend of public and private space and, once aboard, you only have to unpack once. It's a growing area of tourism, with now over 15,000 river cruises from which to choose and close to one million people having taken a river cruise in 2013.

In this chapter, we give you 10 good reasons to take a river cruise and answer some of the burning questions potential rivercruisers might like to ask.

10 good reasons to take a river cruise

1. There's so much to see

River cruising is all about sightseeing, from the key highlights en route to the countryside as you travel

River Countess in Venice.

from one stop to the next. On a typical seven-night cruise on the Danube, you could visit Budapest, Bratislava, Vienna (Wien), Salzburg, Melk and Dürnstein. On a two-week journey through the centre of Europe, you could include major cities including Amsterdam, Cologne (Köln), Nuremberg (Nürnberg), Vienna (Wien) and more.

2. The clear, upfront pricing

The upfront pricing on a river cruise package means that there are few additional costs, making your holiday budgeting simple. Accommodation, all meals (usually including wine, although it may be quite basic), snacks, destination talks, some (or all) excursions, occasional entertainment and, possibly, transfers to get to and from your river cruise are all included, which makes it good value for money.

3. They are small, friendly and comfortable

Rivership size is governed by the length and width of the locks that they need to negotiate. Most riverships carry between 100 and 200 passengers. The atmosphere on board is usually friendly, and fellow passengers tend to have similar interests. On most riverships there is open-seating restaurant dining, which allows you to sit with different people each night and make new friends.

4. It's so easy

Simply embark, unpack and enjoy the scenery as your floating inn takes you from one historic destination to the next. There are no tenders to take to go ashore, and no formalities, and you will no doubt learn something new every day.

5. There's always something to see and do

Unlike ocean cruising, on a river cruise you always have a view of something along the bank, whether an urban landscape or the countryside. On a typical river cruise, you spend half the day ashore and the other half cruising. In addition to enjoying the view from the water, you can listen to talks by guest speakers, and, sometimes, partake in wine- or beer-tasting sessions or cooking demonstrations.

6. You'll most likely have a room with a view

Almost all riverships except three (*Dertour Mozart, Primadonna* and *Rossini*) have outside-view-only cabins, so you'll at least have a window to admire the scenery. Most new riverships now come with balconies, although this is most likely to be a French balcony (doors opening onto a safety railing) due to the size restrictions. (Some suites and cabins come with a full balcony that you can sit out on.)

7. You don't have to look like a tourist on tours

Many river cruise operators provide guides with microphones and passengers with wireless receivers and earphones, so you can hear what is being said without having to crowd around the guide. You won't have to miss the guides' narration, even when they need to speak quietly in cathedrals or other churches.

8. It should all be smooth sailing

Some first-timers worry about seasickness, but there's no need to – the gentle waters of the river are different to those of the ocean, with no waves for a start. Itineraries can, however, be affected by low or high water: not enough water and the riverships can't cruise; too much and they can't get under the bridges (in such cases, comfortable coaches take you to and from the key attractions).

9. Many riverships are surprisingly chic

The newest riverships are very different from those that previously dominated the market, which were mostly over 10 years old. Choose one of the newest examples for your cruise and you can have a balcony, various dining options (eg restaurants in different areas of the rivership, including, perhaps, on an outdoor deck), Wi-fi (sometimes at no charge) and

Pont du Gard excursion in France.

a flat-screen television/entertainment system. Minimalist decor is the norm, although there are exceptions – Uniworld, for example, provides grand hotel-style decor and furnishings and the drawing-room look of yesteryear.

10. You don't have to cook

It's all done for you, and so is the washing up. Additionally, you don't have to make the bed either! Or drive!

Beginners please

Here are the basics you'll need to know before stepping up the gangway for the first time.

Queen Isabel dining room.

Are rivers called he or she?

This depends on their behaviour. The River Rhône, for example, is almost always called he because it can be turbulent, bothersome and rough at times, whereas the Saône is a gentler kind of river – more beautiful and tranquil – and is referred to as she, as is the 'beautiful' Blue Danube (although Napoleon described it as the 'king of the rivers of Europe').

The Rhein (Rhine) is a he, as it is always referred to as 'Father Rhein' (although the adjacent Mosell/Moselle is a she – 'Mother Moselle' although supposedly actually the daughter of 'Father Rhein'). The Mighty Mississippi is called the 'granddaddy of all rivers', and the River Volga is always referred to as the 'dear little mother', even though it is the mightiest river in Europe.

Rivers may also be colourful. The Danube is immortalised in music as being famously blue – although the reality is something different – whereas the Mississippi is brown (the 'Big Muddy'), there's a green river in Utah, a red river in Louisiana, a yellow river in China, and a black river in Brazil.

Enjoying the sun deck on *River Cloud II*.

Are river cruises taken aboard ships or boats?

To set the record straight, river cruises are taken aboard riverships. Ships are always ocean-going. Boats are typically owned for pleasure, with the exceptions of lifeboats, of course, and steamboats (or modern-day replicas), which ply the major rivers of North America. Finally, there are cruise barges, which navigate canals. For more on this, check out the 'What's in a name?' feature box.

Are there differences between river cruise operators?

Yes, both in terms of hardware and software, in the manner in which river cruises are packaged, and the pre- and post-cruise add-ons. Thus, the quality for which the company is known is provided throughout the product and experience, and is not dependent on third-party operators, drivers and guides. A-Rosa Cruises and Emerald Waterways, for example, offer a greater number of active excursions, such as mountain biking for younger passengers, than most.

Are there different classes aboard riverships?

No, everyone is treated equally.

Are there different cabin categories and prices?

Yes. Accommodation is priced according to size and location, from the top deck down. Some suites/cabins have balconies (either full or French ones) or opening windows; cabins on the lower deck have smaller windows. Cabin sizes can vary from a dimensionally challenged 6 sq m (64 sq ft) to an expansive 45 sq m (484 sq ft).

Are excursions available?

Excursions are often included in the overall price of the package, although this depends on the operator. Optional excursions, from helicopter 'flightseeing' and hot-air ballooning to wine tasting and horse riding, are also usually available, although at extra cost. Arrangements can also often be made for you to play golf or tennis.

Are meals included?

Yes. Meals include a self-service buffet breakfast and lunch (with hot food), afternoon coffee/tea, full waiter-service dinner and late-night snacks. In some cases, the rivership's chef purchases produce in local markets for consumption during the cruise. Some operators include beer, soft drinks and wine as part of the package.

How about dining arrangements?

Breakfast (typically 7am–9am) and lunch (usually 12 noon–2pm) are served buffet-style, with open seating (ie you are allotted a table as you arrive for your meal, rather than having a pre-determined one at an agreed set time). Dinner, however, is at one sitting, at a specific time, either at assigned tables, where you may or may not know the person next to you, or in an open-seating arrangement, so you can sit with anyone you want.

Are there any theme cruises?

Several theme cruises come to mind. In Europe, you can experience theme cruises for classical and jazz music, fine food and wine tasting, shopping, Christmas markets and Christmas/New Year celebrations.

Music lovers might enjoy being aboard Mozart cruises on the Danube, while the green-fingered among you might like to see the gardens of the Rhein, including visits to celebrated botanical gardens, arboretums, herbariums and castles and their grounds.

Can I pay by credit card?

Yes, you can use your credit card for bookings, but note that some cruise companies will add a surcharge of up to 3 percent for this.

Are river cruise brochure ratings accurate?

Remember that brochures are designed by company marketing departments to attract and tempt you to take a cruise. According to cruise brochures, every vessel is the 'best in Europe.' Use the brochures to determine which itinerary and cruise attracts you most, but take the ratings with a pinch of salt. As a professional ship tester and evaluation specialist, I go beyond the brochure to bring you accurate, objective Berlitz ratings.

What about safety?

There are numerous regulations regarding the building of riverships. In Europe, those built after January 2007 are required to have two compartments and, in addition to the main propulsion system (forcing the vehicle forwards or backwards), they must also be equipped with a second independent propulsion system (located in a separate engine room) to enable the vessel to move.

Since 2010, riverships longer than 110m (360ft) must have a declaration of sufficient strength by one of three recognised classification societies: Bureau Veritas of France; Germanischer Lloyd; or Lloyd's Register of Shipping (London). In addition, the rivership must remain in a floating condition even if two watertight compartments are damaged and flooded. Finally, most riverships have some basic safety and life-saving equipment, although many of the older (pre-1990) riverships do not have sprinkler systems.

Do riverships have to comply with any environmental regulations or restrictions?

Environmental regulation is the concern of authorities that control various rivers, or sections of rivers, under the auspices of the United Nations. In Europe, for example, the 'Central Commission for the Navigation of the Rhine' has strict emissions controls in force on the river (many are covered in EU directives).

What's in a name?

There is considerable confusion among passengers, rivership operators, cruise/tour packagers and travel journalists regarding the correct name for the different types of vessel, so here is a breakdown, from the largest to the smallest.

Ship

Ocean-going cruise ships can carry boats (lifeboats, search-and-rescue boats and shore tenders). So a ship can carry a boat, but a boat can't carry a ship. Cruise ships sail on oceans and seas (not rivers), generally have a deep hull and can carry between 50 and over 5,000 passengers.

Rivership

A rivership has a flat bottom and is designed for extremely shallow water. Riverships typically travel at speeds of between 10 and 18kph (6–11mph). On board, there is a captain (the driver) and crew, accommodation, all meals and some light entertainment. Riverships have two, three or four accommodation decks, and public rooms include at least a panoramic lounge/bar and a restaurant.

Cruise barge

A cruise barge (also referred to as a hotel barge) is a flat-bottomed craft that draws a shallow draft. They are typically about 30m (100ft) long and about 5m (16.5ft) wide. Although a handful of them are custom built, most are converted cargo-carrying craft. Cruise barges travel slowly (between 3 and 10kph/1.8–6mph), slower than riverships. They normally have only one deck (a few have two decks), which houses cabins and a combination dining room/lounge, and they carry between 6 and 12 passengers, although a few can carry up to 24. Most cruise barges carry bicycles for you to use along the canal towpaths or for exploring the local towns and villages.

Boats

Boats are typically privately owned or rented for pleasure, with the exception of lifeboats or shore tenders carried by ocean-going cruise ships.

Steamboat

This term designates riverships powered by steam engines that drive huge stern-mounted paddlewheels. They ply the rivers of the US, such as the Mississippi.

Narrowboat

Found in England, France, Holland, Ireland, Scotland and Wales, these vessels are so named because the canals, waterways and locks they navigate are extremely narrow. They are usually only 2m (6.5ft) wide. Although there are exceptions, they are usually for use as charter or self-drive craft.

What the brochures don't say

Marketing brochures make river cruises look wonderfully appealing but they can't tell you everything about the experience on board. We cut through the hype to tell you what they don't.

Whether you look at printed brochures or go online and look at the claims made by the river cruise companies, you'd think that all were the best in the world (most of them say they are 'award-winning'). Well, surprise, surprise – they all aren't, of course.

When companies describe their riverships as 'small and attractive' or 'comfortable,' you can rest assured that these will be older vessels, because companies with newer ships always tend to describe them as 'the most luxurious' or 'the most innovative.' Naturally, some companies are probably trying to hide the fact that they are lagging behind in the design stakes.

And when operators talk about having the highest staff to passenger ratio, it should be noted that some riverships have more technical staff than others, while some have more staff on the hospitality side than others, depending on the configuration.

Of the river cruise companies operating in Europe, AmaWaterways, Uniworld and Viking River Cruises

deliver a product that is the closest to what is claimed in the brochures – Ama for its excellent food and service, Uniworld for its opulent cabins and Viking for its Scandinavian minimalism and uniformity, and its large fleet.

So take the hype with a pinch of salt when you're buying and remember to check the small print to be sure of what is and isn't included in the price.

To help you distinguish between companies and feel better informed when choosing your cruise, here are some of the most commonly asked questions by potential river cruisers, with answers to the queries that the brochures gloss over.

Who takes a river cruise?

River cruises tend to appeal to the culturally aware and to those wanting to experience the heart of a country and its people, instead of simply travelling through it. They generally appeal to anyone who prefers travelling in a small group.

Primadonna in Passau.

They are ideal if you want the backup and convenience of an organised tour, with your cruise operator delivering you from A to B, but with greater independence than you would likely get on an ocean cruise, for example.

Isn't it all very regimented?
There are schedules to fit into, of course, as on any other packaged itinerary-based holiday, but while breakfast and lunch are usually an open-seating self-service buffet (you can go at any time during restaurant opening hours), dinner in the restaurant is always at a fixed time. You are under no obligation to go on an included tour if you'd prefer instead to have a relaxing day on the rivership. And you are free, too, to sightsee independently rather than in an organised group, if that is more to your taste – you just need to make sure that you're back at the rivership in time for sailing on to the next destination.

Is the brochure price firm?
As there are limited places on a rivership, they tend to sell out quite far in advance and there's little reason for travel providers to offer discounts. That said, there may be incentives for booking well in advance.

How inclusive is all-inclusive?
Although river cruise companies state that their river cruises are 'all-inclusive', they are actually 'selectively inclusive', based on a packaging price, ie that their selected items are included but there may well be exclusions to this. Depending on the country in which the rivership is marketed, there may be a difference regarding what is or is not included. It is wise to check carefully before booking.

Lower-priced 'all-inclusive' companies usually provide basic brand spirits for drinks and low-cost wines for lunch and dinner (not to mention small wine glasses). Higher-priced 'all-inclusive' companies usually provide better-quality brand spirits for drinks and higher-cost wines for lunch and dinner.

What about the facilities?
River cruise operators constantly try to outdo each other in terms of facilities and gimmicks in order to attract ever-more savvy travellers to the advantages of their products. Examples of this include swimming pools with covers that can be added to convert the pool room into a cinema, 270-degree wraparound windows on luxury suites or free iPads for the duration of the cruise.

Is it difficult to find one's way around a rivership?
No, not at all – five minutes should do it. Most riverships have only two, three or four decks, so it's very easy to get your bearings.

A *Queen Isabel* junior suite.

Who's got the best food?
My top choices in Europe would include AmaWaterways, Viking River Cruises and Uniworld.

What's the dress code?
Strictly casual – river cruising is all about comfort. That said, although there are no tuxedos or ties needed, you're more than welcome to dress more smartly for dinner if you want to.

Can I access the internet on board?
Yes – in theory. Aboard the newest riverships, Wi-fi will be available, subject to interrupted reception due to locks and bridges, and this might be across the whole vessel or just in selected areas. Connections can sometimes also be dropped when your rivership crosses borders between countries, when different telecom systems take over the transmissions and apply different rates. Some upscale lines provide iPads for guests to use, but otherwise you should bring your own tablet or computer.

Is river cruising for solo travellers?
River cruising is designed for couples. Solo travellers are an expensive afterthought, and only a few riverships have single-occupancy cabins (examples include *Ariana, Dertour Mozart, Heidelberg, Statendam* and *Swiss Pearl*). Although you can occupy a double cabin on your own, the fare will usually be higher. However, when river cruises are not sold

A1Vista Cruises operates special cruises for owners and their dogs.

out, opportunities can arise for solo travellers. The best advice is to keep checking.

Are river cruises for honeymooners?

Why not? Most arrangements will have been taken care of before your cruise so all you have to do is show up. Some riverships have double-, queen-, or king-sized beds, although you'll find that, in general, the cabins (and particularly the bathrooms) are compact and the beds are short!

Are river cruises suitable for children?

Although a river cruise is educational, in general, river cruises in Europe are taken by the over 50s. A handful of riverships have cabins with three beds, which are in theory suitable for small families, although cramped.

Are river cruises suitable for disabled passengers?

Not really, although some riverships do have lifts (elevators), typically between the main deck and the restaurant deck and/or stairlifts from the main to the upper (outside) deck. Some have lifts between all decks, and a few riverships have wheelchair-accessible cabins.

Many landing stages are linked to steps leading up to a city or town. In some locations, riverships berth side by side (this may also obscure the view from your cabin), and you may have to cross several of them to get to land.

And it's on land where most problems arise, with many historic continental European cities having cobbled streets, steps with no ramps and few facilities aimed at those with disabilities.

Are there laundry facilities?

Not usually, although a handful of riverships do offer some laundry facilities. If your river cruise is part of a longer holiday, take some washing powder or liquid to clean small, personal clothing items in your cabin. Note that most suite/cabin bathrooms are dimensionally challenged and have little space to hang anything. Most do not have a retractable washing line.

Only one or two riverships currently have ironing facilities.

Will I get seasick on a river cruise?

You shouldn't get seasick, with the possible exception of cruises around the islands in the open sea at the mouth of the River Elbe in North Germany.

Are there medical facilities on board?

Although riverships carry first-aid kits, they do not generally have a doctor or nurse employed on board (unlike on an ocean cruise ship). However, riverships are always close to land, so any emergency medical arrangements can be made quickly, if necessary.

How pregnant can I be when I take a river cruise?

River cruise companies don't allow mothers-to-be aboard past their 28th week of pregnancy. Pregnant women may need to produce a doctor's certificate. Fortunately, you'll never be far from shore, so medical help can be summoned quickly. If you are taking any river cruise, make sure you have adequate medical insurance.

Are animals permitted on board?

No, with the exception of A1Vista Cruises, which operates one or two cruises each year in Europe for owners and their dogs.

Is smoking allowed?

Most riverships are totally no-smoking inside (exceptions include the cigar lounge aboard *TUI Queen*), but allow smoking on the open deck.

Won't I get bored?

No chance. There is always something to see on the river.

What if I don't like it?

I am almost certain that you will enjoy your river cruise experience and the abundant scenic opportunities. If you really don't like your holiday, or if things go horribly wrong, let your river cruise company or travel provider know at the earliest opportunity.

Do river cruise companies have frequent passenger (loyalty) clubs?

Some river cruise operators have a frequent cruisers

club. Examples include: Abercrombie & Kent (Marco Polo Club), Scenic Tours (Scenic Club), Transocean Tours (Columbus Club), Vantage Deluxe World Travel (Platinum Circle) and Viking River Cruises (Viking Explorer Society).

Has any rivership ever capsized?
Not in Western Europe. However, in July 2011, the seriously overloaded rivership *Bulgaria* tragically capsized on a bend of the river in Russia's central region of Tatarstan. Although 79 passengers survived, 119 (many of them children) were confirmed dead.

What happens to old riverships?
Some riverships are sold for use as 'floatels' (permanently moored ships that have been converted into hotels). This might be because the owner no longer wants to operate the vessel, because the engines are inefficient or damaged, or for other reasons (dissolved partnerships, for example). Other riverships simply sit and rust away.

What's the difference between a river cruise and a canal barge cruise?
Canal cruise barges are much smaller, typically catering to a maximum of 12 persons, as opposed to riverships, which can carry up to 200 passengers. They also travel much more slowly than riverships – riverships can sail at up to 20kph (12.5mph), although the typical speed is between 10 and 15kph (6 and 9mph). Cruise barges typically chug along at no more than 5kph (3mph).

Can I eat when I want to?
For breakfast and lunch, there is usually some flexibility on when you can eat, within the restrictions of a 90- to 120-minute time span when the restaurant is open. Generally, you can have your breakfast or lunch at any time within that time slot. Dinner, on the other hand, is always at a set time, typically around 7pm, depending on the itinerary.

Do riverships have room service?
It's not standard, as there simply aren't enough crew members on a rivership to be able to provide it. A handful of vessels are starting to offer this to occupants of suites for breakfast, however. You may also be offered it if you can't leave your cabin due to illness, for example.

Can I bring my own drinks on board?
Most river cruise companies allow you to bring your own drinks on board, but only for in-cabin consumption.

Are tips included?
Gratuities may or may not be included, depending on the river cruise company or tour operator or packager. Some companies have exclusive charters of vessels and may include gratuities in the package price. If the same company offers cruises on 'partner' company riverships, tips may not be included. It's important to read the fine print.

What do ships do about rubbish (garbage)?
Rubbish is offloaded in various ports along the way, depending on the port's regulations.

Dinner time on *River Cloud II*.

Pros and cons

Dream getaway or a claustrophobic holiday nightmare? Here is a list of key pros and cons to help you decide whether messing about on the river is right for you.

River cruises don't come cheap, so it's wise to weigh up the pros and cons beforehand, to be sure this style of holidaying is going to suit. We believe, of course, that the advantages far outweigh the disadvantages – most types of holiday have minuses as well as pluses, after all – but here's our frank breakdown to enable you to make your mind up for yourself.

The advantages of a river cruise

Riverships provide a unique way of seeing the interior of a country. They give a new take on a destination from the one you would get on a wholly land-based tour and totally different, too, from the coastal approach of an ocean cruise.

Riverships allow you to enjoy the ever-changing scenery ('riverscape') at eye level and up close.

With this kind of holiday, there is always the excitement and interest of waking up in a different place each day, usually in the heart of a city or town.

The atmosphere on board is friendly and informal, never stuffy or pretentious.

Riverships lined up in Budapest.

Good food and service are essential elements of any river cruise, with some food sourced from local markets as you travel.

All meals and snacks are provided, and basic table wines may also be included for lunch and dinner, which keeps the additional costs down.

Open dining is standard, meaning you have greater flexibility in terms of where you sit than with the more traditional assigned seating approach of a classic ocean cruise.

The dress code is completely casual.

It's a single currency world on board.

You never have to take a tender ashore – you simply step off your rivership as soon as it is tied up to a pier.

While ocean-going cruise ships have interior (no-view) cabins, almost all riverships in Europe feature only outside-view cabins – nearly all of which have large picture windows. Exceptions include *Dertour Mozart* (four interior cabins), *Primadonna* (eight interior cabins) and *Rossini* (11 interior cabins).

Most excursions are included in the upfront package price, which is good if you want tight control over your budget from the outset.

The entertainment is geared towards the more cultured customer, so if the casinos, bingo games or knobbly knees or wet T-shirt contests that are more typical of ocean cruises fill you with dread, a river cruise may well appeal more.

River cruising provides a sense of continuity that is more difficult to achieve on a bus or coach tour, where constant changing of hotels or lodgings each night means greater disruption. This also saves time in terms of packing, unpacking and settling in.

Some riverships are marketed in several countries, which means that there's an attractive, cosmopolitan mix of travellers on board.

The disadvantages of a river cruise

The flow of water in almost all rivers cannot always be controlled by man, so there will be times when the water level is so low that even a specially constructed rivership, with its shallow draft, cannot travel.

Occasionally (especially on the River Elbe), the water level can become so low (a depth of only a few centimetres) that it is impossible for riverships to move at all. In such cases, you will use the vessel as your hotel, while taking daily bus tours to various destinations that would have been included on your itinerary.

Being part of an organised group tour means that you have less control over the pace of your holiday. Whether too fast or too slow, it can be equally frustrating. It can also mean that you don't get as long as you'd ideally like to spend with the locals.

If you are tall, note that the beds on board most riverships are usually less than 1.8m (5ft 11in) long.

There is generally no room service, as there aren't enough crew members to cope with this.

If your cabin is towards the aft (rear), there may well be the constant humming of a generator, which supplies power for air conditioning, heating, lighting and cooking, etc.

Cabin insulation may be poor, so you may hear noisy neighbours clearly, whether you want to or not.

Mealtimes are strictly followed (all passengers typically eat at one sitting), so there's no choice of dining times, as there is in the ocean-going cruise industry.

In some popular destinations such as Budapest, Bratislava and Passau, several riverships are often tied alongside each other. Passengers on the outermost vessels must cross the others in order to disembark and embark, which is challenging for passengers with poor ambulatory skills.

Non-smokers should note that on the open deck, you may find that smokers are right next to you. The only way to avoid this is to move.

Sailing along the Rhein.

Older vessels (pre-2000) typically have twin beds that are fixed. One (or both) may be a sofa bed that acts as a sofa during the daytime and converts to a single bed at night.

River cruising vs ocean cruising

So how does river cruising compare with its more established cousin, ocean cruising? Here we take a look at some of the key differences.

River cruising and ocean cruising can provide very different experiences – this list intends to help you to work out which style of holidaying might be more appropriate for you.

River cruises provide the kind of up-close inland cruising impossible aboard large ocean-going cruise ships.

The ride aboard riverships is typically silky smooth – there's no rolling about as there is on many of the ocean-going cruise ships.

On riverships, land is almost always in sight; aboard ocean-going cruise ships you may be sailing on open stretches of water for days to reach a destination.

Aboard a rivership, the scenery is at eye level; on an ocean-going ship it isn't, and you may need to take a lift to go up and out to see it.

On a rivership, you simply step on land almost as soon as the vessel ties up. Aboard ocean-going cruise ships, you can be waiting for up to two hours to go ashore in some ports when the ship is at anchor, and you need to take a shore tender. There can be long queues when you return to an ocean-going cruise ship. For rivership passengers it's easy – you simply step aboard.

Aboard a rivership, you dock right in the centre of a city, town or village. Ocean-going cruise ships often have to dock in cargo terminals and other inconvenient places in insalubrious locations some distance from a city or town centre.

Riverships are more intimate than their ocean-going counterparts. They seldom carry more than 200 passengers. Ocean-going cruise ships can carry over 5,000 passengers.

Almost all cabins on a rivership have outside views; there are virtually no interior (no-view) cabins, as are typical on most ocean-going cruise ships.

Riverships often tie-up alongside at night, so you can go off into the local town to enjoy restaurants, concerts and nightlife. Most ocean-going cruise ships sail at night, so you seldom get to experience nightlife ashore.

Rivers are calm and shallow, so there is almost zero possibility of motion sickness, whereas this is likely to be more of a problem on an ocean-going cruise ship.

With ocean cruising, the ship is the destination. In river cruising, the destination is the destination!

Ocean-going cruise ships sometimes have portholes in their dining rooms that you cannot see out of when seated, but aboard rivership dining rooms, there's always a river view through large windows.

On ocean-going cruise ships, most excursions are additional cost items. Aboard most riverships excursions are usually included, although this does depend on the operator, so always check at the outset.

River cruising tends to be more for the seasoned traveller and, generally, to those aged over 50. Ocean cruising caters to a broader clientele, including families and travellers with disabilities.

Life aboard

From what to take with you to how to stay safe once on board, this A–Z gives the lowdown on all the practical basics that you need to be aware of during your cruise.

Air conditioning
Cabin temperature is regulated by a thermostat inside your cabin, so you can adjust it to your liking. Note that you may not be able to turn the air conditioning off completely. At the beginning and end of the summer season – and on Christmas market cruises – heating, rather than air conditioning, is of course provided.

Baggage
Mark your luggage tags clearly with both your name and the name of your rivership. If your whole package is organised through a river cruise operator, they are responsible for getting your luggage from the airport or train station to the embarkation point; if your cruise only includes the sailing, you are personally responsible for getting yourself and your baggage to the rivership on time.

While there is generally no limit to the amount of personal baggage you can take on board, note that

Wrapped up well on the Rhein.

storage space is limited. Towels, soap, shampoo and shower caps are provided on most vessels, so you probably won't have to bring your own.

Beauty salon
Just a few riverships – usually the latest, longest ones – have onboard beauty salons, offering treatments that might include some of the following: haircuts and styling, manicures and pedicures, facials, waxing and, possibly, massages. It's advisable to book appointments as soon as possible after boarding, especially on short cruises. Charges are comparable to those ashore.

Bed linen
European duvets are usually provided, rather than sheets and blankets. Anti-allergenic pillows may also be available. Occupants of suites may get a choice of several different pillows.

Bicycles and walking accessories
On some cruises, bicycles are provided for passenger use. Nordic walking sticks are also sometimes available.

Captain
Most riverships have an open bridge policy, so you can visit the captain at almost any time. Exceptions to this include during poor weather or in hazardous manoeuvring conditions. Check at the reception desk if you're not sure.

Clothing
If you think you might not wear it, don't take it, as wardrobe space is really limited. In the summer, when the weather is warm to hot, pack clothes made of lightweight cottons and other natural fibres. Take a lightweight cotton sweater or windbreaker for the outdoor deck, and sunglasses and a hat. For river cruises in winter (those for Christmas markets, for example) take well-insulated clothing, including earmuffs and thick gloves, because it can be really cold, especially on deck when your rivership is moving.

The dress code is casual, but in the evening what you wear should be tasteful. Men might include a blazer or sports jacket. Comfortable low- or flat-heeled shoes are essential for women. Rubber soles are best for walking on deck.

Comment cards

On the last day you may be asked to fill out a comment card. Be truthful when completing it, as this feedback helps cruise providers to improve on their product. If there have been problems with any other aspect of your cruise, say so.

Communications

Most riverships (although not cruise barges) have direct-dial satellite telephone systems, so that you can call anywhere in the world while on your cruise. Wi-fi may be available in your cabin or selected areas such as the lobby or lounge or library, although the reception can be patchy, especially when going through locks or under bridges. Connections can sometimes also be dropped when your rivership crosses borders between countries, when different telecom systems take over the transmissions and apply different rates. Some upscale lines provide iPads for guests to use, but otherwise you should bring your own tablet or computer. More standard riverships may just provide one or two communal computers with Wi-fi access, mostly with no privacy from passers-by.

Daily programme

The daily programme is a list of any activities and social events plus destination arrival and departure times. It is normally posted up at the reception desk and also delivered to your cabin the evening before the day that it covers. For a sample breakdown of a day on a river cruise, see 'A day in the life of a rivership' (see page 24).

Disabled travellers

River cruising is not ideal for travellers with disabilities. Some riverships do have lifts (elevators) between the main deck and the restaurant deck and/or stairlifts from the main to the upper (outside) deck and a few riverships have wheelchair-accessible cabins, but not all.

Many landing stages are linked to steps leading up to a city or town. In some locations, riverships berth side by side, and you may have to cross several of them to get to land. Anyone in a wheelchair will have to be carried across the riverships (possibly including steps) in order to be placed on the dockside.

And it's on land where most problems arise, with many historic continental European cities having cobbled streets, steps with no ramps and few facilities aimed at those with disabilities. Budapest and Esztergom, for example, are very hilly and cobbled, making wheeling bone-shakingly difficult and uncomfortable. Bratislava is one of several cities to have numerous steps between the docking place at river level and street level, which is much higher.

Disembarkation

Fortunately, this is very straightforward on a rivership. The night before arrival at your final destination, place your bags outside your cabin. They will be collected and off-loaded on arrival. Remember to leave out the clothes you intend to wear on disembarkation day and to retrieve any items you have placed in the personal safe in your cabin or in the rivership's main safe.

Drinks

Some companies provide free bottled water, replenished daily, but many do not. For information on drinks provided with meals and what's covered in 'all-inclusive' packages, see the chapter on dining (see page 20).

Electricity

The cabin voltage is usually 220 volts, but bathrooms may have both 110- and 240-volt (60 cycles) outlets, for shavers only. Hairdryers are normally supplied in your cabin, but, if not, they will be available on request at the reception desk. Most European riverships have a deeply recessed two round pin socket, so you may need to take an adaptor. Check what voltage there is, in case you also need to bring a transformer.

Emergencies

A few words about safety may be given by the cruise manager at the first evening's briefing. Safety instructions – ie what to do in an emergency – are provided in an in-cabin documentation folder. Riverships generally do not carry lifejackets.

Note that most door locks on riverships are operated by an electronic key card. Aboard some riverships, an actual key may be required on the inside in order to unlock the door. It's best to leave the key in the lock, so that in the event of an emergency, you don't have to hunt for it.

Capsizing: This is rare, but riverships do bump into things occasionally due to currents or careless navigation.

Fires: Always make sure that you know the way from your cabin to the nearest emergency exit (typically aft and in the centre of the vessel), which are identifiable by their green signs. Riverships have 'low location' lighting systems, of either the electro-luminescent or the photo-luminescent types, which will lead you to the exits.

In the unlikely event that a fire does break out on your rivership, try to remain calm and think logically and clearly. If there is a fire in your cabin, report it immediately, then leave your cabin and close the door behind you to prevent any smoke or flames from entering the passageway. If you are in your cabin and the fire is in the passageway, feel the cabin door. If the door handle is hot, use a wet towel to turn it. If a fire is raging in the passageway, assess the situation and act as you deem most appropriate. If there is smoke in the passageway, crawl to the nearest exit.

Gyms

Only a handful of riverships have small fitness rooms, typically including a couple of rowing machines, exercise bikes and a few weights, and possibly, although not always, a small infra-red sauna.

Identification cards/passports

When you embark, you hand in your passport (it is used for passport control, as you travel between different countries) and are given instead a personal boarding pass for identification purposes. This sometimes includes your photograph and other pertinent information and must be shown at the gangway each time you board. Your passport will be given back to you at the end of the cruise.

Laundry

Riverships do not generally have laundry facilities. You can always wash small items in your own bathroom, but be aware that there will be very little space to hang anything up to dry. Some riverships might offer a minimal laundry service, although this might be limited to passengers in suites (sometimes those in the Owner's Suite only).

Only a small number of riverships have ironing facilities.

Library

Actually, the so-called 'library' will just be a few bookshelves, usually in the lobby. You'll find a few general-interest books, some destination reference material, and periodicals, as well as board games such as Scrabble, backgammon and chess.

Medication

Although riverships carry first-aid kits, they do not generally have a doctor or nurse employed on board (unlike on an ocean cruise liner). However, riverships are always close to land, so any emergency medical arrangements can be made quickly, if necessary.

Take any medical supplies you need, plus spare spectacles or contact lenses and solution. In some countries it may be difficult to find certain medicines; others may be sold under different names. Ask your doctor for names of alternatives, in case the medicine you are taking is not available. Always take a supply of any medication in your carry-on luggage where flights are involved (eg if you are flying to the start point of your cruise), just in case your hold luggage goes astray. If you are diabetic, ask before you book whether your chosen rivership has an in-cabin refrigerator or mini-fridge to store medication in.

Money

European riverships operate in euros (€), but for the duration of the journey, it's cashless cruising on board, so that you don't have to worry about carrying cash or cards with you. You simply sign for drinks and other assorted services, unless you are on an 'all-inclusive' cruise, in which case most things will be included anyhow. Your final payment at the end of the cruise can be made using major credit cards or cash.

Tipping: If gratuities are not included in the overall package price (they sometimes are and sometimes aren't – check the small print or ask your booking agent to be sure), the accepted standard for gratuities aboard European riverships is €8–10 (£6–8) per person, per day. Tips are given as a lump sum at the end of your cruise and divided equally between all crew members. Companies such as Avalon Waterways, Tauck Tours and Uniworld include gratuities to crew. Others (Saga Holidays, for example) include them on exclusively chartered vessels only.

Pets

With the exception of A1Vista Cruises, which operates just one or two cruises each year in Europe for owners and their dogs, pets are not allowed on board river cruises. Check with the river cruise company as to whether guide dogs would be allowed on a cruise.

Reception desk

Centrally located and manned 24 hours a day, this is the nerve centre of the vessel for general information and help with problems, plus ephemera such as postcards and stamps.

Room service

This is not generally available on riverships, as there simply aren't enough crew members to cope. Some riverships offer room service at breakfast to suites. If you are poorly and confined to your cabin, you may also be offered help in the way of meals brought to your room.

Safety

Bridges: Riverships often pass under very low bridges. In some cases the space between the bridge overhead and the rivership can be so little that if you don't sit down, you run the risk of serious head injury.

Injury: Slipping, tripping and falling can all unfortunately cause injuries on board riverships. This does not mean that vessels of this kind are unsafe, but there are some things that you can do to minimise the chances of injury.

Inside your cabin, note that on many (pre-2000) riverships, there is a raised 'lip' (typically between 15cm/6ins and 30cm/12ins) between the bathroom and the rest of the cabin. Watch out for this, as it's easy to trip over it. On deck, wear sensible shoes with rubber soles (not crepe) when walking on the open deck and don't wear high heels.

Smokers should not throw lighted cigarette or cigar butts, or knock out pipes, over the side of the vessel. The water might seem like a safe place to throw them, but they can easily be sucked into an opening in the side or onto an aft open deck, and start a fire. It is also inconsiderate and environmentally unfriendly.

If you are injured aboard your rivership and want to take legal action against the company running the cruise, note that you need to file suit in the country of registry – so for riverships registered in Switzerland, the lawsuit must be filed in Switzerland (this is known as the Forum Clause). For more details on this, check the small print of your ticket, which will usually state at length the instances in which the cruise carrier will not be held responsible for injury. Note that passengers may not be able to sue a river cruise company in the event of injury or accident on an included or optional shore excursion, since these tours are operated by independent contractors.

Sailing time
At each destination, the vessel's sailing time will be posted at the gangway.

Security
All cabins aboard riverships can be locked. Old-style keys are made of metal and operate mechanical locks; most locks, however, will be electronically coded ones that open with plastic key cards.

Cruise lines do not accept responsibility for money or valuables left in cabins and suggest that you store them in a safe (see 'Valuables').

Alemannia sun deck.

Shops
A small boutique on board, typically run by the reception staff, will offer a selection of maps, souvenirs, gifts and toiletries.

Smoking
Most riverships have complete no-smoking policies inside (an exception to this is the cigar lounge aboard *TUI Queen*), but they do usually allow smoking on the open deck.

Swimming pools
A handful of the newest riverships have swimming pools, sometimes with retractable covers, so that the pool room can be used for other purposes (eg as a cinema) in the evenings (see below).

Television and film
Programming is obtained from a mix of satellite feeds and onboard videos. Some riverships receive live international news programmes, for which river cruise operators pay a subscription fee. Satellite television reception is sometimes poor because riverships constantly move out of the narrow beam of a satellite and cannot track the signal as accurately as a land-based facility.

Films are shown on the in-cabin television system and, on some of the most sophisticated riverships, in a combined pool/cinema room.

Valuables
Most riverships have a small personal safe in each cabin for storing valuables. For extra security, items of special value can also be kept in a safety deposit box at the reception desk – you will be able to access them during your cruise.

Dining

Food is a major part of any successful river cruise. Here we lift the lid on what the dining experience is really like.

Companies put maximum effort into telling you just how fabulous their food is. What is closer to the truth is that you'll be served agreeable food in comfortable surroundings, with the added bonus that you don't have to do any of the cooking, serving or washing up yourself.

In general, river cruise cuisine compares favourably with the kind of 'banquet' food served in a decent hotel. Riverships cannot offer a full-on gourmet experience – despite what the brochures might claim – because the galley ('kitchen' for landlubbers) is small, with batch cooking used to turn out up to 200 meals at a time. At almost any time of the day or night, there is plenty of activity in the galley, whether baking fresh bread at night, preparing meals and snacks for passengers and crew around the clock, or decorating a special birthday cake.

Where to eat

All riverships have at least one restaurant and also offer a second, more casual, alfresco dining option

Restaurant on *River Cloud II*.

in summer. The latest 135m (443ft) riverships may also have an alternative interior dining venue at the aft (rear) of the vessel, giving you a chance to eat in a more intimate setting. All AmaWaterways vessels, for example, have a separate 'Erlebnis' (meaning 'experience') restaurant, where a private chef prepares a high-quality tasting menu. Some riverships also offer lighter fare in a casual bistro area in other parts of the vessel. Note that there's no extra charge to eat in any alternative area – spreading the diners out like this also helps to manage demand in the main dining room from an operational point of view.

On some riverships, there are quite extensive eating options. *Alina* (2011) and *Amelia* (2012) both have two main dining rooms – both of which are full-service restaurants, located at the front of the vessel, one above the other; they also have a steakhouse at the aft of the vessel. Perhaps more new riverships will feature this approach in the future, simply because it provides more options.

Tables for two in the main dining room are a rarity (there are exceptions, such as aboard the Viking River Cruises 'Longships'); most tables seat four, six or eight. When tables are unassigned – called 'open seating' – you can sit with whomever you wish, which means that you can change your dining partners each evening if you want to. On riverships where tables are assigned, it may be difficult to change tables once the cruise has started.

The nitty gritty: It's often the case that the little details all combine to create a greater or worse end product. For example, the restaurants of *A-Rosa Stella*, *Amadeus Silver*, *Avalon Expression*, *Belle de Cadiz* and *Expression Royale* have seats without armrests, which are in my view far less comfortable than those with armrests. Aboard *AmaCello*, *Dertour Mozart*, S.S. *Antoinette* and aboard all the Viking 'Longships' such as *Viking Embla*, dining chairs do have armrests.

Some companies (A-Rosa Cruises, for example) only have placemats on restaurant tables for dinner. Viking River Cruises has placemats for lunch, but tablecloths for dinner. AmaWaterways and Scenic Tours have tablecloths for breakfast, lunch and dinner. AmaWaterways, Dertour Cruises, Scenic Tours, and Uniworld provide linen napkins, whereas many other operators provide only paper napkins. Some operators have paper napkins for breakfast and lunch, and linen napkins for dinner.

River Royale buffet.

Some companies provide fish knives (AmaWaterways and Viking River Cruises, for example). Most riverships catering to North Americans – such as those of Grand Circle Cruise Lines and Vantage Deluxe Cruises – don't have them, nor does A-Rosa Cruises.

AmaWaterways and Viking River Cruises provide proper steak knives, but most others do not.

The food

The cuisine aboard riverships is generally international, although there will be some leaning towards the food of the country or region you are visiting. Gravies and salty cream sauces are fairly standard (sometimes used to mask less-expensive cuts of meat or defrosted ingredients), while light cuisine is not. Portions tend to be small, however.

Aboard budget-priced riverships you can expect portion-controlled frozen ingredients that are simply reheated and plated. On more expensive cruises, you can expect to be served more freshly prepared ingredients, especially fresh fish and better meat

cuts – basically, you get what you pay for. Some companies, such as AmaWaterways, and Uniworld, spend considerably more on food and dining options than others.

River cruise operators work generally closely with their food suppliers to identify and remove any products that contain genetically modified food, with the exception of packages of cereal.

On European rivers, galley standards, food supply, handling and hygiene all come under the auspices of HACCP Certification (Hazard Analysis Critical Control Point).

Breakfast: The first meal of the day, taken between around 7am and 9am, is usually a self-service buffet with a variety of breads, cold cuts of meat and a decent range of French and other European cheeses laid out on a central display table. There may also be an omelette station. (Riverships catering specifically to North Americans tend to offer a greater number of egg dishes.) Hot food items can also be ordered from your waiter. Some riverships (including those of AmaWaterways and Viking River Cruises) may feature a special of the day or other additional menu options.

Aboard some riverships bread and bread rolls may be made on board, even though the bakery section of any rivership galley is tiny; aboard others, these items may be made from frozen dough, or purchased ashore. Many rivership croissants have no taste, because they are made from frozen starter dough and poor-quality butter. Some providers, however, buy from local low-cost suppliers, and some even make their croissants freshly, from proper French flour and d'Isigny butter from Normandy.

Special diets
If you have a vegetarian, vegan or macrobiotic diet, are counting calories or want salt-free, sugar-restricted, low-fat, low-cholesterol food, or indeed have any other dietary restrictions, tell the river cruise company or your cruise booking agent before you make a booking, and ask the cruise operator to confirm that it can handle your dietary requirements. Note that food on many a rivership tends to be liberally dosed with salt, and vegetables are often cooked with sauces containing dairy products, salt and sugar.

The *Avalon Expression* bar.

Lunch: Served between around 12 noon and 1.30pm, lunch is also usually a self-service buffet. The selection usually includes a choice of fresh green salad items with dressings (typically a little unimaginative) and a range of oils (olive, sesame, pumpkin, walnut, etc) that can liven up your salad. The omelette station from breakfast will probably have been converted into a pasta station for lunch. Requests for hot food items are taken by a waiter and cooked to order.

Dinner: Dinner, served from around 8pm, is normally a sit-down meal served at either assigned or unassigned (open-service) tables, although the self-service buffet of A-Rosa Cruises is one exception to this. Served dinners normally consist of a choice of cold or hot starter (appetizer), a choice of three main courses (entrées) – one fish, one meat, one vegetarian – plus dessert and cheese (usually in that order, although cheese might be available at any time throughout the meal). You can expect river fish (other than shrimp/prawns, there will be little in the way of shellfish), and dark red meats such as venison, beef and ox, as well as lighter fare including chicken and other fowl. AmaWaterways uses fresh fish – to my knowledge, this is the only river cruise company to do so.

There may also be an 'always available' selection that includes items such as poached or grilled salmon, chicken or (small) steak, as on AmaWaterways and Viking River Cruises. Candlelight dining and special 'themed' dinners may also be featured. If you have any dietary restrictions, make these known to your cruise provider when you make your booking.

Drinks

River cruise companies often tout that all drinks, including alcoholic beverages, are included in the cruise price. Take a look at the selection in the bar, however, and you may notice brands you've never heard of before. Whiskies available will inevitably be of the blended varieties – ask for a decent single malt whisky and you'll probably have to pay extra. ('It's not included in the included drinks, sir.') And, for that gin and tonic, you may be facing tonic, such as Royal Tonic, that is overly sweet or, alternatively, basic tonic from a hose. As for premium gins – not a chance, although I did experience a fine Black Forest gin called Monkey 47 aboard *AmaCerto* recently.

Wine: Many river cruise companies tout their 'specially selected' wines, sometimes dubbing them 'fine wine' (Uniworld) or 'superb regional and international wines' (Scenic Tours). If you enjoy good vintage wines, expect to be disappointed, however, unless you bring your own (most companies allow you to do this, but only for consumption in your cabin, so not at a meal).

In most cases the wines are very, very young table wines – on a par with the least expensive supermarket wines. And in terms of quantity, most river cruise operators only provide small wine glasses for both white and red wines, although a few (notably AmaWaterways and Scenic Tours) serve large, proper glasses – by this I mean Bordeaux-sized glasses for red wines and Chardonnay-sized ones for whites – and their wines are of a better quality. Measures are up to the waiter. It's not truly unlimited, either: if you read the small print, you will find phrases such as 'Unlimited beverages do not include premium wine and premium spirits' (Uniworld).

Of course, there are exceptions, such as the specialist wine-themed cruises of AmaWaterways, for example, which feature private tastings, exclusive vineyard visits and special brochures on the wine regions of Europe.

Coffee and tea: Riverships have self-service drinks corners, typically with a good-quality push-button espresso/cappuccino machine and a selection of teas. Most companies provide teabags rather than loose tea, although Uniworld is an exception to this. Premium European riverships provide a range of teas from specialist brands such as Fauchon, Ronnefeldt, Tea Forté, Twinings or Whittard. Standard riverships in Europe may provide teas of a lesser quality by companies including Bigelow, Dilmah, Lipton or Pickwick. Coffee varies from the best Italian brands (illy, Lavazza, Segafredo) to the unknown.

Some riverships provide only white sugar for hot beverages, which is a shame, as a choice of white or brown at least is preferable.

Water: Water is usually provided in jugs. These are towel-wrapped aboard some of the premium riverships, but aboard most, they are not.

Excursions ashore

Shore excursions on a river cruise offer everything from helicopter rides and hot-air ballooning to wine tasting, horse riding and musical recitals in historic venues.

Excursions on a river cruise are a highlight for many passengers. When they are included in the cruise fare, it will be reflected in the price, but this does take the pressure off holiday spending. If you are visiting new places and want the value of a good guide, it's best to choose a company where excursions are included. Normally, this will comprise full days of activities when the ship is in port and often a couple of evening events, too.

When river cruise operators plan and oversee optional excursions, they assume that passengers have not been to a place before and aim to show them its highlights in a comfortable manner and at a reasonable price.

Buses or minibuses are usually the principal choice of transport. This cuts costs and allows the tour operator to narrow the selection of guides to only those most competent, knowledgeable and fluent in whatever language the majority of passengers speak, while providing some degree of security and control.

Learn to read between the lines on shore excursions: the term 'visit' should be taken to mean actually entering the place or building concerned, whereas 'see' should be taken to mean viewing from the outside (perhaps even just from the bus, for example).

Excursions are timed to be most convenient for the greatest number of participants, taking into account the timing of meals on board (these may be altered according to excursion times). Departure times are listed in the descriptive literature and in the daily programme (delivered to your cabin and posted at the reception desk), and may or may not be announced over the vessel's public address system. There are no refunds if you miss the excursion. If you are hearing-impaired, make arrangements with the shore-excursion staff to assist you in departing for your excursions at the correct times.

City excursions for larger cities are basically superficial, although they do provide a useful introduction. On most of these tours, Audiovox or Quietvox headsets are provided. These enable the tour guide to communicate by talking into a microphone and passengers to listen wirelessly using tiny earphones, which means that you don't look so much like a tourist and you also have a good chance of hearing all the commentary clearly.

To see specific sights in more detail, or to get to know a city in a more intimate fashion, go alone with a guidebook or with a small group and a private guide. Go by taxi or bus or walk directly to the places that are of most interest to you.

Going solo? If you hire a taxi for sightseeing, negotiate the price in advance and do not pay until you get back to the vessel or to your final destination. If you are with friends, hiring a taxi for a full- or half-day sightseeing trip can often work out far cheaper than renting a car, and you also avoid the hazards of driving. Naturally, prices vary according to destination, but this can be an excellent way of sightseeing, particularly if you can find a driver who speaks your language, and who has a comfortable, air-conditioned vehicle.

Consulting the excursion guide.

A day in the life of a rivership

To give you a flavour of life on board a rivership, here's a sample daily programme. There's also a summary of who's who among the crew.

After arrival at your rivership (usually mid-afternoon), you simply step aboard and check in at the reception desk, where you are given your cabin key. A stewardess then takes you to your cabin and explains everything about it. Your luggage will already be inside the cabin, ready to unpack. While you have dinner in the dining room, your vessel will probably depart.

Each day, when you wake up, your rivership is probably on its way to the next destination or else has already arrived and is tied up at the landing stage, ready for everyone to explore; alternatively, it may be in a lock. Note that all-inclusive excursions are completely optional – you can always just stay on board and relax or go ashore independently.

A typical day on a River Danube cruise

6.30am: Fresh coffee in the lounge for early risers.
7–9am: Breakfast in the dining room.

Breakfast on the deck of *River Cloud II*.

9am: Arrival at the first destination.
9.15am: Leave for the morning excursion – coaches will already be outside, as close to the gangway as possible, ready to take guests on a tour of a historic castle, key town or nearby vineyard.
12 noon: Return from the morning excursion (unless you are in a major city, in which case you would spend a whole day out and about).
12 noon–1.30pm: Lunch in the dining room or a small bistro lunch on the open sun deck (weather permitting).
2pm: Arrival at the second destination.
2.15pm: Departure for the afternoon excursion eg a castle, abbey or monastery, or a historical tour with a museum visit. In a small village (such as Dürnstein, in Austria), it may instead be a simple walking tour escorted by a licensed local guide with in-depth knowledge of the locality.
4pm: Afternoon tea, cakes and sandwiches for anyone not on the afternoon excursion.
5pm: Return from the afternoon excursion.
6pm: Short briefing on the following day's programme (plus information on any changes to the schedule or docking times) in the lounge; pre-dinner cocktails and conversation.
7pm: Dinner of four or five courses is served in the dining room. Guests typically linger over an assortment of cheese and enjoy conversation around the table.
8pm: In the lounge, the resident pianist plays music for dancing or listening to. Occasionally, there might be some additional entertainment from ashore, perhaps a mini-concert (a classical trio of two violinists and a cello, for example), a small *a capella* vocal concert or perhaps some regional folk dancing. There may also be an evening excursion (such as a private concert in Vienna), if your rivership is spending longer than one day in a key destination.
10pm: Late-night snacks are available in the lounge or, if it's warm weather, perhaps outside on the sun deck, followed by a meeting with your pillow. The lounge/bar doesn't usually close until after midnight.

Behind the scenes: how it all works

Riverships are small, and teamwork makes it all happen. Whether you are on or off a rivership, its

Lounge entertainment.

crew works constantly, both on the mechanical side (on the engines, air conditioning, heating and electrical items, etc) or the hospitality side – eg the reception staff dealing with paperwork, acting as the main contact point for passengers, keeping track of who is on board or off the vessel, etc.

Even on the largest (longest) and latest riverships, the maximum number of crew carried will probably be under 50. Some crews are much smaller than this – older-style riverships typically have as few as 18 staff members. They work closely together, and multi-tasking skills come in handy in such a confined environment.

Captain

The captain is the ultimate authority on board. He/she drives the rivership and is responsible for navigation and all things technical. The captain is licensed and insured for the river(s) the vessel sails on and has a deputy who is licensed and able to take over at any time – there is sometimes a lot of night sailing to do, so backup is essential. The captain has a small team of engineers to look after all electrical and mechanical items, including the air conditioning and heating systems.

Hotel manager

The hotel manager is in charge of the overall hotel operation (and all department heads), including all things relating to passenger comfort and satisfaction, the provision of food and drinks (these may be provided by an outside maritime catering company), placing orders for supplies and generally coor-

dinating departments and personnel and communicating with the river cruise company's headquarters, or owner.

Cruise manager

Aboard riverships, the cruise manager makes sure that the route plan is followed, doing the recaps in the lounge, hosting social events, dealing with all the excursions, planning the timing for the next day's programme, and taking care of any other details such as entertainment, library books and reports.

Housekeeping

In the early morning, the cabin stewards and stewardesses will count out the number of fresh towels needed for the cabins in their sections. They will have a stock of sheets and pillowcases available in case any need changing, as well as any toiletries or personal amenities that need refilling or changing.

Executive chef

A hands-on executive chef is responsible for making sure that the team of cooks delivers the food that passengers eat for breakfast, lunch and dinner, as well as food for the crew. The executive chef typically heads up a team of up to eight people in the galley – a small space no larger than a standard-size hotel room. At almost any hour of the day, chefs are busy preparing, cooking, grilling, sautéing or making sauces. During the night, the bakers are busy baking the bread and rolls for the next day, while a pastry chef will be on board to prepare all the cakes and sweet items.

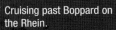
Cruising past Boppard on the Rhein.

Booking and budgeting

Should you book directly with the river cruise company or through a specialist booking agent? Are there any hidden extras to look for when calculating costs? And what about insurance?

We cover the different booking options once you've decided to definitely go on a river cruise – whether to go direct, through an agent or via the internet. We also consider whether there are any hidden costs to look out for when booking, plus whether you should also purchase cancellation, general travel or medical insurance.

Booking direct

River cruise companies, such as AmaWaterways, Avalon Waterways, Viking River Cruises and Uniworld, prefer you to book directly with them because they then don't have to pay commissions to cruise booking agencies. Other firms, however, charter their riverships to tour operators who put together packages including travel, hotel stays and a river cruise, so they do not take direct bookings.

Whether booking direct or via a cruise booking agent, check thoroughly just what is included in any offers, particularly when enticing discounts catch your eye. Make sure, for example, that all port charges, government fees and any additional fuel surcharges are included in the quote.

The internet

The internet may be a good resource tool, but it is not the best place to book your cruise, unless you know exactly what you want. You can't ask questions, and information provided by some river cruise companies is marketing hype. Most sites providing cruise ship reviews have something to sell, and the information can also be misleading or outdated.

Many internet booking agencies are unlicensed and unregulated, so if you do book a cruise with one, confirm with the actual river cruise company that the booking has been made and that final payment has been received.

The internet vs travel agents

Perhaps you've found a discounted rate for your cruise online. Fine, but if a river cruise company suddenly offers special discounts for your sailing, or things go wrong with your booking, your internet booking service may prove very unfriendly. A physical cruise-booking agent, however, can probably work magic in making any discounts work for you. It's called personal service.

Most river cruise companies consider travel agents to be their distribution system (exceptions include Grand Circle Cruise Line and Saga Cruises, who sell direct). Cruise booking agents do not charge for their services, although they earn a commission from the river cruise companies. Consider them to

Riverships have colourful cabin key cards.

Identification and visas

European citizens only need a national identity card to enter European Union countries, but those without them, such as UK and Irish citizens, must have a passport. Visitors from non-European Union countries, such as Australia, Canada, New Zealand, South Africa and the US, must have a full passport and may also need visas – some countries allow you to visit for up to 90 days without one, while others require a visa from day one. You should check this with your tour provider or the consulate/embassy of the country concerned prior to travelling, allowing at least 90 days to get the visa. Also check that your passport is not about to run out, as some countries require at least six months left (from date of entry) prior to the expiry date in order for it still to be valid.

be your business advisor, not just a ticket agent. They will handle all matters relevant to your booking and will have the latest information on any changes of itinerary and any other relevant items.

When you have chosen an itinerary and river cruise company, look for an affiliated agency member of the Cruise Lines International Association (CLIA), or one belonging to the National Association of Cruise Oriented Agencies (NACOA), or the National Association of Career Travel Agents (NACTA). These associations have a full financial bonding scheme to protect passengers from failed river cruise companies.

Reservations

Riverships on Europe's waterways are small compared to ocean-going ships, carrying fewer than 200 passengers, so the most popular river cruises are often sold out a year ahead. Book as far ahead as possible (especially if you want to get the best discounts), and make any special dietary requests known, keeping any correspondence relating to the request.

After choosing a cruise, date and type of cabin, you pay a deposit, typically followed by full payment within seven days (sometimes longer, depending on the river cruise company's conditions). You'll then receive a confirmation invoice. For a late reservation, you pay in full when space is confirmed (when booking via the internet, for example). River cruise companies always reserve the right to change

Queen Isabel exterior.

prices in the event of tax increases, or other costs 'beyond their control.'

After the river cruise company receives full payment, your cruise ticket will be sent by post, or possibly as an e-document. Check to make sure that everything is correct (date, itinerary, etc).

Extra costs

Cruise brochures boldly state that 'almost everything's included,' but in most cases it's not actually true. In fact, for some less expensive cruises (usually with older vessels) 'all-exclusive' would be a more appropriate term. Your fare usually covers the rivership as transportation, your cabin, all meals and snacks, and service on board, and, possibly, shore excursions and tips. Note that even if alcoholic drinks are included, there may be an extra cost for 'premium' brands.

Port taxes/handling charges

These are (usually) included in the cost your European river cruise ticket.

Air/sea packages

If your river cruise price includes air transport, note that flights usually cannot be changed without paying a premium, because river cruise companies may book group space on aircraft to obtain the lowest rates.

If you arrange your own air/train/coach transport, the river cruise company is under no obligation to help you if you don't reach the ship on time. If you are flying overseas, allow extra time (particularly in winter) for possible flight delays or cancellations.

In Europe, air/sea packages generally start at a major metropolitan airport; some may include first-class

Questions to ask a cruise booking agent
1. Is air/train/coach transport included in the cabin rate quoted? If not, what will be the extra cost to get me to my rivership?
2. If I need to make changes to my flight, routing, dates, and so on, will there be an extra charge?
3. Does the river cruise company offer advance booking discounts or other incentives?
4. Have you sailed on the rivership that I want to book or that you are recommending?
5. What is the river cruise company's cancellation policy?
6. Are the shore excursions insured by the river cruise company?
7. Does your agency deal with only one, or several different insurance companies?
8. Is your agency bonded and insured? If so, by whom?
9. How will I know if there are any changes to the advertised itinerary after I have purchased the cruise?
10. Will I need a visa? (Non-European Union citizens only. See 'Identification and visas' box.)

The Iron Gates Gorge on the River Danube.

rail travel from outlying districts. In the US, some river cruise companies include connecting flights from suburban airports convenient to the traveller.

Cancellations and refunds

Do take out full cancellation insurance, if it is not included. Otherwise, if you cancel at the last minute – even for medical reasons – you could lose the whole fare. Insurance coverage can be obtained from your booking agent or from an independent company (it may even be included), and paying by credit card makes sense (there's a better chance of getting your money back, even if the booking agency goes bust).

Cancellation insurance offered by river cruise companies is a 'one-size-fits-all' product, and personalisation is impossible. It will only cover the cruise itself but not any add-ons that you may have arranged on your own, such as non-refundable air tickets.

River cruise companies usually accept cancellations more than 30 days before sailing, but all charge full fare if you don't turn up on sailing day. Other cancellation fees depend on the cruise and length of trip.

Travel and medical insurance

Taking out your own travel and medical insurance is essential, but choose your policy carefully. Note that river cruise companies and cruise booking agents routinely sell travel insurance policies which, on close inspection, appear to wriggle out of payment due to a litany of exclusion clauses, most of which are never explained. Examples include 'pre-existing' medical conditions – ignoring this

little gem could cost you dearly – and 'valuables' left unattended on a tour bus, even though the tour guide says it is safe and that the driver will lock the door. To get the best travel insurance deal, allow time to shop around and don't accept the first travel insurance policy you are offered. Read the contract carefully and make sure you know exactly what you are covered for. Ask for a detailed explanation of all exclusions, excesses and limitations. There may be exclusions for 'hazardous sports'. These could include things typically offered as shore excursions from ships, such as mountain-biking.

Beware, too, of the 'box ticking' approach to travel cover, which is often done quickly at the travel agent's office in lieu of providing expert advice. Insurers should not, in reality, be allowed to apply exclusions that have not been clearly pointed out to the policyholder.

Before you go, check out the procedure you need to follow if you are the victim of a crime, for example if your wallet or camera is stolen while on a shore excursion. If anything of this kind does unfortunately happen to you, always obtain a police report as soon as possible. Note that many insurance policies will reimburse you only for the second-hand value of any lost or stolen item, rather than the full cost of replacement, and you may be required to produce the original receipt for any such items claimed.

If you purchase travel cover over the internet, check the credentials of the company underwriting the scheme. It is best to deal with well-established names and not necessarily to take what appears to be the cheapest deal offered.

What to do if...

Here are some tips to ensure the best river cruise experience possible, and, just in case it doesn't quite go to plan, advice on what to do if you do have a problem.

...you fly internationally to take a cruise.

If your cruise is a long distance from your home, it makes sense (if time and budget allow) to fly to your cruise embarkation point and stay for at least a day or two before the cruise starts. This way you will be better rested and able to adjust to any time changes before your cruise begins. You then step aboard your rivership relaxed and ready for your holiday. As a bonus, you will get to know the departure city/town.

...your luggage does not arrive.

If your holiday package includes flights as well as your cruise, the airline is responsible for locating your luggage and delivering it to the next port. If you have arranged your own flights, you are responsible for picking your luggage up at the airport and transporting it to your cruise. Our tips include placing easy-to-read name and address tags both inside as well as outside your luggage, to increase the likelihood that it will be returned to you if it does go missing, and, if your luggage has been lost during your flight, giving your airline your itinerary and a list of port agents (included with your river cruise documents), so that they can for-

ward it once it has been tracked down. (Keep this list – and contact details for insurance purposes – in your hand luggage, so that it's accessible if your suitcases are lost.)

...you miss your rivership.

If you miss the rivership's departure at the port of embarkation due to late or cancelled flights or connections and you are travelling on an air/sea package, the airline will make suitable arrangements to get you onto your rivership. If you are travelling 'cruise-only', however, and have arranged your own flights, then it is entirely your own responsibility to arrive on time. If you do miss the sailing, contact the rivership's agent immediately – their details will be included in your documents.

...a port of call is deleted from the itinerary.

This can easily happen on a river cruise, perhaps for security reasons or strikes. Remember to read the small print in the brochure before you book. A river cruise company is under no obligation to perform the stated itinerary if they have stated otherwise in the brochure.

Dinner on board in Lyon.

Waiting for passengers to embark.

...you miss the rivership in a port of call.

The onus is on you to get back to your rivership before its appointed sailing time. Miss it and you'll need to get to the next stopping point at your own cost. In Europe, the train network is fortunately so good that this is usually possible, although it's obviously more costly, inconvenient and potentially stressful.

...you leave personal belongings on a tour bus.

If you unintentionally leave something on a tour bus, and you are back on board your rivership, let the staff at the reception desk know. They will contact the excursion operator to ascertain whether any lost property has been found.

...your cabin has no air conditioning or it has heating or plumbing problems.

If there is anything wrong in your cabin, including problems with the plumbing in the bathroom, bring it to the attention of your cabin steward immediately. If things don't improve, complain to the cruise manager. If the rivership is full – and most are fully booked months in advance – it will be difficult to change to another one.

...you are unwell aboard your rivership.

Riverships do not carry their own designated medical team or unit, as ocean-going cruise liners do. Land, however, is always accessible, so arrangements can quickly be made to access medical assistance. Almost all river cruise companies offer insurance packages that include medical cover for most eventuali-

ties. It is wise to take out this type of insurance when you book (see page 29).

Members of European Union/European Economic Area (EU/EEA) countries or those of Swiss nationality should get a free EHIC, which entitles the bearer to state health care at a reduced cost or sometimes for free. It is valid in all EEA countries, including Switzerland. You can apply online at www.ehic.org.uk. Note that EHICs do not cover private health care or repatriation.

...the food is definitely not 'gourmet' cuisine, as stated in the brochure.

If the food is not as described – for example, it promises 'whole lobster' in the brochure, but you only see cold lobster salad once during the cruise, or the 'freshly squeezed' orange juice on the breakfast menu is anything but – inform the maître d'.

...you have a problem with a crew member.

Go to the manager and explain the situation. It's his/her job to resolve issues of this kind, although they are hopefully rare, since river cruise companies try to hire the best crew members they can.

...you're unhappy with your cruise experience.

If the cruise doesn't meet your expectations or performs less well than the brochure promises, let your booking agent and the river cruise company know as soon as possible. Be certain to read the small print, however – after you've done so, it'll probably seem as if passengers don't have many rights after all.

River cruise companies

This list of the key river cruise providers includes background information on each company, including whether it has its own fleet of riverships, plus essential characteristics of its cruises.

Whether you want to cruise along the mighty Volga, the castle-rich Rhein or the famously 'blue' Danube, there's a wide array of itineraries, destinations, operators and riverships from which to choose. To help differentiate, here is a summary of the main river cruise providers, with background information and details of key features of their cruises.

A-Rosa Cruises

German company A-Rosa Cruises began operating its own river cruises in 2002, although the company was established in 1969 as Seetours, when it chartered riverships in Russia. Seetours was founded by Alf Pollak with financial backing from Holland America Line, for whom Pollak was the general sales agent in Germany. The company – which became A-Rosa Cruises in 2003 – is based in Rostock, Germany, and also operates spa resorts in Austria and Germany.

The onboard dining concept is different to most, in that there is no formal meal service – instead, all

A-Rosa Stella at Chalon-sur-Saône, France.

meals are provided in a self-service buffet style, with no tablecloths. Extra-cost 'all-inclusive' drinks packages are available.

Abercrombie & Kent

Abercrombie & Kent was founded in 1953 in Chicago, Illinois, by the father of Geoffrey Kent, the company's current president, and was originally set up as an operator of safari tours in Africa. It began offering river cruises in 1978. The company, which caters principally to North American and British passengers, charters or books into a variety of river-cruise operators' vessels and tailors the river cruise holiday package (including pre- and post-cruise hotel stays and travel services) to its clientele. Abercrombie & Kent also provides high-quality ground handling and meet-and-greet personnel for its river and barge cruises.

AmaWaterways

Founded in 2002 as Amadeus Waterways (the company changed its name in 2008), AmaWaterways has helped to redefine European river cruising. Owned by modern river cruise industry pioneer Rudi Schreiner, cruise industry executive Kristin Karst and former owner of Brendan Worldwide Vacations, Jimmy Murphy, the company has riverships with spacious cabins, 82 percent of which have French balconies. Each passenger is given a pocket-sized travel guide, complete with detailed information on the route. AmaWaterways spends more on its food and wine and on food service training than almost any other river cruise company.

APT (Australian Pacific Touring)

Founded in Melbourne, Australia, in the 1920s by Bill McGeary, APT River Cruises is part of the APT Group. Still a family-owned company, run by Rob and Lou McGeary, it added European river cruises to its portfolio for its Australasian clients in the 1990s, although its offering has really taken off in the last 10 years or so. APT is a partner of AmaWaterways, whose riverships are used for its European river cruise programmes.

Avalon Waterways

Originally founded in 1928 by Antonio Mantegazza, who used his rowing boat to take passengers across Lake Lugano in Switzerland, the company became

Avalon Waterways in 2003, under the umbrella of privately held company Group Voyages Inc. Now based in California, the company includes well-known tour operator brands Globus and Cosmos. Today, the group consists of more than 30 tourism and aviation businesses.

Avalon owns and operates its own vessels, including twin-cruisers (riverships comprised of two sections). Gratuities and all drinks (except premium brands) are included in the cruise price.

CroisiEurope

CroisiEurope was founded in France in 1976 by the late Gérard Schmitter as Alsace Croisières and originally ran lunch and dinner cruises (river cruising proper started in 1982). Alsace Croisières became CroisiEurope in 1997, in order to reaffirm its commitment to Europe. The company, which is presently run by Gérard Schmitter's four offspring, has its headquarters in Strasbourg, France, with another French office in Lyon and a Belgian office in Brussels. The fleet consists of more than two dozen riverships, some of which are owned, some chartered.

The company specialises in river cruising for French-speaking passengers. Most of its riverships have the same layout, cabin sizes, features and facilities in two grades: 'Prestige' and 'Excellency' (equivalent to 'standard' and 'standard-plus'). Negatives include the deck lounge chairs, which are white plastic patio-style ones and not particularly elegant (stainless steel or aluminium ones are generally more comfortable and stable as well as smarter). The company also runs gastronomic theme cruises several times each year, including dinners ashore with notable French chefs.

Dertour Cruises

One of the leading travel and tourism companies in Austria and Germany, Dertour is part of the Rewe Group, which was founded in Cologne in 1927 and specialises in retail, travel and tourism. It has a large client base and charters and operates riverships from several different owners. It also sells the river cruises of other operators.

Emerald Waterways

This company, which debuted in 2014 with two brand new riverships, is a division of Scenic Tours. It is a lower-priced alternative to its parent company's Scenic Cruises (about 20 percent lower, but with fewer choices included), and is aimed at a younger audience, with excursions that are more active. The company's riverships each feature an indoor pool, which can be covered and converted into a cinema at night.

Excellence River Cruises

Based in Basel, Switzerland, this company is owned by the long-established travel agency and tour pack-

Avalon Artistry II interior.

ager Reisebüro Mittelthurgau and is part of the Twerenbold Reisen Group (founded by Werner Twerenbold), which has its own deluxe tour buses and several riverships in Europe.

Grand Circle Cruise Line

Grand Circle Travel was founded in New York in 1958 by Ethel Andrus, a retired schoolteacher. She founded the American Association of Retired Persons (AARP – today an extremely large organisation for retirees and senior citizens) and served its members until 1982. Grand Circle Travel was purchased in 1985 by Alan Lewis and moved to Boston. Its first privately owned rivership was *River Symphony* in 1998. The company was sold in 2007 to private equity firm Court Square Capital Travel.

Grand Circle Travel caters exclusively to North American retirees, with its own riverships in Europe under the Grand Circle Cruise Line brand. It also offers an extensive array of pre- and post-cruise optional stays and tours. The deck lounge chairs are rather inelegant white plastic ones, which spoils an otherwise contemporary product.

Nicko Tours

Based in Stuttgart, Germany, this company was founded in 1992 by Ekkehard Beller to market and operate river cruises with chartered riverships. It first started with river cruises in Russia, but added the Rhein in 2002. In 2005 it launched the first 'twin-cruiser' rivership *(Flamenco)*, with French balconies for each cabin. Switzerland-based financial investment company Capvik became a major investor in Nicko Tours in February 2013.

Noble Caledonia

Noble Caledonia was founded in London in 1991 by Christer Salen and Andrew Cochran, as an outgrowth of the successful ocean-going expedition cruise company Salen Lindblad Cruising (presently known as Quark Expeditions). Noble Caledonia started offering river cruises in 1992, catering mainly to its large UK client base.

Noble Caledonia is known for its creative packaging of hassle-free river cruises in many parts of the world, including Europe, Russia, China, and Burma. The company has exclusive charters and also books into other operators' riverships; it tailors the river cruise holiday to its mainly British and North American passengers. Extras such as transfers and baggage handling are included in its attractively packaged, good-value river cruises. The company always has one or more representatives aboard each cruise.

Phoenix Reisen

Phoenix Reisen, based in Bonn, Germany, was founded in 1974 by Johannes Zurneiden and started offering river cruises in 1991. The company has both exclusive charters and also books into other river cruise operators' vessels and tailors its river cruises to its mainly German-speaking passengers, for whom typically such extras as transfers and baggage handling are included in attractively packaged holidays.

The company does not own its own riverships, but relies on the operating and product delivery standards of those on board the vessels under charter, although Phoenix Reisen always has one or more representatives aboard each cruise.

The riverships may not be the very best available (deck lounge chairs are white plastic ones, for example), but they are comfortable and offer good value for money.

Premicon

The Munich-based financial service and investment company was formed in 1998 for the purpose of investing in cruise ships and riverships, purchasing its first two riverships the following year. Today the company owns about two dozen riverships and has investments in one ocean-going cruise ship *(Astor)* and real estate in the US. The company does not operate the riverships itself, but charters them to various river cruise operators (such as Avalon Waterways, TUI Cruises and Viking River Cruises) or tour operators (including Phoenix Reisen and Transocean Tours).

Scenic Tours

Founded in Australia in 1986 by Glen Moroney, Scenic Tours markets its river cruises principally to Australian, British and New Zealand travellers. The river cruises are fully inclusive, including gratuities and onboard drinks. The company owns and oper-

ates several riverships in Europe, all featuring butler service. See also Emerald Waterways (see page 33).

Scylla Tours

Based in Basel, Switzerland, the family-run Scylla Tours was founded in 1973 by André Reitsma. The company has well-run vessels featuring smart, traditional interior design, fittings and soft furnishings, combined with balcony cabins. Vessels owned by Scylla Tours are typically chartered to non-competing tour operators such as Phoenix Reisen, Transocean Tours and Uniworld for their own dedicated markets, rather than being operated by Scylla Tours. Deck lounge chairs are made of stainless steel or aluminium, which is more elegant and comfortable than plastic.

Tauck Tours

Based in Connecticut, US, this company was founded in 1925 by Arthur Tauck as a tour packager and operator to take participants on life-enriching tours. The company charters riverships owned by Swizerland's Scylla Tours but operated under the Tauck Tours brand name. Tauck is known for its attention to its care of clients and provides more staff (at least four per rivership) from the US aboard its vessels than most other river cruise operators, to the benefit of its mainly North American clientele. On excursions, sightseers are split into three or four smaller groups, using the 'Quietvox' system (where you wear an earpiece into which tour information is conveyed) for guided tours.

Transocean Tours

Based in Bremen, Germany, Transocean Tours was founded in 1954 by Wolfgang Blaum, Herbert Drewes and Hans Heidelk. It started offering river cruises in 1980 and for many years, chartered riverships in Europe and Russia, principally for its German-speaking passengers. Basic table wines are usually included for lunch and dinner. Note that deck lounge chairs are typically just white plastic ones.

Travelmarvel River Cruises

A division of APT, this company introduced two chartered riverships (but not from AmaWaterways) for 'all-inclusive' river cruising at reduced prices for its mainly Australasian passengers.

Uniworld Boutique River Cruises

Uniworld was founded by Yugoslavian travel entrepreneur Serba Ilich in 1976. The company started offering river cruises in Europe in 1994 and was one of the first companies to charter Russian riverships exclusively for American passengers.

Based in Encino, California, Uniworld has its own European river cruise line, Global River Cruises (which itself owned 75 percent of Holland River Line

– established as a Swiss-owned company and based in Basel, Switzerland). While most of its riverships in Europe are nearly new, some features are a little basic – the plastic chairs on deck, for example. Also, dining room chairs typically have no armrests. The company's passengers are typically all English-speaking.

In 2004 Uniworld was purchased by The Travel Corporation (founded by South Africa-born Stanley Tollman), the parent company of Trafalgar Tours, Contiki Tours and several others, including Red Carnation Hotels. Some of Uniworld's riverships are owned, while some are chartered from other owners.

Vantage Deluxe River Cruises

Vantage Deluxe World Travel was founded in 1983 by Gordon Lewis, whose son, Henry, is the present president (his brother Alan Lewis is president of Grand Circle Cruise Lines). The company headquarters are in Boston, US. The fleet presently consists of several owned and chartered riverships.

The company, which sells direct instead of marketing via travel agents, caters exclusively to North Americans and specialises in trips for solo travellers. It has its own fleet of smart riverships in Europe. Dining is in an open-seating arrangement. Smoking is not allowed inside any of the riverships – only outside on the open decks.

Vantage operates self-serve buffet breakfasts and lunches, with dinner served at your table. Low-salt, low-fat, gluten-free and diabetic menu selections are available. However, the food is fairly average, with little choice of main courses (entrées) for dinner. The deck lounge chairs are white ones. Tips and drinks

(except for the Captain's Dinner evening), are not included, but land excursions are.

Viking River Cruises

Viking River Cruises was founded by a Scandinavian and Dutch consortium headed by Torstein Hagen (formerly connected with the long-defunct oceangoing Royal Viking Line) and Christer Salen (formerly of Salen Lindblad Cruising – the ocean-going expedition cruise company now called Quark Expeditions). The company has grown fast from small beginnings in 1997 when it chartered a single Russian rivership. The company then purchased Aqua Viva, a French operator, with two vessels.

In 2000, in a major coup in European river cruising, Viking purchased KD River Cruises, Europe's oldest established rivership operator, with the landing stages (a valuable asset) included in the purchase. The UK's Travel Renaissance, founded in 1977 by Graham Clubb (for many years Viking's UK general sales agent) was purchased by Viking in 2005.

Some riverships cater exclusively to North Americans; others cater to European and international passengers. An ambitious new-build programme saw several new vessels constructed specifically for North American passengers and introduced in a period of just two years.

The company deservedly prides itself on the consistently high standard of its product, cuisine and service. Pluses include, aboard the newest riverships, smart, comfortable deck lounge chairs made of stainless steel or aluminium, and pocket-sized travel guides, with information on the route, for each passenger.

Passengers returning to *Belvedere*.

Design and layout

An overview of the different types of riverships and what to expect to find inside. To finish, there's a detailed breakdown of eight riverships from different cruise companies.

River cruise companies try to attract customers by adding ever-more bells and whistles to their newest riverships and constantly challenging designers to create new ways of providing practical and attractive cabins and suites, dining rooms and lounges and bars.

The brochures lead us to expect floor-to-ceiling windows and doors that open onto some kind of balcony, but they don't tell us about the mosquitoes that can invade the Danube in the afternoon or that riverships must tie up alongside each other in busy ports (blocking the view), or that a balcony is fairly useless when a rivership moves up and down in the many locks. While a balcony of some sort may be desirable, consider how much you will use it compared with the premium it costs. Since the main purpose of a river cruise is to experience the destinations, a balcony may not actually be necessary.

Overview

Riverships are long and low in the water, with fold-down masts in order to negotiate low bridges. The navigation bridge can also be raised and lowered hydraulically, and all side railings can be folded down so that the uppermost (open) deck is completely clear of all obstructions.

Public rooms common to all riverships include a dining room and an observation lounge/bar. Some may also have a (tiny) shop and beauty salon, a fitness room and a small sauna. Most have a good amount of outdoor deck space for viewing the scenery and hosting food-and-drink-themed events such as the once-per-cruise midday 'Frühschoppen' (Bavarian-style brunch).

There is only so much the designers can cram into the hull of a rivership, but there has been a burst of creativity during the past couple of years, driven by the increased demand for premium facilities. The latest 135m (443ft) riverships for Emerald Waterways, for example, also have a dual purpose area at the aft of the vessel containing a small indoor heated pool, with a retractable cover that converts the area into a cinema.

The standard length of European riverships used to be 110m (360ft). The newest riverships however, are 135m (443ft) long – the maximum possible for the locks on the Rhein–Main–Danube system.

Cabin on *Avalon Expression.*

Design

Depending on the river on which they operate, European riverships have either two or three accommodation decks. This is due mostly to the restrictions placed on a vessel's dimensions by the locks and bridges on the various rivers. Almost all riverships are built on a single hull (monohull) arrangement, except *Primadonna* and *Dertour Mozart*, both of which operate exclusively on the Danube.

Primadonna has two hulls. *Dertour Mozart* has a double-width monohull with two sets of bows that give the impression of having twin hulls. While the increased width provides more room, the hull has to flex more to accommodate the strong currents and water movement encountered in some parts of the river. *Dertour Mozart* and *Primadonna* are limited to the River Danube because the river's locks can accommodate the larger size.

As a result of their long, low-slung design, riverships have a limited amount of space for public areas. There are just two principal public rooms: a dining room and an observation lounge (main lounge). There are, however, variations and differences between vessels, such as the location and position of the bar within the lounge, the possible addition of a small dance floor and upright or baby grand piano, and the degree of comfort and user-friendliness built into the design.

Every inch of space aboard riverships is utilised to the full, and innovative design thinking, such as that used by Viking River Cruises, has created new levels of comfort and user-friendliness that will make it increasingly difficult for older vessels (ie those built before 2000) to compete. As noted above, the newest riverships are also 25m (82ft) longer than the standard older ones.

Rivership types

There are two main types of rivership: monohull, and twin-cruiser. Riverships are traditionally built on a monohull, with or without a slightly modified split-front with bullnose (or 'Cadillac') front.

The twin-cruiser was a design innovation when first launched in 2005 in the shape of the *Flamenco* (presently operated by Nicko Tours). At time of writing there were just eight of this type in service. As is apparent from the name, a twin-cruiser consists of two sections: firstly, there is a long accommodation block, restaurant, galley and lounge, built as a separate unit that is bolted onto a smaller aft section; then there's a tractor (propulsion) unit at the back, housing the engines, engineering, propulsion and steering equipment. The rear section includes a hydraulically operated navigation bridge that can be adjusted according to the height of the bridges encountered en route.

The rear power 'barge' pushes the front accommodation 'barge' section. The captain has a forward view over the whole of the vessel. It's neat in theory (and should also mean that the front, lived-in section is quieter), but unfortunately doesn't really work well for a rivership, because docking often requires multiple manoeuvres (docking and undocking), when other riverships are using the same dock facilities.

Cabins and suites

You may see different words used for what is essentially a cabin, or a large cabin, or a suite. These include 'stateroom', which is often used by North American companies for normal cabins. Then there are suites, which should comprise a lounge or sitting room separated from a bedroom by a solid door, not just a curtain. Smaller 'suites' are sometimes termed 'junior' or 'deluxe' suites, but these are simply larger cabins than standard. There tends to be a greater choice of accommodation on newer riverships than older ones, from standard cabins to owner's suites. Basically, the more you pay, the more space you get. However, on a seven-day cruise, you probably won't spend much time in your cabin, so a suite may be a waste of money. If you take a longer cruise (for example 14 days from Amsterdam to the Black Sea), it may be worth the extra expense.

When you're booking your cruise, if you're early enough, you may have some say in which cabin you get – try to avoid the ones located directly under or adjacent to the galley, as these can be extremely noisy, particularly early in the morning when the chefs are preparing breakfast.

Although rivership cabins are small compared to most hotel rooms, with limited cupboard and drawer space, they are functional and practical. Virtually all cabins have outside river views, except very few interior (no-view) ones. Cabins on the lowest deck may have only small windows, while those on the deck(s) above feature larger picture windows, some of which can be opened.

A number of the latest riverships (examples include *Avalon Illumination*, *Avalon Imagery* and *Avalon Poetry II*) have cabins that are placed in a sideways arrangement that allows for a full-sized bathroom, with a bath and even two washbasins (as on some ocean-going ships). The biggest advantage of this is that the bed faces the river, so you wake up each morning with a great view (unless the rivership is in a lock, in which case you may feel like you are in a darkened lift). This design first came on the market in 2007, in the shape of the 104-passenger *Premicon Queen* (presently *TUI Queen*).

Cabin ceilings (some are nicely indented one-piece ceilings, while others are plain ceiling panels) tend to be rather low, and the beds are typically shorter and narrower than you may be used to at home. Much to the horror of *feng shui* practitioners, ships' designers often place large mirrors opposite the bed to give the illusion of space. (Some riverships do not have a full-length mirror in cabins, though – *Viking Europe*, for example.)

Aboard some of the older (pre-2000) riverships, it is common to have twin beds that are fixed and can't be pushed together – this is not great for romantics, but it does, of course, provide 'snoring' and 'no-snoring' beds. Examples of this include *Der Kleine Prinz, River Adagio, River Aria, River Concerto, River Harmony, River Melody, River Rhapsody* and *Swiss Ruby*. Some cabins, including those on the *River Ambassador*, have twin-sized beds that cannot be separated, while others (often on newer vessels) do have double beds or twins that can be placed together. Still others have two beds in 'L'-shaped configurations. Some rivership singles are lower and/or slimmer than a standard single.

Some older riverships – including the vintage *Amsterdam* (1948), *Rigoletto* (1987), *Cezanne* (1993), *River Harmony* (1999) and *River Rhapsody* (1999) – have fold-down beds that convert into sofas or push away into a recessed wall during the daytime, giving extra space in the cabin. While they are practical and space-efficient, they are ideal for couples who would prefer a double bed on holiday.

Note that some beds have mattresses inside a bed frame instead of on top of it, with square, not round, corners. The problem here is that passengers have very little room to move in and hence often knock their legs on the sharp corners, which can be very painful.

The bed linen aboard most riverships is 100 percent cotton, but aboard some it may be a 50 percent cotton/50 percent polyester mix. One rivership, *Serenity 2*, has Tempur (memory foam) mattresses, but most riverships have premium or standard mattresses.

In terms of facilities, most cabins feature a personal safe, a minibar, a television and an alarm clock/radio. On the more upmarket riverships, especially if you have a suite, you may have more impressive gadgets such as a personal iPad and fancy audio systems for the duration of your journey.

Balconies: A private balcony – that revered bit of space that lets you make contact with the outside – costs more, of course. It does provide a sense of exclusivity, but watch out for the mosquitoes. A full balcony is one on which you can sit outside and enjoy the scenery. A 'French' or 'Juliet' balcony features a floor-to-ceiling sliding glass door that opens to safety railings, but this design only allows you to stick out your nose (or toes) and smell the fresh air

In 2010, Viking River Cruises introduced a new design (a series of over 30 Viking Longships) with several suites featuring both a full balcony and a French balcony. Other companies, including AmaWaterways, also have riverships with both full and French balconies, due to a double-width cabin layout.

Bathrooms: Expect bathrooms to be functional rather than sumptuous – there simply isn't room on a river cruise vessel to accommodate the luxurious touches you would find in a hotel suite or in the top suites on board an ocean-going ship. A typical bathroom includes a washbasin, toilet and shower, while baths are available in some suites. The older riverships usually have shower curtains, while newer ships have the more stylish and streamlined glass doors. Some bathrooms have fixed-head showers, while others have flexible hoses. Some riverships, such as *Viking Freya*, have heated floors, while S.S. *Antoinette* has heated towel rails; most riverships have neither of these, however. Towels are normally supplied on board, so you don't have to bring them

A trio of Viking 'longships'.

AmaCello in Cochem, Germany, on a winter cruise.

with you. The size varies considerably from one rivership to another – examples include 142 x 102cm (56 x 40ins) on Viking River Cruises, 132 x 71cm (52 x 28ins) on AmaWaterways and 102 x 71cm (40 x 28ins) on Scylla/Tauck Tours.

Observation lounge/bar

At the front of most riverships there is a lounge/bar, with large panoramic windows for river viewing – especially important for sightseeing en route at the beginning and end of the cruise season in Europe, when it may be too chilly for some passengers to stay on the outside deck for long. Within the lounge, there will be a bar, which is best placed at the back of the room to leave more space for prime river viewing in the front section. (If the lounge bar is towards the front of the panorama lounge, as on the *Cezanne*, *Der Kleine Prinz* and *Excellence Royale*, for example, only the bartender has good views, while passengers sitting on bar stools face inwards.)

Restaurants

Most riverships have one main restaurant, with large river-view windows, plus, in summer, an area outside for casual, alfresco dining. Some of the newer models do also have an extra interior area for dining but this is quite a new innovation. The principal difference in the present design of rivership restaurants lies in the layout of the buffet display counter. Note that tables that are located adjacent to the doors or open entrance to the galley can be noisy, and should be avoided if possible.

Other facilities

Some riverships may also have a small plunge pool, a diminutive sauna and massage room and a gym, although few passengers actually find time to use these facilities on a busy one-week cruise. Some of the newer riverships, notably *Emerald Sky* and *Emerald Star*, incorporate the dual purpose swimming pool/cinema room.

A number of riverships have squared-off fronts, which allows the designers to accommodate a dining terrace. These usually have fully opening glass doors that allow a total alfresco option – the 'Viking Longships' incorporate this feature. And, for the very well-heeled, one rivership – *Queen Isabel* (DouroAzul) – even has a small helicopter landing pad on the sun deck.

The top deck

The most important area for many passengers is the open top deck. This runs almost the full length of the vessel. In, or close to, the front is the navigation bridge (pilot house), which is cleverly constructed so that it can be lowered hydraulically into the deck below to avoid obstacles such as low bridges. Any of the canopies and side railings on the top deck are also designed to be folded down, while chairs and sun loungers simply remain on deck all the time.

Most riverships have a life-size chess game or sunken small pool – a plunge pool rather than somewhere to swim. When the top deck is in use, it provides a wonderful vantage point from which to watch the constantly changing scenery. It's also a

Self-service buffet aboard one of the A-Rosa Cruises riverships.

social place, where you'll meet your fellow travellers and enjoy drinks and snacks.

In terms of the quality of the hardware on deck, there can be quite a difference between vessels. The open sun deck aboard *River Cloud II* and *Royal Crown*, for example, is laid with real teak wood, but most riverships have blue or green fake turf (when it gets wet it's just soggy underfoot), or a rubberised decking material that is made to look like wood.

White plastic patio-style deck chairs are typical of budget-priced river cruise operators. The more upmarket operators, such as AmaWaterways, Scylla Tours and Viking River Cruises, provide better-quality – and more stable and comfortable – stainless steel or aluminium chairs for the open upper deck.

Panorama (observation) lounges at the front of the vessel typically have large chairs, sofas and low coffee tables, as well, unfortunately, as a number of functional pillars that obstruct sightlines (exceptions include the *River Cloud II* and *Royal Crown*), the result of old shipbuilding techniques. Although the pillars prevent the flexing that can occur in the longest riverships, the designers and builders need to re-think in terms of passenger comfort.

Key rivership examples

At the end of this book is a comprehensive list of some 280 riverships, each with a summary of key features. Here, however, I have chosen a rivership from each of eight different operating companies to describe in detail. Use this more detailed analysis to work out which of the cruise providers you might like to travel with, then consult the list at the back of the book for details of their full portfolio of riverships.

Note that the beam is the measurement of the rivership at its widest point.

The riverships covered below, in alphabetical order, are:

A-Rosa Bella (A-Rosa Cruises)
AmaCerto (AmaWaterways)
Dertour Mozart (Dertour)
Primadonna (Nicko Tours)
River Navigator (Vantage DeLuxe World Travel)
Royal Crown (Various Tour Operators; built as *River Cloud*)
Saxonia (Scylla Tours)
Viking Embla (Viking River Cruises)

Features/points common to all are that the navigation bridge retracts, and all side railings fold down, allowing the rivership to sail under low bridges. In addition, smoking is permitted only on the open deck.

Of the eight riverships chosen, *AmaCerto* and *Viking Embla* are of the latest type (see page 36), ie around 25m (82ft) longer than the standard older ones. Notably, *Viking Embla* crams 95 cabins (190 passengers) into the same space as *AmaCerto*, which has only 82 cabins (164 passengers). It's not difficult to guess which one feels less crowded… Of the eight examples given, the number of passengers to crew members varies between 4.0 and 3.2 to 1, which is important, of course, as it has an impact on service.

Using the Berlitz scoring system explained later in this book (see page 108), the rivership with the greatest number of points out of these eight examples is *AmaCerto* (AmaWaterways), which did particularly well for the high quality of its food and service.

A-Rosa Bella (A-Rosa Cruises)
Built: 2002
Length: 124.5m (408.4ft)
Beam: 14.4m (47.2ft)
Passenger cabins: 100
Crew: 50
Passenger to crew ratio: 4 to 1
Decks: 3 + open sun deck
A-Rosa Bella is easily recognisable by a pair of bright red, pursed lips holding a rose on the bows – the logo of the *AIDA* ocean-going cruise ships that are part of the Carnival Corporation. On board, there are two full accommodation decks, plus a few cabins on the third deck. All 48 cabins on Deck 2 feature French balconies, while 46 cabins on the lower decks have picture windows that can be opened. The cabin decor is contemporary, casual and minimal. Two single beds are convertible to a queen-sized bed. Other features include a vanity/writing desk and a television. The brightly coloured bathrooms have shower enclosures, washbasins and toilets. Storage space for toiletry items is very limited. Some cabins have pull-down berths for a third person, which is useful for families with children, although it does make the cabin very cramped. Soundproofing is just so-so.

The main public room is the AIDA Lounge, which has whimsical decor and large panoramic windows, plus a novel bar arrangement whereby passengers face each other instead of facing the barman, as aboard most riverships.

The Markt Restaurant is open throughout the day. The self-service buffet displays are adjacent to, although separate from, the dining room. The restaurant has a small 'show' galley, where you can watch the chefs at work, an open grill and open seating, so you sit where and with whomever you wish. There's no sit-down dining service, no menu, no assigned seating and no tablecloths – just placemats on bare tables. The cutlery is placed on tables in a rack from which you help yourself (this is a rather unhygienic arrangement because anyone can touch the utensils). The bistro-style restaurant, located aft, has panoramic windows on three sides and doors that open on to an open aft deck for alfresco eating. Again, there are no tablecloths, only placemats. A second, smaller café bar, where you can get machine-dispensed teas/coffees, is located at the entrance to the Markt Restaurant.

A Fitness/Wellness Centre (SPA-ROSA Active) is a doughnut-shaped gymnasium that is tucked in underneath the small plunge pool on the open deck above; the area includes a small dry sauna and a steam room, a massage room and changing areas. Fitness checks and muscle-function tests are available. Treatments include massages and facials, and a range of Ligne St Barth products is available for purchase. There are also 50 trekking bicycles for passengers (free of charge). A gratuities box is provided (tips are shared by all crew members).

The open sun deck is covered with rubberised decking and fake green turf, while the deck lounge chairs are white plastic ones.

AmaCerto (AmaWaterways)

Built: 2012
Length: 135m (442.9ft)
Beam: 11.4 m (37.4ft)
Passenger cabins: 82
Crew: 49
Passenger to crew ratio: 3.3 to 1
Decks: 3 + open sun deck with pool/hot tub

Like its rivership sisters *AmaPrima*, *AmaReina* and *AmaSonata*, *AmaCerto* has music-themed deck names (violin, cello and piano), perhaps due to the company's original name – Amadeus Waterways. A wheelchair-accessible glass lift runs between all three indoor decks.

The *AmaCerto* has four suites, each of which has a large bathroom with tub and separate shower enclosure; one suite is wheelchair-accessible. Only 17 cabins on the lowest deck have twin windows – all 61 others have either one or two balconies, usually both a full balcony, with stainless steel railings, wood floor and two chairs, and a French balcony with a wooden floor, off the lounge area, usually with a full-length

mirror adjacent. They feature nicely indented ceilings with hidden lighting (no panelled ceilings here), wooden cabinetry and wardrobes (one with a full-length mirror on an inside door), two chairs, a coffee table, a writing/vanity desk with large mirror opposite the bed, telephone, Audiovox system for excursions, internet-connected television and good soundproofing. There are two nice long single beds that can be pushed together into a queen-sized bed. Next to these are two-drawer bedside tables, reading lamps and an alarm clock. Premium bedding and plush down duvets are provided, and there's a choice of pillow types.

The rectangular-shaped bathroom has large white marble tiles, a toilet, large washbasin and a large shower enclosure with both a large overhead 'sunflower' shower head and a hand-held shower hose. There's also a magnified shaving mirror and a long shelf with plenty of space for personal items. A range of personal toiletries is provided, as is a cotton bathrobe. The main lounge has a bar – located aft – with a high, indented ceiling and comfortable seating; there is also a small central dance floor and a self-service drinks station. Adjacent is a boutique, and a library with two fake fires. Towards the rear are the reception desk and the main entrances. Fresh flower arrangements everywhere help create to a warm, homely atmosphere.

The dining room has several alcove-style seating areas in a 'double-centre' section (ie with the left and right centre sections split), which is hidden from the self-service buffet counter, while other seating is at or adjacent

A typical cabin bathroom aboard *AmaCerto*.

The interior lobby of *Primadonna*.

to window-view tables, with seating at tables for four, six or eight. There's also a 12-seat private venue called the Wine Room within the main restaurant. At the aft of the vessel is a very popular alternative restaurant called 'Erlebnis' (the name is German for 'experience'), found aboard all AmaWaterways' European riverships. It has five tables and 28 seats and features a set menu that is bordering on gourmet. A drinks station, with mugs rather than teacups, is located at the rear of the main lounge. Also to the rear is a fitness area with windows looking out to the port side; equipment includes two Exercycles with video screens, a rowing machine and a walking machine. On the open sun deck, a large iron-shaped plunge pool is located directly behind the navigation bridge, as are storage cabinets for more than 25 bicycles plus a walking track, while at the front is a bar and sunken seating area with large wicker-style armchairs and sofas. From the range of food and special menus on offer, including one gourmet 'Chaîne des Rôtisseurs' menu (named after the society devoted to fine food), together with some high-quality Austrian and German wines (no cheap supermarket wines here), it is clear that this company spends far more per passenger per day than any other river cruise company (although Scenic Tours' wine selection is also very good). *AmaCerto* is about as good as it gets.

Dertour Mozart (Dertour Cruises)

Built: 1987
Length: 120.6m (395.6ft)
Beam: 22.8m (74.8ft)
Passenger cabins: 100
Crew: 50
Passenger to crew ratio: 4 to 1
Decks: 3 + open sun deck
Dertour Mozart is a very spacious vessel, built in 1987 for the Donau-Dampfschiffahrts-Gesellschaft (then

known as DDSG and later as the Köln–Düsseldorfer Deutsche Rheinschiffahrt, or KD line), and acquired in 1993 by the now-defunct Peter Deilmann River Cruises. It was the forerunner of the rush to build larger and better riverships, within the size constraints of the rivers and locks, and was hailed as the most luxurious rivership at that time. The front of the vessel appears to be split into two sections, giving it the look of a catamaran despite the hull actually being a single structure, or monohull, which adds to its strength. The rivership is extra wide because it was built to operate only on the River Danube, which has broader locks than most rivers.

There are two accommodation decks, the upper of which features cabins with a French balcony. There is no lift between decks. Some cabins are intended for single occupancy. Unusually for a rivership, this one has five interior (no-view) cabins, each with three berths, making them suitable for a small family travelling together.

Most cabins, however, have two parallel beds. Some are in an L-shape; 10 cabins have adjoining doors, so that two cabins can be made into a comfortable suite, with 'his and hers' bathrooms. The cabins measure a generous 18.8 sq m (203 sq ft), while suites measure 37.7 sq m (406 sq ft). All have dark wood cabinetry, lots of cupboard space, a sofa, a table for drinks, a vanity desk with mirror, a telephone, a television and Wi-fi connection. Beds have European duvets and feather pillows. There are no personal safes in the cabins or suites, but safety deposit boxes are available at the reception desk. Bathrooms are practical units, with a washbasin, toilet and shower enclosure. The cabin soundproofing is reasonable.

Public rooms are the main lounge and the dining room. The lounge has large, front-facing panoramic windows, with a bar at the back. There is a baby grand piano on the port side, to allow for maximum views to the front. A walk-around promenade deck allows you to go around the forward lounge and past the dining room. There is one sitting for all meals, and this is at assigned tables. The restaurant has window-side tables and a central self-service buffet display. Although dinner is served by waiting staff, you can also help yourself to salad items.

One deck below, a small heated swimming pool occupies the forward space, from where swimmers can see the river ahead. On the port side is a massage room. There is also an infirmary and a qualified doctor on board – an unusual addition, so good to note if you have health issues but still wish to cruise.

The open sundeck is covered with fake green turf and has white plastic chairs for lounging.

Although international passengers are welcome, the language on board is German. The vessel also flies the German flag.

Primadonna (Nicko Tours)

Built: 1998 (originally named *Delphin Queen*)
Length: 113.3m (371.7ft)
Beam: 17.3m (56.7ft)
Passenger cabins: 76
Crew: 47
Passenger to crew ratio: 3.2 to 1
Decks: 3 + open sun deck

Built specifically to fit the wider-than-average locks on the Danube, *Primadonna* – which was renamed from *Delphin Queen* in September 2001 – is double the width of most riverships and hence very spacious. Passenger capacity is 196. Unusually for a rivership, it has a wide two-deck-high interior promenade, a little like a much-reduced version of the 'Royal Promenade' on some Royal Caribbean International cruise ships; this is useful as a space for a pavement-style café or for exhibition space.

There are three interior decks, all with a mix of cabin types and public rooms. There are three cabin sizes: 8 sq m (86 sq ft); 12 sq m (129 sq ft); and 16 sq m (172 sq ft). Although they are not large, the cabins have outside views through big picture windows. Two decks of cabins have private balconies that are creatively angled; each has its own small two-person bench seat and floor-to-ceiling glass windows. Note that cabins 405, 406, 407, 408, 410 and 412 – all located on the lowest deck – are directly under the galley and are subject to noise in the early morning; for this reason, they are the smallest and least expensive cabins. Adjacent to a glass-walled lift, for passengers with limited mobility, are four cabins with extra-wide doors, a large bed and a sofa bed. In addition to the lift, there's also a sit-on stair-lift on two aft stairways up to the open-air sun deck.

All cabins have wood-panelled walls, twin beds (electrically operated foot and head sections can be independently raised and lowered), bedside reading lights, televisions that swivel so that they can be seen from the bed or the lounge chairs, cordless direct dial telephones, personal safes, individual climate control, illuminated wardrobes, minibars plus switches to turn announcements on or off. The bathrooms are fully tiled and include a shower enclosure, toilet, shelves for personal toiletries, a hairdryer, cotton bathrobe and towels. The cabin soundproofing is fairly good.

Public areas include an open-air sun deck covered with fake turf and with white plastic chairs for lounging, an observation lounge, an entertainment/lecture salon and a dining room, where dinner is for all passengers at one sitting, at tables for four or six. Breakfast and lunch are self-service buffets, while dinner is a served meal. In addition, mid-morning *bouillon*, afternoon tea and a late-night snack are usually provided.

The reception desk in the glass-floored lobby is open 24 hours a day. Any tips given are pooled and divided among all crew members.

River Navigator (Vantage Travel)

Built: 2000
Length: 110m (360.8ft)
Beam: 11.4m (37.4ft)
Passenger cabins: 72
Crew: 36
Passenger to crew ratio: 3.7 to 1
Decks: 3 + open sun deck

River Navigator's standard cabins have quite plain decor, brightened up with rich soft furnishings, for example colourful bedspreads. They are compact, measuring approximately 14sq m (150 sq ft). Deluxe suites are 21 sq m (225 sq ft) and have a small lounge area, minibar and coffee/tea maker, French balcony, plus better-quality linens and nicer artwork than standard cabins. There's one owner's suite, which has all the facilities of the deluxe suites plus amenities and services including private airport transfer, laundry service, audio system and a sofa in the sitting area. The cabins on the upper 'Navigator Deck' feature twin beds that convert to a queen-sized bed and have floor-to-ceiling sliding glass doors that open to a French balcony. The cabins on the middle deck feature large picture windows, while those on the lower deck have smaller windows.

All cabins are equipped with a television, telephone, private bathroom with toilet, washbasin, shower enclosure and inbuilt, wall-mounted hairdryer. They have little space for toiletries. The beds in all cabins convert to sofas for daytime use. The cabin soundproofing is quite good.

The two main public rooms are the lounge – with piano music each evening – and the dining room, with large picture windows. For meals, there is one open sitting. There's also a small gift shop and a reading room, with books, magazines, cards and games.

On the open sun deck, which is covered with fake blue turf and has a sun awning, seating is arranged in clusters.

Royal Crown (Various tour operators)

Built: 1999 (originally built as *River Cloud*)
Length: 110m (360.8ft)
Beam: 11.4m (37.4ft)
Passenger cabins: 45
Crew: 20
Passenger to crew ratio: 4.5 to 1
Decks: 2 + open sun deck

The former *River Cloud* was introduced in 1999 as a top-of-the-range rivership – the height of *eau couture* at the time – with the Art Deco style of the 1930s. The open sun deck has a very elegant look, with real teak decking and hardwood steamer-style chairs and tables, together with sun umbrellas; there's also a life-size chess board game on deck.

The cabins measure 12–19 sq m (129.1–204.5 sq ft). Except for the six Royal Suites, the largest of the accommodation on board, most cabins are small but well appointed, with half-height wood panelling along the walls and a large arched panoramic window, one-piece ceiling, rich, polished rosewood cabinetry, two beds with European duvets and cotton pillows, television, radio, telephone, refrigerator and individual climate control. Bathrooms are fully tiled, with anodised gold and brass fittings and include a toilet, washbasin and large shower enclosure. Cotton towels and a hairdryer are supplied. The cabin soundproofing is excellent.

The main salon has dark wood ceiling accents, a dance floor, baby grand piano and bar, and no pillars to obstruct sight lines. The dining room, located in the mid-aft section, has stylish Art Deco-style arched windows and rosewood-accented ceilings and wall decoration; the dining chairs are slightly more luxurious than normal, with armrests.

Breakfast and lunch are self-service buffet-style affairs, while there is table service at dinner, which is also served by candlelight. Dining is in one sitting, with assigned tables. Table wines are usually included for lunch and dinner, although this depends on which company has the vessel under charter. A small premium wine list is also available, although this is at extra cost. The food is creative and attractively presented, but menu choices are limited, because the galley is small. A late-morning 'Frühschoppen' (brunch-style meal of sausages and beer) is featured with each cruise, with Bavarian Weisswurst (white sausage) a favourite inclusion at this.

Other facilities include a 24-hour reception desk, a small shop, a library, a hair salon and a small fitness room with sauna. There's also a promenade deck outdoors.

Any tips given are pooled and divided among all crew members.

Saxonia (Scylla Tours)

Built: 2001
Length: 82m (269ft)
Beam: 9.5 (31.1ft)
Passenger cabins: 44
Crew: 23
Passenger to crew ratio: 4 to 1
Decks: 2 + open sun deck

Saxonia is a small rivership, but it's really the ideal size for travelling along shallow rivers and tributaries such as the Elbe, Mosel, Neckar or Saar. All cabins are a compact 12 sq m (129 sq ft), although they do have good-sized river-view windows. Cabins on the upper deck have larger windows, some of which can be opened, while the cabins on the lower deck have two non-opening windows.

Inside the cabins, practical fold-down ('Murphy') twin beds pull down from the wall for night-time use – during the day, these can be pushed back up and hidden from view to give a more spacious feel. European goose-down duvets are standard. The walls are decorated with bird's-eye maple wood panelling, and fittings and furnishings include a walk-in wardrobe (it's tight, but there are two rows for hangers, plus two trays on the back of the cupboard door for toiletries, etc), a full-length mirror, hairdryer, personal safe, television, alarm-clock radio, telephone, refrigerator, individual climate control and a single 220-volt electrical (two-pin European plug) socket.

The bathroom has a toilet, white washbasin with blue/black marble surround, separate shower enclosure and 220-volt shaver socket. Cotton towels are provided.

The observation lounge has a ship's bow-shaped bar in the front, although this gets in the way of what could otherwise be good forward views. On the floor, there's the same carpet (blue with a gold motif) that owners Scylla Tours places aboard all its riverships – the effect is both appealing and practical.

In the centre of the lobby, a wrought-iron staircase with a brass handrail goes between the upper and lower decks. It branches into two as it heads towards the lower decks, but take care, as the steps on the lower portion are narrow.

The decor in the dining room creates a restful atmosphere, and wrought-iron-and-etched-glass room dividers give a cosy feel. A self-service buffet station is located in the middle of the room. Dining is in a single sitting, at assigned tables, so you could be seated with people you don't know.

The open sun deck is covered with rubberised decking, while deck lounge chairs are of the white plastic variety.

Viking Embla (Viking River Cruises)

Built: 2013
Length: 135m (442.9ft)
Beam: 11.4m (37.4ft)
Passenger cabins: 95
Crew: 48
Passenger to crew ratio: 3.9 to 1
Decks: 3 + open sun deck

New in 2013, *Viking Embla* is one of a series of 190-passenger 'Viking Longships' introduced between 2012 and 2014. Each is designed in such a way as to be able to provide suites with both a full balcony and a French balcony on one side of the vessel and spacious cabins with French balconies on the other side, plus a few cabins without balconies, on the lowest deck.

The Longships stretched the talents of Viking's interior designers Yran and Storbraaten (famed designers of Seabourn's ocean-going ships), who have created the impression of rooms full of light, with the blonde wood and light colours that are typical of Scandinavian Minimalism.

The vessel's front end has a squared-off aspect instead of being pointed, and this provides extra space for viewing and eating out of doors. It features an 'Aquavit Terrace and Café', with glass walls, nine tables and overhead heaters for when the weather is a trifle cool. Eating here is all about the view – indeed, if you sit here, you'll reach things before the captain does, as the bridge, or pilot house, is located further back! In the centre there is a black granite buffet counter, displaying lighter fare than the main restaurant. Floor-to-ceiling glass walls separate the outside from an interior winter garden-style section – another good example of just what can be achieved by creative design.

The restaurant, which is located at the front of the vessel, one deck below the Aquavit Terrace, has a lot of tables for two, unlike on most riverships, where passengers dine at group tables. It has a light, open feeling, with a central, permanent, well-designed central hot/cold buffet counter.

A two-deck-high atrium lobby with glass sides, a glass ceiling and sliding glass doors lets in plenty of natural light. The atrium's lower level features a small moss 'garden' (with plastic flowers) under an open-tread stairway that softens the otherwise minimalist, uncluttered look of the area. There's also a small library corner.

The central accommodation corridor is actually set off-centre, in a patented design, so it's not in the middle, as one might expect. Its position means that the designers have found the extra space needed to include balconies that are large enough to take seats.

There are two luxury 'Explorer' suites, named after famous Norwegian adventurers, in the aft section. Each suite has a lounge with 270-degree views and a small rear-facing balcony with rubberised decking, a completely separate bedroom and a separate bathroom.

There are also seven 'Veranda' suites, with different gradings according to their size. These feature two full rooms with a veranda off the living room and a French balcony off the bedroom.

The standard cabins actually have more storage space than the suites. The bed and 'lounge' areas are quite modest, although they do have balconies. The cabin soundproofing is very good, and all cabins have their own mini-refrigerators.

The open sun deck is covered with rubberised decking and green fake turf, while the aluminium deck lounge chairs are more upmarket than usual.

Another plus point to note is that free Wi-fi is accessible across the whole vessel. Eco-friendly hybrid engines on the vessel produce very low vibration levels and give a smooth ride. The open top deck has solar panels neatly tucked into each side to help produce usable electricity. On the down side, tips are not included in the main package price.

Viking Embla, near Vienna.

Cruising past Marksburg Castle on the Rhein.

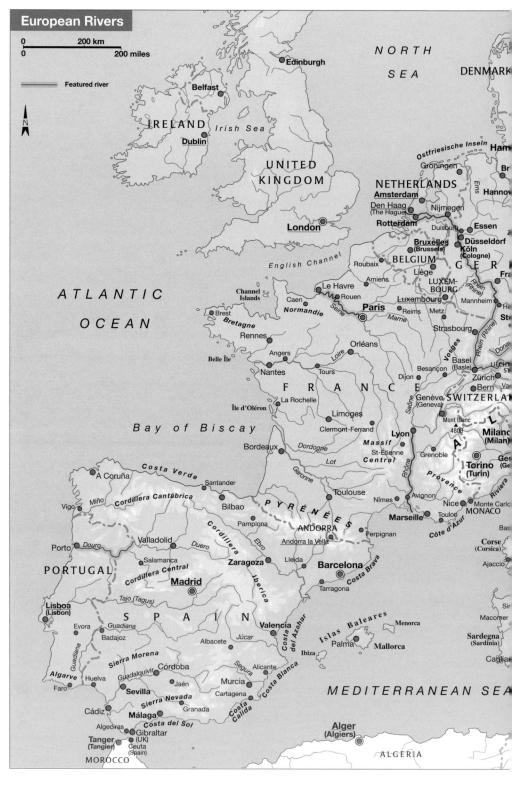

European Rivers

N

NORTH SEA

DENMARK

Edinburgh

Belfast

IRELAND   *Irish Sea*

Dublin

UNITED KINGDOM

London

Ostfriesische Inseln   Ham

Groningen   Br

Ems   Hannov

NETHERLANDS

Amsterdam

Den Haag (The Hague)   Nijmegen

Rotterdam   Duisburg   Essen

Bruxelles (Brussels)   Düsseldorf   Köln (Cologne)

BELGIUM   **GER**

Roubaix   Liège   Fra

Amiens   LUXEM-BOURG   *Rhein (Rhine)*

Mannheim   He

Luxembourg   St

Metz

Reims   Mannheim

English Channel

Le Havre   Rouen

Caen   *Seine*   **Paris**

Normandie   *Marne*

Strasbourg

Vosges   *Donau*

ATLANTIC OCEAN

Channel Islands

Brest   *Bretagne*

Rennes

Belle Île

Nantes

Angers   *Loire*   Orléans

Tours

F R A N C E

Dijon   Besançon   Basel (Basle)   LIECH-ST

Zürich

Bern   Va

SWITZERLA

La Rochelle

Île d'Oléron

Limoges

Clermont-Ferrand

Massif Central

St-Étienne

Lyon

Genève (Geneva)

Mont Blanc 4800

A   **Milanc (Milan)**

B a y   o f   B i s c a y

Bordeaux   *Dordogne*

Lot

Grenoble

Ge

Torino (Turin)

Garonne

Toulouse

Nîmes   Avignon

Rhône

Provence

Nice   Monte Carlo

Ge

Marseille   Toulon   **MONACO**

Côte d'Azur   Bas

Corse (Corsica)

A Coruña   *Costa Verde*

Santander

Vigo   *Miño*   *Cordillera Cantábrica*

Bilbao

P Y R É N É E S

Pamplona

ANDORRA

Andorra la Vella

Perpignan

Riviera

Ajaccio

Porto   *Douro*

Valladolid   *Duero*

Salamanca

Zaragoza   Lleida

Ebro

Barcelona

Costa Brava

Tarragona

Sir

Macomer

PORTUGAL

Cordillera Central

Madrid

Cordillera Ibérica

Sardegna (Sardinia)

Caglia

Lisboa (Lisbon)

Evora

Tajo (Tagus)

Guadiana

Badajoz

S P A I N

Albacete

Júcar

Valencia

Costa del Azahar

Islas Baleares

Menorca

Palma   **Mallorca**

Ibiza

M E D I T E R R A N E A N   S E A

Algarve   Huelva

Guadiana

Sierra Morena

Córdoba

Sevilla

Guadalquivir

Jaén

Murcia   *Costa Blanca*

Alicante

Segura

Cartagena

Faro

Cádiz

Sierra Nevada

Málaga

Granada

Costa Calida

Algeciras

Costa del Sol

Gibraltar (UK)

Tanger (Tangier)

Ceuta (Spain)

MOROCCO

Alger (Algiers)

ALGERIA

Europe's rivers and waterways

A guide to the main river cruise routes and ports of Europe, accompanied by diagrammatic maps. Major ports of call come with our list of top sights.

Europe is the world's most developed and best-organised region for river cruises, and it is the heart of the European continent that is in most people's minds when they consider a river cruise. The earliest European river cruises were on the Rhein (Rhine), and later the Danube, and it isn't hard to see why. Accessible and wonderfully scenic, a trip on these great waterways instantly transports the passenger into old Europe, providing a constantly changing perspective on its history and landscapes.

A river cruise provides a unique perspective on the historic landscapes through which these waterways wend their way, past historic cities, medieval towns, fabled villages, forbidding castles, soaring cathedrals, monasteries, churches, romantic châteaux, forests, hills, gardens, vineyards and industrial backdrops (commerce is still conducted along these rivers and waterways, so the scenery, while often magnificent, can also be industrial at times). River cruises can be combined, too, with other interests, from music – in the shape of an evening concert, attendance at a festival or through connections with a celebrated local composer – to tasting events for food and wine aficionados to film nights and more.

River Cloud II by Budapest's Parliament Building.

Major European waterways

But on to the rivers themselves… The Rhein is justly famous for the fabulous scenery along its middle course between the German cities of Mainz and Koblenz, an utterly romantic riverscape of brooding castles perched atop steep hills covered in vineyards. Its major tributaries – the Mosel (Moselle in English), Neckar and Main – are also well-established cruise rivers. Most Danube cruises concentrate on the stretch between Passau on the German/Austrian border via Vienna and Bratislava to the Hungarian capital, Budapest – although there is also plenty of interest along the upper course in southern Germany (now linked to the Rhein via the Main–Danube Canal), as well as the lesser-known lower reaches that traverse the Balkans en route to the Black Sea. The Elbe, running from the Czech Republic through eastern Germany to the North Sea, is the other popular river of Central Europe, and itineraries along it typically explore the beautiful cities of Prague and Dresden.

Other waterways

Away from these major rivers, there is a variety of lesser-known waterways to explore, including the Douro in northern Portugal, the Po in Italy, and the Rhône and Seine in France. A wide range of barge cruises and other trips are also possible – barge cruising is especially popular in France.

Key highlights and kilometre details

Along most (although not all) European rivers, you'll notice white marker boards with black numbers at every navigable kilometre. These generally mark the distance from the river's source to the estuary, although on the Danube it is the other way round.

What follows in this section of the book is an overview of the key highlights you'll see on your cruise, by river, with kilometre details included, if they are likely to be marked.

Sample itineraries

There are many different possible itinerary combinations on European river cruises. Here are some examples of varying lengths, taken from various river cruise brochures.

7-day cruises

Amsterdam to Mainz (Rhein, Mosel)
Amsterdam, Rotterdam, Xanten, Cologne (Köln), Bernkastel, Cochem, Koblenz, Rüdesheim, Mainz
Amsterdam to Amsterdam (Elbe)
Amsterdam, Volendam, Enkhuizen, Kampen, Deventer, Arnhem, Dordrecht, Rotterdam, Amsterdam
Chalon-sur-Saône to Arles (Rhône, Saône)
Chalon-sur-Saône, Mâcon, Trévoux, Lyon, Vienne, Tournon, Viviers, Avignon, Arles
Frankfurt to Frankfurt (Oder)
Frankfurt, Kostrzyn, Gorzów, Kostrzyn, Hohensaaten, Świnoujście, Szczecin, Frankfurt
Paris to Honfleur (Seine)
Paris, Melun, Conflans, Vernon, Rouen, Les Andelys, Caudebec, Honfleur
Venice to Cremona (Po)
Venice, Casalmaggiore, Cremona, Mantua, Pontelagoscuro, Polesella, Chioggia, Venice
Passau to Passau (Danube)
Passau, Dürnstein, Vienna, Esztergom, Budapest, Bratislava, Melk, Grein, Passau
Hamburg to Dresden (Elbe)
Hamburg, Tangermünde, Magdeburg, Wittenberg, Torgau, Dresden, Bad Schandau, Dresden
Potsdam to Potsdam (Elbe)
Potsdam, Genthin, Magdeburg, Dresden, Wittenberg, Magdeburg, Brandenburg, Potsdam
Hannover to Potsdam (Elbe)
Hannover, Braunschweig, Magdeburg, Torgau, Pillnitz, Königstein, Litoměřice, Bad Schandau, Dresden, Meissen, Wittenberg, Burg, Brandenburg, Potsdam
Stralsund to Stralsund (Elbe)
Stralsund, Vitte/Hiddensee, Greifswald-Wieck, Swinemunde, Wolgast, Peenemunde, Lauterbach, Zingst, Stralsund
Berlin to Prague (Elbe)
Berlin, Magdeburg, Dessau, Wittenberg, Torgau, Meissen, Dresden, Bad Schandau, Usti, Prague

10-day cruises

Amsterdam to Basel (Rhein, Mosel)
Amsterdam, Arnhem, Cologne, Koblenz, Zell, Trier, Bernkastel, Alken/Winnigen, Rüdesheim, Worms, Speyer, Strasbourg, Basel
Frankfurt to Mainz (Rhein, Main, Neckar)
Frankfurt, Nierstein, Mannheim, Heilbronn, Bad Wimpfern, Eberbach, Heidelberg, Ottmarsheim, Basel, Strasbourg, Pittersdorf, Mainz
Frankfurt to Prague (Elbe, Oder)
Frankfurt, Küstrin-Kietz, Oderberg, Potsdam, Magde-

The Douro Valley, Portugal.

burg, Wittenberg, Meissen, Dresden, Pillnitz, Königstein, Litoměřice, Melnik, Prague
Frankfurt to Frankfurt (Elbe, Oder, Warthe)
Frankfurt, Küstrin-Kietz, Hohensaaten, Lunow, Stettin, Stralsund, Zingst, Vitte, Dranske Bug, Lauterbach, Wolgast, Stettin, Küstrin, Landsberg, Frankfurt
Frankfurt to Frankfurt (Mosel, Main, Rhein, Saar)
Frankfurt, Mainz, Rüdesheim, Braubach, Koblenz, Cochem, Piesport, Trier, Saarburg, Merzig, Remich, Thionville, Metz, Pont-à-Mousson, Nancy

14-day cruises

Amsterdam to Vienna (Rhein, Danube)
Amsterdam, Cologne, Koblenz, Rüdesheim, Mainz, Wertheim, Würtzburg, Hassfurt, Bamberg, Nuremberg (Nürnberg), Roth, Kelheim, Regensburg, Passau, Melk, Dürnstein, Vienna
Amsterdam to Prague (Rhein, Elbe)
Amsterdam, Xantem, Münster, Braunschweig, Potsdam, Brandenburg, Magdeburg, Wittenberg, Meissen, Dresden, Pillnitz, Königstein, Litoměřice, Melnik, Prague
Amsterdam to Budapest (Rhein, Danube)
Amsterdam, Cologne, Koblenz, Rüdesheim, Mainz, Aschaffenburg, Miltenburg, Karlstadt, Würzburg, Schweinfurt, Bamberg, Nuremberg, Reidenburg, Kelheim, Regensburg, Melk, Dürnstein, Vienna, Ezstergom, Budapest
Passau to Constanţa (Danube)
Passau, Dürnstein, Vienna, Budapest, Kalocsa, Mohacs, Vidin, Rousse, Constanţa
Trier to Budapest (Mosel, Rhein)
Trier, Bernkastel, Cochem, Koblenz, Rüdesheim, Aschaffenburg, Miltenburg, Wertheim, Würzburg, Bamberg, Nuremberg, Berching, Regensburg, Passau, Melk, Vienna, Budapest

16-day cruise

Passau to Vilkovo to Passau (Danube)
Passau, Bratislava, Budapest, Kalocsa, Mohács, Iron Gate Gorge, Giurgiu, Olteniţa, Vilkovo, Somovit, Oriachovo, Iron Gates Gorge, Budapest, Esztergom, Vienna, Dürnstein, Passau

River Danube

Winding its way from the foothills of the Alps to the distant shores of the Black Sea, this majestic waterway has long been a powerful transportation route and is a perennial favourite for river cruises.

The Danube has shaped the history of central Europe over many centuries, as an important transportation route and economic lifeline between the heart of Europe and the Balkans, although, commercially, it is less busy than the Rhein (Rhine). It has halted armies at its banks and been the inspiration for musical serenades, interludes and waltzes. Yet despite Johann Strauss's famous *Blue Danube* waltz, the river, its bed thick with sediment, is actually a murky brown, not blue – although some claim that it can have an azure sheen in the spring and autumn sunshine.

Europe's second-longest river after the Volga, the Danube flows through a range of scenery on the long journey from its source in the Black Forest to the vast delta on the Black Sea, cutting through the wooded hills of Bavaria to the steep terraces and castles of the wine-growing country of Lower Austria, then on to the edge of the Hungarian steppes and into the Balkans. The river has carved deep gorges across ancient mountain ranges, while in other places, meanders across broad, marshy plains. Sightseeing opportunities are numerous, from medieval monasteries to castles, fabulous museums and unspoilt national parks.

Towns and cities of particular interest include Regensburg and Passau in Germany; Linz and Vienna in Austria; Bratislava in Slovakia; Budapest in Hungary, and Vidin in Bulgaria. Other highlights include Dürnstein and Melk in Austria's alluring Wachau Valley and historic Esztergom in Hungary. Most cruises spend at least one night in Vienna and Budapest.

Visitors have a huge choice of itineraries, but the most rewarding is to cruise the river's entire length. There's something fascinating and addictive about the Danube, a promise of discovery and mystery as it flows eastwards through ever-more exotic lands. For many passengers, it is a first into the former Eastern Bloc. Take a shorter voyage as far as Budapest, and you'll find yourself looking longingly at the barges and cruise vessels continuing their journey through the Balkans towards the Black Sea, and vowing to come back and explore Serbia, Romania and Bulgaria.

The course of the Danube

The source of the mighty Danube is marked by an ornate fountain and ornamental pool in the gardens of the Fürstenberg Palace at Donaueschingen in the hills of the Black Forest in southwestern Germany, where the two source streams, the Breg and the Brigach, unite. From here to its marshy delta on the distant Black Sea coast of Romania, the river flows through six countries and forms the border with three more, covering a distance of some 2,888km (1,794 miles). Along the way, some 300 tributaries join the river to bolster its flow. This lengthy course can be divided up into three sections.

The Upper Danube runs for approximately 1,000km (620 miles), stretching from its source to the 'Hungarian Gate', the point near the Slovakian border at which the river crosses into the wide Carpathian Basin. Along this section of the river there is considerable inclination of the river bed, and a rapid current. The first navigable point is at Regensburg.

The Middle Danube is approximately 940km (580 miles) long. From the Hungarian Gate it courses east across the plain until, at the Great Bend, it runs into the hard granite of the Börzsöny and Cserhát Hills,

Rivership on the Danube at Passau.

and swings suddenly south to Budapest. The Danube then meanders across the Great Hungarian Plain, clipping the northeastern corner of Croatia before surging across the plains of Vojvodina in northern Serbia to reach the dramatic Iron Gates Gorge on the Serbia–Romania border. Here, the river cuts through the southern spur of the crescent-shaped Carpathian mountain range.

The Lower Danube is approximately 950km (590 miles) long. The river here is broad, shallow and marshy as it forges across the Wallachian Plain (forming the border of Romania and Bulgaria) to the large delta by the Black Sea.

Main–Danube Canal

In 793, Charlemagne had the vision of establishing a navigable waterway between the Danube and Main rivers, to be called the 'Fossa Carolina'. Thousands of Charlemagne's workers began to dig a navigable trench between the Rezat and Altmühl rivers. But the project failed due to incessant rain and the resulting 'invasion' of water. One section, now called the Karlsgraben, still exists today.

Charlemagne's vision was finally realised on 25 September 1992, when the 170km (106-mile) Main–Danube Canal was finally opened, providing the means for larger craft of up to 3,300 tons to navigate all the way from the North Sea to the Black Sea. The construction of the canal, linking the rivers Rhein, Main and Danube, is one of Europe's largest transport-engineering projects.

Costing 4.7 billion German marks at the time to build, the canal runs through rural Bavaria and rises 406m (1,332ft) via 16 locks, with up to 24m (78ft) lifting height. It was cleverly constructed to blend with the surrounding landscape, and it looks more like a river than a canal. Some 75 million German marks were invested in nature reserves and conservation projects. The canal is 55m (180ft) wide and 4m (13ft) deep, and flows into the Danube at Kelheim in Germany.

Highlights from Bamberg (Germany) to the Black Sea (Romania)

There are many permutations of river cruises on the Danube and many tour operators selling them, but the key stops are summarised below. These are the highlights that can be seen as you cruise downstream, from Bamberg to the Black Sea. Note that, along the Danube, distances are measured not from the source to the estuary, as is customary in Europe, but from the estuary to the source. Another thing to note is that it is possible for the water level of the Danube to be too low for navigation, particularly during the warm, dry summer months, so it's worth checking with your travel provider to make sure that

the water levels are sufficient for your cruise. Conversely, the water level may be too high for vessels to pass under the bridges of the upper section of the Danube beyond Passau.

Bamberg, Germany (Km 3–6.4)

Known for its symphony orchestra and tasty smoked beer *(Rauchbier)*, this medieval city has narrow, winding streets lined with Baroque patrician houses. The old town, the 11th-century cathedral and the *Bamberg Reiter* (Bamberg Horseman) statue were declared a World Heritage Site by Unesco in 1993. The river Regnitz runs through the middle of the city, joining up with the Main 3km (2 miles) downstream.

The tombs of the Holy Roman Emperor Heinrich II and Pope Clement II are housed in the magnificent cathedral. The old Town Hall, or Rathaus, sits in the middle of a twin-arched bridge over the river and is a most impressive sight, and old fishermen's cottages can be seen close by on the river bank. In Schillerplatz, you can see E.T.A. Hoffmann's House, dedicated to the poet, musician and caricaturist, author of *The Tales of Hoffmann*. Bamberg is also known as the home of several well-known breweries.

The scenery as you head south towards Nuremberg is craggy and forested, giving the area the name 'Fränkische Schweiz' (Franconia's Switzerland).

Nuremberg (Nürnberg), Germany (Km 67.8-72)

Half-timbered houses, cobbled streets and Gothic churches with intricate spires and grand gateways are all part of the architectural heritage of Bavaria's second-largest city, as is the almost intact 5km (3-mile) city wall with its 80 defensive watchtowers. Most of the sights are contained within the walls and are easy to find on foot, although you'll need to take a taxi, public transport or the ship's shuttle service for the 15-minute drive from the suburban dock to the old town.

One of the best views of the city and surroundings can be had from the medieval Kaiserburg (Imperial Castle), an imperial residence for 500 years. The famed post-World War II trials of Nuremberg took place at the Palace of Justice.

Peter Henlein invented the world's first pocket watch in Nuremberg in 1510, and the world's first globe was also made here. You can see examples of early watches on display at the German National Museum of Art and Culture (Germanisches Nationalmuseum), the largest museum of its kind in the German-speaking world. Another highlight is the Albrecht Dürer House (Albrecht-Dürer-Haus), with its multimedia show depicting the life of the German painter, printmaker, draughtsman and art theorist, generally regarded as the greatest German Renaissance artist.

In 1835, Germany's first railway line was opened between Nuremberg and Fürth. Today, the Transport Museum (DB Museum) houses many locomotives, wagons and railway accessories.

It's also worth paying a visit to the Schöner Brunnen, a fountain on the Hauptmarkt. This towering, ornamented treasure was carefully covered during World War II to protect it from Allied bombing. A wrought-iron fence encloses it, and there is a bronze ring looped around one part of the fence. Turning this ring three times is supposed to grant the turner's wish. Needless to say, there is usually a line of visitors waiting to be photographed doing just that.

Nuremberg gained notoriety during the 20th century, first as the site of the Nazi party rallies, but later

---

Did you know...?

…that the Danube is the only major European waterway to flow from east to west?

…that the Romans called the Danube the Danuvius, from which its present name is derived?

…that the Greeks sailed up the Danube, in the 7th century? They got as far as the Iron Gates, where the rapids prevented them from further progress.

…that the Danube delta is a paradise for birdwatchers, with over 250 species including the last ibises and pelicans in Europe?

…that in 1989 an unprecedented 50,000 people assembled outside parliament in Budapest? They were part of the environmental movement protesting against plans for the construction of a hydro-electric dam on the River Danube.

…that in 1812, in Vienna, a vessel named *Caroline* became the first steam-driven vessel on the Danube? Its introduction was significant, and meant that, for the first time, vessels could move upstream under their own power. Prior to this date, all riverships moving upstream could only do so by being towed

– first by men, then by horses, then by locomotives; hence the term 'towpath'. Many towpaths still exist along both sides of the Danube, and today provide excellent pathways for cycling and walking.

…that the great wine route of the Wachau spans some 32km (20 miles) along the banks of the Danube, in Austria? The steep, terraced vineyards soak up the summer sun, yet the nights are cooler, making an ideal climate for a balanced wine, although the work of harvesting the grapes is a tortuous one. Many growers own small parcels of land – a hectare or two – and so making wines from the variety and quality of grapes provided is not an easy task for the region's wine makers.

…that in 2002 the Danube reached its highest level for over 500 years?

…that only about 30 percent of the Danube is truly free flowing?

…that sailing between Bamberg and Kelheim in Bavaria takes you over the Continental Divide?

Regensburg's Cathedral Square.

when the famed post-World War II trials took place (from 20 November 1945 until 1 October, 1946) at the Palace of Justice. Nuremberg was chosen because the Palace of Justice was spacious (it had 22,000 sq m/236,813 sq ft of space, with about 530 offices and about 80 courtrooms; war damage to it was minimal; and a large, undestroyed prison was part of the complex) following agreement between the four major powers at the time, although Russia had initially wanted the trials to be held in Berlin.

Regensburg, Germany (Km 2381–2377)

Founded by Marcus Aurelius over 2,000 years ago, Regensburg is one of the best-preserved of all European medieval cities, having escaped the bombing of World War II, and is the oldest city on the entire length of the Danube; the first Roman camp here has been dated by historians to AD 70, and parts of the original Roman wall can still be seen. The city's 12th- to 14th-century Patricians' Houses are architecturally fascinating, and are reminiscent of the medieval tower-houses of San Gimignano in Tuscany. Riverships dock close to the centre, within walking distance of the main sights, and tours are usually a half-day, with free time afterwards.

Visit the Stone Bridge, built between 1135 and 1146 and, with 16 arches, a masterpiece of medieval engineering. The cathedral, regarded as the best example of Gothic architecture in Bavaria, has some superb stained-glass windows in its twin towers, which were added between 1859 and 1861 at the request of King Ludwig I of Bavaria, and a tranquil 15th-century cloister.

The heart of the city is Neupfarrplatz, which presents Regensburg's history in microcosm. Over the years it has been the home of Roman officers, the Jewish quarter, the marketplace, the scene of riots and protests, and of the mass burning of books by the Nazis. Between 1995 and 1998, massive excavations revealed Gothic and Romanesque synagogues, remains of the old Jewish houses and a treasure trove of gold coins.

Some 11km (7 miles) downstream from Regensburg, just outside Donaustauf, look out for a white classical temple with Doric columns on the hillside, approached by a grand staircase. This is Valhalla (Walhalla), home of the gods in German mythology – in this case, built by Ludwig I in the 1830s as a kind of Teutonic Hall of Fame, and a copy of the Parthenon in Athens.

Passau, Germany (Km 2210)

The starting point for many cruises on the Danube, Passau, located 290m (950ft) above sea level, marks the border between Germany and Austria. Ships dock right in the centre, although new berths for four riverships have been constructed at Landau, about 2km (1.25 miles) downriver from Passau, to ease the congestion that occurs at weekends, when many passengers embark and disembark.

Somewhat fancifully dubbed 'the Venice of the Danube' because of the three rivers that converge

The pretty town of Melk.

here (it is also sometimes called Dreiflüssestadt – the city of three rivers) and the Italianate style of the architecture, Passau has been a bishopric for 1,200 years. St Stephen's magnificent Baroque-style cathedral houses the world's largest cathedral organ; it has 17,774 pipes in three banks, and 233 registers, or stops. Liszt wrote his *Hungarian Coronation Mass* for this cathedral in 1857.

Passau's location as the confluence of the three rivers, the Danube, Ilz and Inn, means it often suffers from flooding. The tower of the town hall shows the high-water marks, the highest recorded being in 1501, 1595 and 1954.

Linz, Austria (Km 2139-2127)

Although the Renaissance and Baroque centre of the city, which is the provincial capital of Upper Austria, is attractive (Linz was designated a 'European City of Culture' in 2009), Linz is an industrial city, known for its chemical and metallurgical industries. The classic *Linzer Torte*, with a pastry base, redcurrant jam filling and crisscross pattern on the almond-encrusted top, was invented here by Bavarian baker Konrad Vogel in 1822. You can taste the real thing in one of the many street cafés in the beautifully preserved Old Town.

The cobblestoned main square is also the site of the Trinity Column – a 20m (66ft) -high white marble Baroque-style sculpture by Sebastian Stumpfegger to a design by Antonio Beduzzi; erected in 1723, it is dedicated to commemorate the dangers of war (1704), fire (1712) and the plague (1713).

Riverships dock next to the Lentos Art Museum – a magnificent glass structure housing a superb art collection.

Linz is also known for its connections with the composer Anton Bruckner, who was born at Ansfelden (now a suburb of Linz) in 1824, and died in 1896 in Vienna. Mozart also lived here for a while in 1783 as a guest of Count Thunn, during which time he composed his *Linz Symphony*. Alterdom, the magnificent baroque cathedral is where Anton Bruckner served as organist.

Melk, Austria (Km 2037.5–2037)

The mustard-yellow Benedictine Abbey of Melk, perched on a steep hill overlooking the river and visible from afar, is one of the highlights of a Danube cruise. It was founded in the year 1089 by Leopold II and dominates the town, though at the same time blending in beautifully with the surrounding landscape. It was completely reconstructed in Baroque style in the early 18th century by its architect, Jakob Prandtauer, who died before its completion. The imposing abbey was completed by Prandtauer's relation and assistant, Joseph Mungengast.

The imperial rooms of the abbey once accommodated such renowned figures as Emperor Charles VI and Maria Theresa, Pope Pius VI and Napoleon – all presently immortalised in a permanent wax museum. Paul Troger frescoes can be found in the library, which houses over 2,000 manuscripts. A Gutenberg Bible, which was on display here for many years, has since been sold, and can now be viewed in the Yale Library in the US. The balconies command sweeping views of the Danube. A short organ concert is typically held for anyone on a shore excursion. The organ, built by Gregor Hradetzky (Krems), has three keyboards, 45 registers (stops) and 3,553 pipes.

Dürnstein, Austria (Km 2008)

Beyond Melk, the Danube carves its way through the beautiful, Unesco-protected Wachau Valley, a 30km (18-mile) section of steep, terraced slopes of vineyards and forested hills, which turn incredible shades of red and gold in the autumn. It is regarded by many as one of the most scenic stretches of the river. In its midst is Dürnstein, discernible from some distance away because of the jagged outline of the ruined castle on the hilltop, and the unusual Wedgwood-blue-and-white Baroque monastery tower squatting like a giant pepperpot on the river bank.

A steep one-hour walk/climb from Dürnstein itself leads to the Babenberg Duke Leopold's Kuenringerburg Castle. Richard the Lionheart was incarcerated here for more than a year in the 12th century. He was released after paying an incredible 100,000 marks – truly a king's ransom in those days. There's not much of the castle to see nowadays, but the views along the Wachau Valley and over the town below are breathtaking.

Krems, Austria (Km 2003–2002)

This university town, together with its former sister town of Stein (both are located close to Dürnstein at the eastern end of the Wachau wine-growing district), grew wealthy as a result of trade in iron, grain, wine and salt. The town is an important example of successful restoration work and the centre has been a Unesco World Heritage Site since 2000. Krems was the home of the painter Martin Johann ('Kremser') Schmidt, who created numerous works in the churches of Austria.

One nearby attraction is the Stift Göttweig, an abbey set on a hillside. Its playful Benedictine architecture – its corner towers, onion domes and pastel-coloured facade – has earned it the title of 'Austria's Monte Casino', after the Italian abbey where the Benedictine Order was first established.

Vienna (Wien), Austria (Km 1933–1928)

Vienna (Wien), located 170m (558ft) above sea level (it used to flood regularly in the winter), is built in a very strategic location, at the junction of routes from both east to west and north to south.

For centuries, the city was the seat of the mighty Habsburg dynasty, and is also the birthplace of Schubert, and of much of the music of Mozart (he composed his greatest operas and symphonies here), Beethoven and Strauss. The city exudes romance at any time of year, with its beautiful parks and Baroque palaces, elegant shops and legendary coffee houses. Most cruises spend at least one night here, giving plenty of opportunity to see the sights, attend a performance at the opera, listen to the Vienna Boys' Choir or admire the white Lipizzaner horses at the Spanish Riding School.

The Danube does not pass through the centre of Vienna – instead it runs through the northeast part of the city. Most river cruise vessels stop at the Vienna Shipping Centre (Schiffahrtszentrum), about 3km (2 miles) from the old centre. The compact, historic centre is encircled by the Ringstrasse, inside which most of the main sights are located. The following is a list of the city's top attractions:

Stephansdom: St Stephen's Cathedral, with its distinctive roof, is one of Vienna's most famous landmarks and one of the greatest Gothic structures in Europe. The interior is rich in woodcarvings, altars and paintings. Climb the steps of the south tower for a breathtaking view of the city.

Museum Quarter: The Museums Quartier is a giant cultural complex including the Museum of Modern Art (MUMOK) and the Leopold Museum, with its wonderful collection of 19th- and 20th-century art, including work by Egon Schiele, Gustav Klimt and Oskar Kokoschka. At the centre of the complex, the Kunsthalle holds temporary exhibitions.

Staatsoper: Vienna's magnificent opera house was constructed in the 1860s, and rebuilt in 1945 after

---

Christmas market cruises

There's nothing quite like a river cruise in Europe at Christmas, when the twinkling fairylights and the seasonal aromas of cinnamon, gingerbread, roasting chestnuts and *Glühwein* (mulled wine) at Christmas markets in most cities and towns along the Danube, Rhein (Rhine) and Elbe really put you in the mood for the holiday.

Along the Danube, Vienna has a number of Christmas markets, and the window dressing of the stores along the wide Kärntnerstrasse is among the best in the world. The city's Christmas decorations are beautiful, too. Nuremberg hosts perhaps the most famous Christmas market of all. Located in the old walled section of the city, it is the oldest in Germany, dating back to the 17th century. Rows of specially constructed stalls provide the old-world setting and a magical atmosphere.

Along the Rhein, Cologne's magnificent Gothic cathedral provides an impressive backdrop to that city's Christmas market. Rüdesheim's Christkindlmarkt (Christmas market) is one of Germany's largest, with more than 100 stalls. Regensburg, often a starting or finishing point for several riverships, has its Christmas market in the town's delightful square.

AmaWaterways, CroisiEurope, Uniworld and Viking River Cruises are among the companies that offer cruises to the Christmas markets of Europe.

suffering a direct hit in a bombing raid. It was inaugurated in 1869 with Mozart's *Don Giovanni*. The main facade is elaborately decorated with frescoes depicting *The Magic Flute*. Once a year the stage and orchestra stalls turn into a giant dance floor for the Vienna Opera Ball. If your rivership stays overnight in Vienna, you could consider an evening out at the opera, although you may need to reserve well in advance for this.

Secession Building: The Secession Building was built as a 'temple of art' to plans by Joseph Maria Olbrich in 1897. Gustav Klimt designed the *Beethoven Frieze*, on display on the lower floor, a visual interpretation of Beethoven's *Ninth Symphony*. The cubic foyer is crowned by a dome of 3,000 gilt laurel leaves. Over the entrance is the motto 'To Each Time its Art, to Art its Freedom', a riposte from the Secession artists to the conservative Academy of Fine Arts.

Schloss Schönbrunn: A short distance from the inner city lies the Schönbrunn Palace, the imperial summer residence. Leopold I wished to build a palace to rival Versailles but financial difficulties stalled his plans. It was not until 1743 that Empress Maria Theresa employed Nikolaus Pacassi to build the fabulous palace we see today. In the formal grounds are the Baroque zoo, the Palm House and the graceful Gloriette, a neoclassical colonnade perched on the crest of a hill.

Prater: The Prater, an open fairground and amusement park, is a favourite place of relaxation for the Viennese. Its main attraction is the Riesenrad, the giant Ferris wheel that was immortalised in the 1949 film *The Third Man*. This extensive stretch of parkland and woodland extends for almost 5km (3 miles).

Karlsplatz: Otto Wagner's two wonderfully elegant entrance pavilions for the Stadtbahn on Karlsplatz date from 1894 and are prime examples of Jugendstil (Austrian Art Nouveau). For the designs of the pavilions, he combined a green iron framework with marble slabs and gilded sunflower decoration, and pioneered a new form of architecture in which functionality and simplicity of ornament were the priority.

Kunsthistorisches Museum: Several famous artists helped create the interior of the Kunsthistorisches Museum. A huge number of art treasures amassed by the Habsburgs are on display, including a fine collection of ancient Egyptian and Greek Art, and works by many of the great European masters.

Belvedere: The Belvedere, a palace of sumptuous proportions, was built between 1714 and 1723 for Prince Eugene of Savoy. It is in fact two palaces, the Upper and Lower Belvedere, joined by terraced gardens. Today it houses three museums containing works of Austrian and European art and sculpture.

Hofburg: The Hofburg was the winter residence of the ruling Habsburgs. Within the confines of this vast and impressive imperial palace are the Spanish Riding School and the sleek Lipizzaner horses, and the Burgkapelle, where the Vienna Boys' Choir sing Sunday Mass. Notable collections housed here are the Collection of Court Porcelain and Silver and the Imperial Treasury, containing crown jewels and ecclesiastical treasures. The palatial National

Vienna at night.

Bratislava's 16th-century castle with earlier fortifications.

Library, also in the complex, contains more than 2 million manuscripts, printed books, maps and musical scores.

Bratislava, Slovakia (Km 1869)

Located right at the heart of central Europe close to Slovakia's borders with Austria and Hungary, Bratislava has changed its identity, and its name, more times than it cares to remember. In Habsburg times, the city was Pressburg to the Germans and Pozsony to the Magyars. Renamed Bratislava after the creation of Czechoslovakia following World War I, it emerged from the communist years to become capital of the new state of Slovakia in 1993. An ambitious rebuilding and restoration programme has transformed the city. The picturesque old town is clustered around a low hill on the left bank of a broad stretch of the river. The Danube is wide here – about 300m (984ft) across.

Highlights include the castle, built in the 16th century on top of earlier fortifications, the picturesque Old Town with fabulous Baroque palaces, St Martin's Cathedral, with an unusual spire topped by a tiny Hungarian crown, St Michael's Gate, the city's only surviving medieval gateway, and Pálffyho Palace, where, in 1762, the six-year old Wolfgang Amadeus Mozart gave a performance. This distinguished building now houses the Academy of Fine Arts.

Esztergom, Hungary (Km 1718.5)

Formerly the Roman settlement of Gran, Esztergom is located in the foothills of the Pilis Mountains, right on the border with Slovakia. Esztergom is famous for its vast, neoclassical cathedral, flanked by a red-brick castle, which towers over the city. The giant dome is one of the world's largest and can be seen for miles around. The castle itself was the seat of government for Hungary's kings and queens for more than 300 years when the Hungarian lands further south were held by the Ottoman Turks, while the town was the centre of the Catholic Church in Hungary, which flourished during the reign of Louis I (1342–82), a role it retains today. The Gothic-style cathedral was built in the 19th century to replace its predecessor, ransacked by the Turks in 1543 after they pushed northwards, although the red-marble Bakócz Chapel inside survived. Both Beethoven and Liszt performed here.

Budapest, Hungary (Km 1647)

Budapest is the perfect destination for river cruises, because the Danube flows right through the heart of the city for some 10km (6 miles), with Buda (and Obuda) on the west bank and Pest on the east bank connected by eight bridges. Riverships dock in a superbly convenient (and also picturesque) location in the very heart of the city.

Often referred to by the local inhabitants as the 'Pearl of the Danube', Budapest goes beyond the at-

Viennese coffee houses

The Viennese coffee-house tradition is deeply rooted in the country's culture and history, dating back over 300 years. Gentry and intellectuals mingled in the shady and fashionable *Kaffeehaus*. People take their coffee seriously here and there are names for every shade, from black to white. Coffee is served in a wide variety of ways, often with the addition of alcohol or whipped cream, though always with an obligatory glass of water.

tractions of its fabulous, romantic riverine setting. It is the cultural heart of the nation and a city of international standing, yet it still possesses some of its late 19th-century flair and romance. Nostalgia can be found in the sumptuous spas offering the simple pleasure of bathing in thermal waters, and in the grand old coffee houses, still frequented by artists of all backgrounds and interests.

Budapest marks the starting point for the second half of river cruises (typically of 14 days or more) that travel all the way to the Danube Delta at the Black Sea.

City highlights include the following:

Parliament Building: Strongly reminiscent of the Palace of Westminster in London, the Parliament Building (Országház) is one of Budapest's most famous sights. The neo-Gothic pile, which was completed in 1902, extends along the Danube for some 268m (292 yds).

Chain Bridge: When it was completed in 1849, the Chain Bridge (Széchenyi Lánchíd) linked the two halves of the city, Buda and Pest, for the first time (there are now eight Danube bridges in the Hungarian capital, as well as more on the outskirts). Count István Széchenyi, the 19th-century reformer and innovator, brought in engineers from Great Britain to construct the graceful span, which is beautifully floodlit at night.

Gellért Hill: Rising steeply from the Buda riverfront, the craggy, wooded heights of Gellért Hill (Gellért-hegy) can be seen from almost anywhere in the city (not least from where the riverships dock). Naturally, the views are tremendous, extending as far as the distant Matra mountains on the Slovak border on a clear day.

Heroes' Square: At the end of Andrássy út, one of Pest's major thoroughfares, is the wide open space of Heroes' Square (Hősök tere), with its 36m (118ft) Millennium Monument, erected in 1896 to mark 1,000 years of the Magyar state. The square is flanked by the Palace of Art and Museum of Fine Arts and behind the former is the world's largest hourglass, the Timewheel, unveiled in May 2004 to mark Hungary's admission into the European Union. Some 8m (26ft) in diameter, the structure 'turns' once a year to send the sand running anew.

Váci utca: Long, narrow and pedestrianised for much of its length, Váci utca (pronounced vah-tsee ooh-tsa) is a busy and fashionable shopping street, which also has a range of bars, cafés and restaurants. At its northern end is the square of Vörösmarty tér. At No. 7 is one of the city's main meeting places and home to Gerbeaud, doyen of the city's prosperous café society since 1884 and a major tourist attraction in itself.

Museum of Fine Arts: Hungary's pre-eminent art gallery, the Museum of Fine Arts (Szépművészeti Múzeum) has a huge collection, focusing on European art from 1300–1800. Highlights include works by the Spanish school including El Greco, Goya and Velázquez.

Matthias Church: The focal point of the old town of Buda, high above the river, the Matthias Church (Mátyás-templom) is named after Hungary's most popular medieval king, Mátyás Corvinus Hunyadi (1458–90). The Habsburg emperor Franz Josef I was crowned king of Hungary here in 1867. The unusual geometric patterns on the roof, the stained-glass windows and other details date from the 19th century, but parts of the building are far older. Outside the church in Trinity Square (Szentháromság tér) is the mighty equestrian statue of St Stephen.

Fisherman's Bastion: Overlooking the Danube and just in front of the Matthias Church, the fairytale spires and turrets of the Fisherman's Bastion (Halászbástya) afford the classic view of Budapest. Built onto the castle walls in the early 20th century purely for ornamental reasons, the monument's name is a reference to the fishermen who heroically defended the ramparts here against invaders in the 18th century.

Hungarian National Museum: The large Hungarian National Museum (Magyar Nemzeti Múzeum) is the most important museum in the city. St Stephen's Crown, the symbol of Hungarian sovereignty, was returned here in 1978, having been stolen by the Wehrmacht in World War II. Inside, amid monumental architectural and ornamental details, the whole story of Hungary unfolds – from prehistory right up to the 21st century. On display are prehistoric remains, ancient jewellery and tools, Roman mosaics, a 17th-century Turkish tent fitted out with grand carpets, and a Baroque library. There is some notable royal regalia, although the crown, orb, sceptre and sword have been moved to the Parliament Building.

Central Market Hall: A good place for souvenirs is the upstairs section of the cavernous Central Market Hall (Nagy Vásárcsarnok) at the Pest end of Freedom Bridge.

Gellért Baths: At the southern edge of Gellért-hegy, the Gellért Baths (Gellért gyógyfürdő) comprise medicinal baths as well as regular swimming pools, all decorated in opulent Art Nouveau style. The unisex indoor pool has a vaulted glass ceiling and Roman-style carved columns, while the thermal baths feature marble statues, fine mosaics and glazed tiles.

Kalocsa, Hungary (Km 1515.4)

Kalocsa is a pretty town in the middle of the Puszta region, located on a terrace overlooking the Danube, 10km (6 miles) from the river itself (passengers are taken by coach) and famous for growing the paprika that gives Hungarian goulash its distinctive flavour. It's an important agricultural and tourism centre, surrounded by pepper fields, and the shops are packed with paprika souvenirs, from painted eggs to colourful pottery and embroidered linen.

Some 1,000 years ago, Kalocsa was the seat of the archdiocese, and the Archbishop's Palace, whose permanent exhibition of ecclesiastical relics and treasure is open to the public. The House of Folk Art Museum and the Károly Visky Museum feature the colourful local painting for which the region is famous, while for something different, the world's only Paprika Museum documents the history of paprika production in Hungary, from growing to different pepper types and the processing technique.

Belgrade (Beograd), Serbia (Km 1170)

Belgrade, capital of Serbia (and of the former Yugoslavia), is strategically located on the southern edge of the great Carpathian Basin, at the confluence of the River Danube and River Sava, and has a turbulent history. It is one of the oldest cities in Europe and nowadays forms the largest urban area in southeastern Europe after Athens. The ravages of communism and damage from the war in 1999 are still visible, and the city is noticeably less colourful (and wealthy) than Budapest, but vibrant nonetheless, with a busy, pedestrianised centre.

Budapest's Chain Bridge and Parliament Building.

Lower Danube

Iron Gates Gorge (Km 949.7)

The Iron Gates (Porţile de Fier) are a highlight of any Danube itinerary. The river cuts through the southern spur of the Carpathian Mountains where they meet the northern foothills of the Balkan ranges, forming an emphatic natural boundary between Serbia and Romania. The 'true' Iron Gates is in fact a single narrow gorge, which boats enter at Km 949, but the name is generally given to the entire stretch of river between Km 1,059 and Km 942 – a series of gorges linked by wider stretches of river. There are towering cliffs on either side, although these are less impressive than they were before the river level was raised in the 1970s. Parts of the river bed here are among the world's deepest, with depths up to 60m (196ft).

At the eastern end of the Iron Gates, at Km 942, is the enormous Djerdap Hydro-electric power station complex. There are actually two power stations (one belonging to Serbia and the other belonging to Romania), two double-level locks, and a barrage supporting a railway and road bridge. The whole project involved much resiting of infrastructure, the reconstruction of 13 river harbours and the relocation of many inhabitants (8,400 within Serbia and 14,500 within Romania) at the time of its construction, which, when completed in 1972, had cost an estimated $500 million. The dam has raised the Danube's water level by some 33m (100ft), and removed the treacherous currents and whirlpools at a stroke. On the negative side, the higher water has hugely diminished the grandeur of the landscape, obliterated a number of historic towns and villages (notably the Turkish island enclave of Ada Kaleh, a short distance downstream from Orşova), and the river's diminished flow is no longer sufficient to flush pollution – chemical toxins and other waste – downriver and out to sea.

The first gorge is the Golubac, 14km (9 miles) in length. The town of Golubac was flooded by the power-station project, but nine massive towers – the ruins of a castle that was, for more than two and a half centuries, a base for the Turks for their raids to the north and west until they left in 1688 – can still be seen on the Serbian side. After a broader section, the second gorge – the Gospodin Vir – extends for a further 15km (10 miles). Beyond is the famous Kazan gorge, 19km (13 miles) long, where the river flows between towering cliffs soaring 700m (2,300ft) through a chasm only 150m (492ft) across.

Vidin, Bulgaria (Km 790)

Vidin, on the Bulgarian side of the river, occupies the site of an old Celtic settlement and is one of the country's oldest towns, dating back to Roman times. The dramatic fortress of Baba Vida, built in the 14th century, is the best-preserved example of medieval architecture in the country and looms impressively on the bank of the Danube as you approach. In fact, the whole town used to be famous for its fairytale minarets, towers and domes, although its skyline suffered from the building of ugly concrete apartment blocks during the communist era. Most tours combine Baba Vida with a visit to the amazing village of Belogradchik, cut directly into sandstone rock.

Bucharest (Bucureşti), Romania

There is no kilometre marking for Bucharest, the capital of Romania, but that's because the city is actually located somewhat inland from the river (about a one-hour coach journey from Rousse). A visit to Nicolae Ceauşescu's truly monumental Parliament Palace, the world's second largest administrative building (after the Pentagon), may be included on your excursion itinerary. Just a handful of the 3,000 rooms can be visited. You will probably also the see Revolution (formerly Royal Palace) Square, where the famous riots started that led to the collapse of the communist dictatorship in December 1989.

Rousse (Ruse), Bulgaria (Km 495)

Rousse is the largest and most important river port in Bulgaria, set in gorgeous, rolling countryside brilliant with sunflowers in summer and golden wheatfields in autumn. The city itself was once the garrison of the Roman Danube fleets and was known as Sexaginta Prista – 'Sixty Ships'. Today, it's an industrial centre, and across the river you can see the grim-looking factories of Giurgiu in Romania.

The Iron Gates Gorge.

Most of the attractions are outside the centre. A short drive away is the Rusenski Lom National Park, where a tributary of the Danube has carved a sheer-sided gorge through the uplifted limestone. Tours include a visit to the imposing Basarbovo Monastery, sprawling across a steep hilltop.

Giurgiu, Romania (Km 493)

Capital of Giurgiu County, southern Romania, the city is located about 65km (40 miles) south of Bucharest. Romanian crude oil is loaded here for shipping, via a pipeline that connects it with the oil fields of Ploesti. A bi-level, combined highway and railway bridge, the 2,224m (7,296ft) -long Friendship Bridge (Km 489), one of the longest bridges in Europe, which connects Romania with Bulgaria, was opened in 1954.

Olteniţa, Romania (Km 430)

This little town is home to a building yard for riverships. In former times, however, it was a quarantine station.

Constanţa, Romania (Km 0)

The official end of the River Danube. This port city, reached via the Danube–Black Sea Canal, is the capital of southeastern Romania, is the country's principal seaport and its most important commercial centre, and is located about 200km (125 miles) east of Bucharest. It is slowly being modernised. At journey's end in Constanţa, riverships tie up at the Gare Maritime in the heart of the city.

The Rhein and its tributaries

The Rhein (Rhine) is a magnificent river for cruising, with its vineyard-clad slopes and generous peppering of romantic castles. The Mosel, Neckar, Main and Saar tributaries hold plenty of interest too.

'Old Father Rhein', as the Germans lovingly call it, is Europe's most important commercial waterway, flowing for some 1,320km (820 miles) from source to estuary. The Rhein (Rhine) has long been Europe's busiest river, with some of the densest shipping traffic in the world, yet its waters and turbulent past have inspired poets and romantics for centuries. The mystery of the river comes alive in the folklore tales of Lorelei and the Nibelung, the music of Wagner and Beethoven, and in the countless legends surrounding the fairytale castles and fortresses that line its banks.

Although it is essentially seen as a German river, the Rhein crosses several international boundaries, passing through no fewer than six countries – Austria, France, Germany, Liechtenstein, the Netherlands and Switzerland – on its journey from the Alps to the North Sea. Although the stretch known as the Middle Rhein, or the Romantic Rhein, with its towering cliffs, castles, vineyards and dense forests, is the best-known section, the river has many other faces as it flows along the German–French border, or cuts a course across the flat, agricultural landscapes of the Netherlands in the final stages of its journey north.

Together with the Bodensee (Lake Constance), the Rhein forms a reservoir of drinking water for approximately 30 million Germans. It irrigates mile upon mile of vineyards. It has been an essential transport route through Europe since prehistoric times and has given rise to a string of prosperous towns and cities along its banks. A cruise on the Rhein is rarely without something to draw the eye. Heavily laden barges chug their way north or south, pleasure cruisers ply the waters from one beauty spot to the next, and hikers, swimmers and cyclists enjoy the river's banks and beaches. In parts, there is abundant birdlife to spot, spectacular castles to identify and bridges, statues and monuments all charting the river's history.

On the Rhein at Cologne.

Did you know...?

…that the name 'Rhein' comes from the Celtic word *renos*, meaning 'raging flow'?

…that there are more castles in the Rhein Valley than in any other valley in the world?

…that since 1855 there has been a signal-box for river shipping at the top of the Mice Tower (Mäuseturm) near Schloss Ehrenfels (Ehrenfels Castle) on the Rhein, just downstream from Rüdesheim?

…that the composer Schumann (1810–56) attempted to drown himself in the Rhein in 1854? He lived in Düsseldorf for four years and was appointed conductor of the municipal orchestra in 1850.

…that the Roman Emperor Caracalla used to go to the spa at Baden-Baden to cure his rheumatism?

…that salmon once thrived in the Rhein? Sadly, dams and industrial pollution have all but killed salmon fishing. In 2001, despite €20 million having been spent on breeding wild salmon, only 60 fish were detected in the river; some €50 billion was spent in cleaning up the polluted river. Compare this with the more than 250,000 wild salmon recorded caught on the Rhein in 1885 and you can see why wild salmon (so much better tasting than the farmed variety) are now a rarity.

…that the first stone bridge across the Mosel was built in 1363 for pilgrims on their way to Rome?

…that in Switzerland, 25 percent of all freight arrives by water?

…that the German for 'lock', as in watergate, is *die Schleuse*?

The course of the Rhein

The source of the Rhein is a mountain brook that trickles out from the craggy Gotthard Massif in southeastern Switzerland. This is where two small streams, the Hinterrhein and Vorderrhein, unite to form the Alpine Rhein (Alpernrhein). The waters then flow along the borders of Liechtenstein and Austria and into the beautiful sweep of Lake Constance, emerging from the other side of the lake to tumble over the Rhein Falls, Europe's biggest waterfall, near Schaffhausen in Switzerland, where the river plunges 21m (69ft). The river is joined here by the Aar, doubling its volume.

The next stretch, known as the High Rhein (Hochrhein), forms the Swiss–German frontier. At Basel, the river executes a sharp right turn, the 'Rhein Knee', to head northwards, cutting a course through a broad valley along the French–German border. Close to the city of Karlsruhe, the French border is left behind and the river enters its German heartland. After holding a northerly course for some distance, it twists to the west between Mainz and Bingen, an area known as the Rheingau, before forcing its way through the Binger Loch (Hole of Bingen), a steep gorge which marks the beginning of the Middle Rhein (Mittelrhein), or Romantic Rhein. The river then flows northwest through the Uplands (Rheinisches Schiefergebirge) along its most scenic stretch with steep vine-clad slopes, deep gorges and dramatic castles towering over the water.

Below Bonn the river becomes the Lower Rhein (Niederrhein). It then travels through the flat territory of Germany's heavily industrialised Westphalia and the neighbouring Netherlands, where it divides into a number of delta arms, the principal ones being the Lek and the Waal, before finally disgorging into the North Sea.

The Rhein is fed by a number of tributaries, the most important being major rivers in their own right, such as the Main and the Mosel. River cruises operate on both of these, usually in conjunction with the Middle Rhein, and also on the pretty Neckar, which flows through one of Germany's biggest tourist attractions, the city of Heidelberg.

Castles on the Rhein

There are many castles and castle ruins along the banks of the Rhein, most dating to the Middle Ages or earlier, and legends, deeds of chivalry, internment and torture of every kind are connected with almost every one of them. Many were built by the feudal lords to protect their land; others were built to take advantage of the views of the traffic on the Rhein and later became toll-collection points. Between Mainz and Bonn, especially in the narrow slate gorge

Rheinstein Castle.

between Bingen and Koblenz, a distance of only 56km (35 miles), there are more castles than in any other river valley in the world.

The following castles can all be clearly seen from a rivership as it motors quietly along the Rhein. Many are in excellent condition and have been converted into hotels, although some have fallen into ruin.

Bonn to Koblenz

Km 647.6 (right): Godesburg Castle
Km 645.3 (left): Königswinter Castle
Km 643.7 (left): Drachenburg Castle and Drachenfels Castle (ruin)
Km 640 (right): Rolandseck Castle (ruin)
Km 623.9 (left): Arenfels Castle (now a hotel)
Km 621.9 (right): Rheineck Castle (now a hotel)
Km 618 (left): Hammerstein Castle (ruin)
Km 592.3 (left): Ehrenbreitstein Castle (now a youth hostel)

Koblenz to Bingen

Km 585.2 (left): Lahneck Castle
Km 585.2 (right): Stolzenfels Castle (now a hotel)
Km 580 (left): Marksburg Castle
Km 556.9 (right): Rheinfels Castle
Km 556.5 (right): Sterrenberg Castle and Liebenstein Castle
Km 555.9 (left): Katz Castle (now a hotel)
Km 549.1 (right): Schönburg Castle
Km 546.5 (left): Gutenfels Castle
Km 543.1 (right): Stahleck Castle (with a water-filled moat and inner wall)
Km 541 (right): Fürstenberg Castle (ruin)
Km 539.8 (left): Nollig Castle (ruin)
Km 539.4 (right): Heimburg Castle
Km 537.4 (right): Sooneck Castle
Km 534.5 (right): Reichenstein Castle (in use today as a hotel)
Km 533 (right): Rheinstein Castle
Km 530.4 (left): Ehrenfels Castle (ruin)

Rhein and tributaries

Key cruising routes

There are four principal routes for river cruises along the Rhein: from Cologne to Mainz; along the Rhein and Mosel, from Koblenz to Trier (from the source to the mouth); along the Saar, from Trier to Mettlach; and along the Neckar, from Ludwigshafen (opposite Mannheim) to Stuttgart.

Principal tributaries

The Main: Some 524km (325 miles) long, the Main starts at Kulmbach from the confluence of the brooks known as the White and Red Main, which have their sources in the Fichtel Mountains and in the Franconian Alb. The riverships typically cruise on the section between Frankfurt and Würzburg, passing forested hills, lush meadows and historic towns.

The Mosel (Moselle, in English): At 535km (332 miles) long, the Mosel is the longest of the Rhein's tributaries. It is narrower and, some say, prettier or more intimate than the Rhein. It rises in the Vosges Mountains at some 735m (2,410ft) above sea level. Mosel means 'little Maas' in French, a reference to the fact that, in prehistoric times, its bed joined that of the Maas. The river was only developed into a navigable waterway as recently as 1964, an event made possible by the signing of a contract between France, Germany and Luxembourg, following which a system of 14 locks was constructed.

The Mosel twists and turns in a series of sharp bends as it cuts its way through a deep valley, the sides lined with steeply terraced vineyards, before merging with the Rhein at Koblenz, at an altitude some 676m (2,218ft) lower than its source. On its journey it forms the border between Luxembourg and Germany for a distance of 36km (22 miles). The Mosel is navigable from Thionville in France to Koblenz, a distance of 270km (165 miles).

The Neckar: This is one of the longest tributaries to flow into the Rhein. Its source is in the Baar in a region between the Black Forest and the Swabian Alb (the region in which the Danube also has its source), to the east of the Rhein in Baden-Württemberg, north of Lake Constance. The river is 367km (228 miles) long and navigable for 203km (126 miles), although some stretches have canals that enable cargo

Ships' castles

A castle, in the construction terminology of ocean-going ships, is a structure or area that is raised above the main deck, for combat or work purposes (similar to early fortress turrets). You'll find the forecastle and sterncastle – or aftercastle – at the bow and stern of a vessel. The first known castle aboard a vessel was in Roman times, when they were placed amidships (in the centre) to afford vantage points in skirmishes at sea.

An Amsterdam canal.

vessels to make their way through the 26 sets of locks as far upstream as Plochingen.

The Neckar flows through some of Germany's most beautiful countryside, castles guarding every curve of the river, and vines and forests sloping right down to the banks. The whole valley is one of Germany's great summer playgrounds, with pleasure boats, canoes, punts and dinghies out on the water, and cyclists and hikers enjoying the scene from the banks.

After a journey of 367km (228 miles) past great towns and cities including Stuttgart and Heidelberg, the river cuts briefly across the flatter, more industrialised Rhein plain and disgorges its contents into the major river at the city of Mannheim.

The Saar: Another of the Rhein's longest tributaries, the Saar flows through France and Saarland on its way from the Vosges mountain range to the Mosel. Some 246km (153 miles) long, it is navigable from Dillingen to the confluence in Konz. It was integrated in 1989 into the European waterways network with additional locks and canals. One of these canals cuts off a magnificent horseshoe-shaped loop of the river near Mettlach. The hill (called Cloef) adjacent to the river provides an excellent vantage point for photographs of this spectacular bend.

Highlights between Amsterdam (The Netherlands) and Basel (Switzerland)

Amsterdam, The Netherlands (Km 0)
At the start of the Rhein Canal is cosmopolitan, easygoing Amsterdam. The city lies near the sea on the narrow land strips between Lake IJssel and the North Sea. The River Amstel runs through the centre of the city, which consists of a horseshoe-shaped network of over 100km (62 miles) of man-made canals that connect about 90 islands and 400 stone bridges.

Whether you arrive by air, or by train, the riverships berth close to the central railway station, along the Oosterdokskade or Ruijterkade Oost (oceangoing cruise ships sail from a different terminal in Oosterlijke Handelskade).

The city is one of Europe's most enjoyable destinations, unique in many ways – not least for its balance of past and present. Perhaps no community has ever had such a glorious explosion of wealth and culture as Amsterdam during the 17th century, the city's Golden Age, yet this is a place that has always looked forward rather than back. The modern city is exuberant, with a tremendous range of cultural life from world-class art galleries to wacky street theatre.

Here are its highlights:

Canal ring: Amsterdam's horseshoe-shaped network of canals is the city's most distinctive feature and a must-see for visitors – lined with tall, elegant mansions from the 17th and 18th centuries. The canal ring (Grachtengordel) encompassing the three parallel waterways of Herengracht, Keizersgracht and Prinsengracht is the most scenic stretch.

Maritime Museum: This excellent museum (Scheepvaartmuseum) documents and celebrates Amsterdam's illustrious maritime history.

Rijksmuseum: Home to arguably the greatest collection of Dutch art in the world, the Rijksmuseum is housed within a magnificent Victorian Gothic building that has recently undergone a vast programme of renovations; it finally re-opened in April 2013.

The collection is varied, but most visitors come to see the works of the Dutch masters from the 15th to the 17th centuries. Among the collection are 20 works by Rembrandt, including *The Night Watch*. Johannes Vermeer is well represented, as is Frans Hals, the founding artist of the Dutch School, along with a collection of Dutch artists who were influenced or schooled by the masters. The museum also has a collection of work by non-Dutch artists, including Rubens, Tintoretto and El Greco, along with porcelain, furniture, sculpture and decorative arts, and Asiatic art.

Van Gogh Museum: The world's largest permanent collection features a selection of paintings by Van Gogh hung in chronological and, to a degree, thematic order – though the location of individual works may change from time to time.

Royal Palace: Dominating Dam Square in the heart of Amsterdam is the 17th-century Koninklijk Paleis (Royal Palace). The rather heavy exterior belies an elegant series of rooms inside with some notable works of art. The square itself is a hub of activity and meeting point.

Anne Frank House: A staircase leads into the backrooms where Otto Frank, his family and friends hid for two fraught years, from 1942 until August 1944. The house is a monument to all the victims of Fascism and anti-Semitism and something of a place of pilgrimage.

De Looier antiques market: A vast indoor antiques market selling anything from memorabilia to handmade pottery, and old dolls and toys.

Utrecht, The Netherlands (Km 31)

The fourth-largest city of the Netherlands is also the capital of Utrecht Province in the country's central section. Magnificent churches abound here (Domkerk, or St Martin's Cathedral, St Jacobuskerk, St Janskerk and St Pieterskerk), and there's also a large, historic university, founded in 1636.

Amsterdam–Rhein Canal (Km 913.4)

The canal, which opened in 1952 and is 72km (48 miles) long, connects the city and port of Amsterdam with the Lek River, making Amsterdam an important port for the trans-shipment of cargo. Considered to be the most heavily used canal in Europe, it has four locks.

(Start of the Rhein kilometre markings).

Düsseldorf, Germany (Km 744.2)

The capital of North Rhine-Westphalia and its administration centre, Düsseldorf is best known for its iron and steel production and as a centre for banking. It is also famous for its beer, with a number of microbreweries and some hundreds of pubs in the atmospheric Altstadt (Old Town), and for its shopping, particularly along the Königsallee.

The Fine Arts Museum is worth a visit, as is the Ceramic Museum, and the Lambertus Basilica, begun in 1288 (its spire is twisted), and the Castle Tower, which houses a museum of navigation. The city has long been famous for its Christmas market. The Bolkerstrasse, one of the city's liveliest streets, was the birthplace of the poet Heinrich Heine, author of *Die Lorelei* (see page 72).

Cologne (Köln), Germany (Km 688)

Cologne (Köln) is one of the most important traffic junctions and commercial centres in Germany and the most important economic centre on the Rhein.

Katz Castle and Lorelei rock.

Riverships berth at landing stages in the heart of the old town centre, with its fine river-front promenade and views along the Rhein.

It's a busy modern city with a strong sense of historical heritage. Already established as an important centre in Roman times and resurgent in the Middle Ages, today's city centre is still dominated by its glorious twin-towered cathedral. Repeatedly bombed in World War II, Cologne preserved its historic street pattern when it was rebuilt and, although most buildings are modern, much of its traditional atmosphere survives. It's a lively place, best experienced for those with stamina during the merrymaking of Karneval (Lenten Carnival) time. The historic core of Cologne is large, bounded by the semicircular boulevard of the Ring running along the line of the old city walls, although the epicentre of city life is to be found in the busy squares around the cathedral. Shoppers will enjoy walking the Hohe-Strasse, close to the docking area.

Cologne is also noted for its very own 'Original' Eau de Cologne toilet water (its brand name is 4711, which was the maker's former address).

Dom: With its awesome dimensions, the cathedral (Dom) is the unmistakable landmark of the city, its two mighty towers the defining symbol of Cologne's skyline. Construction began in 1248 and resumed in 1880, the final result remaining true to the original plans. A winding staircase of 509 steps leads to a viewing platform 95m (312ft) up in the south tower, where the view amply rewards your efforts.

Fischmarkt: There are few reminders today that the people of Cologne once bought and sold fish, but adjacent to the river is the city's old harbour area and the former fish market. The late-Gothic buildings surrounding the square, now lined with bars and restaurants, have been preserved in their distinct, original style.

Römisch-Germanisches Museum: Containing treasures from over 2,000 years ago after the Romans had established their camp of Colonia here, the city's Roman-Germanic Museum was built over the famous Dionysus Mosaic.

Wallraf-Richartz Museum: Cologne's oldest museum showcases art from the 14th to the 20th centuries. The collection represents every period and school, from Dutch and Flemish masters to French Impressionists, with works by Dürer, Rembrandt, Rubens, Degas and Cézanne, among many others.

St Gereon Church: This medieval church is known for its intricate floor mosaic of David and Goliath and its unique decagon-shaped dome. It contains the tomb of St Gereon and other martyrs.

Bonn, Germany (Km 654.8)

The Rhein flows through the suburbs of Bonn, the former German capital. The Romans named it Castra Bonnensia 2,000 years ago, when it formed

Cologne at night.

part of their Rhein Valley defences, although its real development did not begin until the Middle Ages. The city became the residence of the electors and archbishops of Cologne in the 17th century, and was the capital of West Germany before reunification and the eventual reinstatement of Berlin as the home of government in 1999. Today, Bonn is a university town, and has several museums on the riverbank in the 'Museum Mile', including the Kunst- und Ausstellungshalle (Art and Exhibition Hall), with exhibitions of art, technology, history and architecture, and the Kunstmuseum (Museum of Art).

Beethoven was born in Bonn in a house that, since 1890, has been a museum (Beethovenhaus). You can see original handwritten manuscripts, his instruments (including a piano complete with amplified sound to allow for his deafness), listening horns and life and death masks.

Drachenfels Castle, Germany (Km 643.7)

According to legend, it was at the foot of the sheer Drachenfels (Dragon's Rock) cliff that Siegfried, the hero of the *Nibelungen Saga*, slew the dragon and then bathed in its blood in order to render himself invulnerable. The castle is now a ruin, and is reached by funicular from Bad Godesburg. The view is magnificent.

Rolandseck Castle (Km 640)

Rolandseck was originally a fortress that also served as a customs station. It is now in ruins, but old archways can still be found on the grounds, the principal one being Rolandsbogen (Roland's Arch). The Rolandsbogen got its name from the legend of the young knight Roland, who is said to have looked yearningly down from this window at the Nonnenwerth convent, on an island in the middle of the Rhein, where his beloved was incarcerated. She had taken her vows because she had believed that he would not return from the Crusades. He did come

The curious Pfalzgrafenstein Castle.

home, but she was not allowed to leave the nunnery, and the couple died apart, their love unfulfilled. It is said that a tunnel led from the castle to the Nonnenwerth convent, but the castle was destroyed in the 17th century, and the last remaining archway of the ruin collapsed in 1839. The poet Ferdinand Freiligrath had the idea that the Rolandsbogen should be restored – and it was, in 1840. It now rests some 150m (500ft) above the Rhein, covered in a thick growth of ivy.

Andernach, Germany (Km 613.3)

Known as 'Backerjungenstadt' ('city of baker's apprentices') because legend has it that it was once under siege, and baker's apprentices threw bees' nests on the attackers from the city walls. Its historical town hall, with its Jewish baths, can be visited.

Ehrenbreitstein Castle, Germany (Km 592.3)

Located opposite the mouth of the Mosel, where it flows into the Rhein at Koblenz, this squat, solid-looking fortress was built around 1100 on a site that is 116m (380ft) above the water, with incredible views over both rivers, the Eifel Hills and the city of Koblenz. It was acquired in 1152 by the Electorate of Trier and expanded, becoming a fortress around 1500 with the addition of more fortifications. By 1750, after several breaches by the French, the fortress was made impregnable by the brilliant architect Balthasar Neumann. Today, the castle houses the National Collection of Monuments to Technology, and also serves as a youth hostel. Ehrenbreitstein Castle is also one of the sites for the annual Rhein in Flames celebration (see page 71).

Koblenz, Germany (Km 591.5, Rhein/ Km 0.30, Mosel)

A former Roman trading settlement, Koblenz grew up at the confluence of the Rhein and the Mosel and lies on the massif of the Middle Rhein Highlands. It is bordered by North Rhine-Westphalia to the north, Hesse to the east and Saarland to the south. The Rhein cuts it diagonally from southeast to northwest.

Stolzenfels Castle, Germany (Km 585.2)

Located just south of Koblenz and surrounded by thick forest, this handsome, imperial yellow castle was originally built in the 13th century to defend the nearby silver mines. The castle was destroyed by the French but rebuilt in 1852 by the Prussian Crown Prince Friedrich-Wilhelm IV, in neo-Gothic style. In the castle's chapel, important works from the period of High Romanticism can be found in the murals. It is one of the best-known castles along the Rhein.

Marksburg Castle, Germany (Km 580)

This beautiful, mystical castle is the only one in the entire Rhein Valley never to have been destroyed, and is easily the most visited, as it gives the best insight into medieval life. It dates back to 1150, towering majestically 170m (557ft) above the town of Braubach. The original founder, one of the nobles of Braubach, named it after St Mark. A successor, Eberhard von Eppstein, had the castle extended and further fortified in 1219, and it was occupied after 1220 by vassals of the Counts Palatine. In 1283, the castle was acquired by the counts of Katzenelnbogen.

At the end of the 19th century it passed to the German Castles Association, which has its headquarters and archives here. The library houses over 12,000 volumes. A tour of the castle will take you through not only the citadel itself, but also the impressive kitchens in the Gothic Hall building. There is a gruesome torture chamber in the cellar of the older hall building, where a great assortment of grisly instruments of torture can be viewed.

A complete replica of the castle can be seen today in an amusement park in Japan. It appears that the Japanese offered to buy the original ruin, have it dismantled and shipped to Japan, for 250 million marks, but were refused by the German Castles Association – hence the replica.

Boppard, Germany (Km 570.5)

A charming river-front city, Boppard (of Celtic origin) is located at one of the bends in the Rhein. It has a medieval town hall, Roman castle (eight of the original 28 towers still exist, as do the medieval town gates), several convents, stylish villas and half-timbered houses. Grapes (mostly Riesling) are grown on slopes that are among the steepest in Germany – these are used by 14 full-time cooperatives that obtain more than 500,000 litres (approximately 110,000 imperial gallons) from the cultivation.

Liebenstein Castle and Sterrenberg Castle (Km 566.5)

Not far from Boppard are the ruins of two 12th-century castles, Sterrenberg and Liebenstein, built close together. These were inhabited by two brothers who hated each other so much that they erected a wall between the castles. The story goes that they made up their differences, and for fun, decided to wake each other with an arrow shot every morning. Inevitably, one killed the other by mistake with a badly aimed arrow.

Lorelei, St Goarshausen, Germany (Km 554.6)

Nobody can pass through the medieval wine-growing village of St Goarshausen without learning the legend of the Lorelei (see box). Here, the river carves its way through a steep, narrow gorge, with its bed descending to 25m (82ft) in places, winding around jagged rocks and creating powerful whirlpools, which have sucked many a ship below the surface. The gorge, with its 132m (433ft) cliffs, is so narrow that the railway line that runs alongside the river has been cut into rock tunnels. A bronze statue of the maiden Lorelei looks down on the river from where, as related by the famous poem written by Heinrich Heine in 1824, the mysterious nymph would once appear, captivating sailors with her beauty and her hypnotic singing before luring them onto the rocks to their death. The poem *Die Lorelei*, set to music in 1837, is seen as the epitome of Rhein Romanticism. A visitor centre stands on the top of the rock today, although the entrance fee is hardly worth it, as there is little inside (it's much better to cruise past the rock).

Pfalzgrafenstein Castle (Km 545)

This is undoubtedly one of the most curious castle creations in the world, a six-storey tower clinging to a tiny island in the middle of the swirling waters and resembling a ship. The castle was erected in 1326 by King Ludwig I of Bavaria purely for collecting customs duties from passing vessels on the Rhein. Anyone who couldn't pay would be sent down a rope to the 'dungeon' – a platform floating at the bottom of a deep well. Since 1946 it has been the property of the state of the Rheinland-Palatinate. Although it has been repaired and restored, purely for tourism purposes, the castle was in use as a signal point for Rhein shipping until the 1960s.

Reichenstein Castle, Germany (Km 534.4)

In the 19th century, Reichenstein was called Falkenburg Castle. It was erected to protect the property of Cornelimunster Abbey near Aachen in the 11th century. It has been destroyed and rebuilt several times, the last time in 1899. Nowadays, it is in use as a hotel.

Rheinstein Castle (Km 533)

Originally constructed as an imperial castle for customs and toll collection, it also protected the surrounding estates. One of the oldest castle buildings on the Rhein – it dates back to the 9th century – it has an astounding position: the steely-grey castle appears to be part of a huge, jagged slab of rock high on the hillside.

Rheinstein belonged to the archbishops of Mainz, who named it after their patron saint, Bonifatius, although its original name was Vogtberg. It fell into ruin in the 16th century, and in 1823 Prince Friedrich of Prussia paid 100 Reichsmarks for what was left of it, renaming it Rheinstein. His great-granddaughter sold it in 1975, in an advanced state of dilapidation,

---

Rhein in flames

Time it right and you could be part of the fabulous 'Rhein in Flammen' (Rhein in Flames) celebration, which typically takes place in August each year. There are, in fact, three such celebrations, but by far the best is on the section of river between Boppard and Koblenz. Almost 100 riverships take part each year, strung one behind the other in convoy, like a string of sausages (the river police organise this), and measuring over 3km (1.8 miles) in length.

As the convoy moves from Boppard to Koblenz, past numerous towns and villages along the way, fireworks light up the night sky, with all the local towns and villages vying to create the best display. On reaching Koblenz, the convoy stops and turns round to face Ehrenbreitstein Castle (see page 70), the magnificent fortress across from the mouth of the Mosel River. The castle is gloriously lit in red spotlights, with smoke rising all around it, so that it seems to be on fire. It is an unforgettable sight. For more information, see www.rhein-in-flammen.com.

to an Austrian singer from the Tyrol. It is now pre-served thanks to donations from tourists, a society founded by the singer and income from its rental.

Mäuseturm, Germany (Km 529)

Below the mouth of the Nahe, close to Rüdesheim and Bingen, a slender red-and-yellow tower looking like something out of a Disney cartoon perches on a small island. The legend relates how the original tower was built by the evil, hard-hearted Archbishop Hatto of Mainz in 1208 as a reinforcement for the customs castle, Ehrenfels, which stands in ruinous state on the opposite hillside. The tower's strategic position allowed the archbishop to fleece passing traffic on the Rhein. To bolster his income, peasants were levied a corn tithe, which he collected in a large barn in Mainz. After a bad harvest, the hungry popu-lace went to Mainz and asked for grain. Archbishop Hatto, having promised to help, then proceeded to lock them up in his tithe barn and set fire to it.

Everyone inside perished, but the story goes that some mice escaped. The archbishop departed to his castle on the island by boat from Bingen, opposite Rüdesheim, but the mice followed him... and then ate him alive, even though he had had his bed sus-pended by chains from the ceiling, so that it was well above the floor.

The edifice thus became known as the Mice Tow-er (Mäuseturm), although its actual title was once Mautturm (Customs Tower). Under France's King Louis XIV, the castle was burnt down, although fortu-nately it was restored by the King of Prussia in 1855 and used as a signal tower for shipping, to warn ships of the treacherous whirlpools and rocks of the Hole of Bingen. It remained in this manner until 1974, when the channel was deepened, and, since then it has been inhabited only by bats, and, so the legend goes, the ghost of the evil archbishop.

Rüdesheim, Germany (Km 526.7)

This was the terminal point of the old 'Merchant Road' that originated in Lohr and circumvented the waterfalls that once made this stretch of river treach-erous. It is famous for its wine growing districts on the Rüdesheim Hills, located at the foothills of the Niederwald Forest and Taunus Mountains. A cable car will take you to the top of the Rheingau hills, where the famous Niederwald Denkmal monument – a statue of Germania built to commemorate the founding of the German Empire in 1871 – is located.

Four castles were constructed to protect this im-portant merchant centre and traffic route, one of which, Bromserburg, belonged for a while to the Knights of Rüdesheim; today it is a wine museum. A number of taverns and drinking houses line its nar-row streets, particularly Drosselgasse.

One fascinating attraction in Rüdesheim is Sieg-fried's Mechanisches Musikkabinett (Siegfried's Mechanical Instrument Museum). This unusual mu-seum, located in the Bromserhof (parts of which date back to the 15th century), is famous for its outstand-ing collection of priceless mechanical musical instru-ments. All 250 instruments have been collected from the period spanning 150 years prior to 1930 and have all been restored. Siegfried Wendel, the museum's owner, is always on hand and frequently plays some of the instruments for visitors. It is open from March to December.

The Lorelei

Near St Goarshausen, at one of the most notorious bends in the Middle Rhein Valley, the Lorelei is a large, almost perpendicular slate rock 130m (427ft) high that produces an echo. In days of old, so it is told, noblemen occupied the area in order to squeeze taxes from passing traffic – from every vessel and merchant needing to travel beyond its grasp.

Back then, Lorelei herself, a siren, could be seen occasionally on the hilltop. Echoing through the landscape, a mysterious voice belonging to the maiden chanted the now-famous poem, as fishermen passed within her grasp. She lured them on to the craggy rocks, and to a fate unknown.

The charming maiden's beauty and reputation spread throughout the land, until one day it reached the ears of the son of the Duke Palatine. Yearning for passion, the young man left his father's palace in secret and journeyed by boat to win the maiden's heart. It is said that at sunset he and his followers reached the gorge and were spellbound by the singing of the Lorelei. He caught a glimpse of her hair and enchanting figure at the top of the steepest cliff.

Magically, the strength to row vanished from their arms as they stared at the figure. It seemed as if the boatswain had lost

memory of his duties. The young prince, somewhat impatient, jumped into the waters to reach the lovely maiden and take her hand. With a cry of 'Lorelei', he sank into the busy, swirling waters, never to be seen again.

The Duke ordered his son's betrayer to be captured. The rock, soon surrounded by the Duke's revengeful soldiers, became a silent witness. One captain took the bravest of his soldiers with him to the top of the hill. 'Unholy woman, now you can pay for your sins,' he commanded, blocking the monster's path to her grotto. 'That does not lie with you,' she replied and cast her pearl necklaces into the floods below. They rose out of the water – as high as the cliff top – and carried the fairy away into the grey evening night. Lorelei was never seen again, but if you go today to the rock and stare at it, a manifold echo may taunt you.

The Lorelei has been the subject of a number of literary works, including, most famously, Heinrich Heine's 1824 poem, which has been set to music by more than 20 composers. Although Heine made the poem famous, he was not its creator. That honour goes to the German romantic poet Clemens Brentano who, in 1801, included the ballad of Lore Lay in his novel, *Godwi*.

Christmas market in Düsseldorf's Altstadt.

Mainz, Germany (Km 498.5)

Mainz, located on the west bank of the Rhein opposite the mouth of the river Main, is over 2,000 years old (it was founded as the Roman camp Moguntiacum). It is the capital city of Rheinland-Pfalz (Rhineland-Palatinate), and has a history as seat of electors and bishops. Much of the city was devastated by bombing in World War II and has been rebuilt. In the Old Town, visit the six-towered cathedral, originally constructed in AD 975 and a highlight of ecclesiastical architecture in the Upper Rhein region.

Mainz is also home to the Gutenberg Museum, which tells the history of printing. The city is also one of the main centres of the Rhein wine trade. There are several museums and palaces to explore, but one sight not to miss is St Stephen's Church, with its stunning stained-glass windows by the French painter Marc Chagall.

Worms, Germany (Km 443.2)

One of the oldest cities in Germany, Worms was originally inhabited as an imperial residence on the banks of the Rhein and the centre of the Burgundian Empire that was destroyed by the Huns. Today, the city is known as a wine-trading centre. The vineyards surrounding the city produce the grapes used for making 'Liebfraumilch', a trade name for the much-maligned semi-sweet white wine that is from the Palatinate, Rhein-Hesse, Nahe and Rheingau wine-growing regions. Passengers typically disembark at Worms to take a tour (by bus) to Heidelberg (see page 76).

Mannheim, Germany (Km 415–425)

The city was founded in 1606 in a circular layout that covered only the peninsula at the strategic confluence of the Neckar and the Rhein. The city, which developed from the fortress that is aligned with the Rhein, was created by the Palatine Elector Frederick IV and has grown into a modern finance and insurance centre. It also has a university.

Speyer, Germany (Km 400)

This is typically used as a short stop so that passengers can leave the vessel to take a tour to Heidelberg (see page 76), although Speyer has a few noteworthy sights, including an immense Unesco-protected cathedral, one of the most important Romanesque buildings from the time of the Holy Roman Empire, and the Jewish baths. The city was burned down on the order of Louis XIV in 1689. After it was returned to Germany in 1816, it became the government seat of Bavaria Palatinate until 1845.

Gambersheim Locks, France (Km 309)

The Gambersheim locks are a relatively recent construction, put into operation in 1974. They are operated from Strasbourg and are the largest inland waterway locks in France. There are two chambers, each with a length of 270m (885ft), and the locks are in operation 24 hours a day, all year round (it takes about 15 minutes to pass through them). About 20 million tons of goods pass through the locks each year, as well as numerous riverships.

Strasbourg, France (Km 294.3)

The medieval city of Strasbourg is the seat of the Council of Europe, the European Commission on Human Rights and the European Science Foundation, and is also capital and cultural centre of the Alsace region of France. The port is the largest on the Upper Rhein, and a large network of docks provides freight and other services.

Strasbourg's centre is surrounded by the River Ill, and is mainly pedestrianised, particularly the area

The Rhein in Flames celebration.

known as Petite France, where the river splits into a number of canals. At the end of Petite France, look out for the Ponts Couverts, a series of wooden foot-bridges dating back to the 13th century (but no longer covered).

The focal point of it all is place Gutenberg, named after Johannes Gutenberg, the inventor of the print-ing press, who lived here during the 15th century and whose statue stands at the centre of the square. A highlight of any visit is the massive hulk of the Cathédrale de Notre Dame, the tallest medieval building in Europe, its viewing platform reached by a wearying 332 steps up inside the tower. It's worth the climb for the vista of the Black Forest (and, in the other direction, the Vosges Mountains) beyond the colourful roofs of the old town. At noon, crowds are drawn to the astronomical clock inside the cathedral, adorned with a Parade of the Apostles, which dates from 1838.

Many river cruises start and end in Strasbourg, and the Gare Fluviale is located adjacent to the rue du Havre, a short walk from the heart of the city on an arm of the Ill.

Basel, Switzerland (Km 165–169)

Basel, the navigable limit of the Rhein, is the start-ing point for many cruises. The city has grown up either side of the river, with the industrial Kleinbasel section to the north and the lovely old part, Grossba-sel, on the south bank. Basel has a real international flavour; it is, after all, where three countries – France, Germany and Switzerland – meet. Situated at the 'knee' of the Rhein, it is the location of the oldest university in Switzerland, together with some 30 mu-seums and an inviting old town – a jumble of me-dieval buildings along the hilly river bank (a short walk from the cruise boat landing stage). Basel is also steeped in Roman history.

The focal point of the city is the Rathaus (Town Hall) and marketplace, around which are several late Gothic, Renaissance and Baroque guildhalls. The 13th-century Romanesque Münster (Cathedral) is an unusual shade of red, its slender towers built from sandstone quarried from the nearby Vosges Mountains.

There are several museums worth visiting, includ-ing the Kunstmuseum, where you can view two Picasso paintings (The Seated Harlequin and Two Brothers), purchased by the people of the city in 1967, together with four others the artist donated.

Basel is famous for its music festivals and in-dustrial trade fairs, the most famous being the Autumn Fair, which has been held each and every year since 1471.

Highlights on the Mosel

Moselkern, Germany (Km 34)

This small, sleepy hamlet provides a stopping point for riverships, so that passengers can take a tour to Burg Eltz, a castle set not on a hillside but deep in the forest. The castle is unusual in that it is really a col-lection of three houses. A drawbridge-like entrance from a steep winding forest road helps to add to the atmosphere.

Cochem, Germany (Km 51.3)

One of the loveliest and most picturesque of all the towns along the Mosel, Cochem is located at the beginning of a 20km (13-mile) bend in the river. The walled Old Town is laced with narrow alleys. The skyline is dominated by the Imperial Castle, which has a rectangular keep *(donjon)* and numerous small towers. Worth a look is the Capuchin monastery, built in 1623, and restored for use today as a cultural centre. The Baroque Town Hall is also of note, as are the old gabled houses overlooking the Market Fountain. The Mosel Wine Week takes place here in mid-June each year, and the wine taverns along the river front have 'green wine' (very young wine) available all year round. Behind the waterfront are more taverns, which are recommended for their friendly atmosphere.

Bernkastel-Kues, Germany (Km 129.4)

Bernkastel-Kues is comprised of two villages (Bernkastel and Kues), one on each side of the Mosel (and joined by a bridge) at the confluence of the Tiefenbach (meaning 'deep stream'). The riverships dock on the Kues side. This is big wine-growing country, and the Middle Mosel Wine Festival is staged here in the first week in September. There is also a Wine Museum in the town. The ruins of a fortress called Lanshut dominate the town, which is filled with gorgeous half-timbered houses; the lowest floor of many houses is typically smaller than the upper floor because taxes used to be charged based on the amount of ground the house covered. During winter Christmas market cruises, the picture-postcard setting is magical.

Trier, Germany (Km 181.5–191.4)

Trier is the principal city of the Mosel Valley and the oldest in Germany; growing up around a ford used by the Germanic-Celtic Treveri tribe before being officially founded in 16 BC by the Roman Emperor Caesar Augustus, who named it Augusta Treverorum. Trier, which lies in the Middle Rhein Highlands, is bordered by Luxembourg and Belgium to the west, North Rhine-Westphalia to the north and Saarland to the south.

One of the best-preserved and most important Roman edifices in Germany is the 2nd-century, four-storey Porta Nigra (Town Gate), built of sandstone (originally without mortar) and today protected as a Unesco World Heritage Site. You can visit the Constantine Baths, and other remaining Roman relics such as a 20,000-seat amphitheatre and Roman bridge. A cross dating from AD 958 can be found in the Stadtmuseum (town museum); there is a replica in the market square, while close by is the Petrus Fountain, constructed in 1595. It is also famous as the birthplace of Karl Marx (1818–83), whose house still stands in Bruckenstrasse.

Trier is at the heart of the Mosel wine-producing region and close to one of the area's largest breweries: Bitburger. It is also known for its Christmas market.

Nancy, France (Km 149.2)

Five palaces, two fountains, a triumphal arch, a cathedral and a grand square are among the attractions backdrop of this delightful town, which is located in an important manufacturing region of France. At its heart is place Stanislas, a vast, impressive square with splendid iron gateways, gilded lanterns and a huge

Sunset in Petite France, Strasbourg.

fountain with wrought-iron screen (features that were introduced by the former, exiled King Stanislas of Poland). On one side of the square is the Musée des Beaux-Arts, home to a collection of paintings from Old Masters to the 20th century. Other highlights include the rose-filled Parc de la Pépinière.

Highlights on the Neckar

Heidelberg, Germany (Km 22.7)

Heidelberg, located just over 20km (13 miles) upstream on the Neckar from Mannheim, is the epitome of German Romanticism, nestling on the south side of the river and set against the forested hills of Oldenwald, and dominated by a sprawling red-sandstone castle complex. This venerable city is the old capital of the Electorate of the Palatinate, although its history goes back a good deal further than that – some 600,000 years, in fact: the jawbone of *Homo heidelbergensis*, the oldest human remains discovered in Europe, was found near here. Thousands of years later, Celts and Romans settled the area. Count Palatine Ruprecht I founded Germany's oldest university here in 1386, and for 500 years the Electoral College, which was responsible for electing the German kings, was based in the city. Heidelberg Castle, constructed with a moat and several keeps, is considered to be the most magnificent castle ruin in all of Germany, and attracts several million visitors a year.

The castle took 400 years to build and encompasses many different architectural styles. It was destroyed by the French during the Wars of Succession between 1689 and 1693, then subsequently rebuilt only to be destroyed again in 1764 when freak lightning struck and burnt it to the ground. Today, some parts lie in ruins, while other sections have been restored to be used for concerts and banquets or to house museums. The whole complex can be reached on foot by steps and walkways that lead up to it from the city, spread along the river below, or via a funicular railway. Highlights include the Friedrich Wing, with impressive statues of the German kings, and the Heidelberg Tun, one of the world's largest wine vats. The castle houses a fine restaurant with views over the castle courtyard. Try the local duck speciality – you'll receive a handwritten card from the chef showing the number assigned to the portion of duck you have just eaten.

Within the castle complex, the Otto Henry Palace is a richly decorated Renaissance building constructed in 1556. Although only the facade remains, it is a splendid reminder that this was the first such Renaissance building to be built in northern Europe. Inside is the Deutsches Apotheken-Museum, containing old medical instruments and medicine bottles.

The city below is full of wonderful Baroque and Renaissance buildings, and remains an important university town, its population swelled by 28,000 students, so there's always a lively buzz during term-time. Other things to see include the Heiliggeistkirche (Church of the Holy Ghost), the wonderful Renaissance facade of the Hotel Ritter and the Old Bridge (the Karl Theodore Brücke) over the Neckar, which the writer J.W. von Goethe believed to be one of the wonders of the world, thanks to its breathtaking view.

Eberbach, Germany (Km 57.4)

This market town is home to one of the best-kept medieval monasterial establishments in all of Germany,

Heidelberg.

The loop in the Saar at Cloef.

the Eberbach Abbey (Kloster Eberbach). The abbey was built in two stages, from 1145 to 1160, then from 1170 to 1186. Architectural scholars will enjoy the remarkable monks' dormitory, which was built as a double-naved, ribbed vaulted room with a slightly rising floor; columns were shortened accordingly, and the finished article provides the illusion that it is much longer than it really is (approximately 85m/279ft).

Bad Wimpfen, Germany (Km 100)
Located at the mouth of the River Jagst, Bad Wimpfen is a saline health spa that is extremely popular with German health seekers. From the river, there is a superb view of the old Staufer Palace, with its spires, Romanesque arcades and red roof. The town itself is extremely pretty, with richly decorated half-timbered houses and narrow streets.

Stuttgart, Germany (Km 179–189)
Wealthy in financial and cultural terms, Stuttgart is the capital city of Baden-Württemberg. It is known as the spiritual home of Mercedes-Benz, building of which was started here by two remarkable pioneers, Gottlieb Daimler (1834–1900) and Karl Benz (1844–1929). At night, the famous trademark of Mercedes – a three-pointed star within a circle – can be seen illuminated high above the city.

Definitely worth a visit for automobile-lovers is the Mercedes-Benz Museum, with over 100 vintage and veteran cars on display. Also worth seeing is the Linden Museum, with its many sections displaying ethnological collections from around the world and the Staatsgalerie, one of Germany's finest art collections. The city itself has a handsome centre with many 16th-century buildings.

Highlights on the Saar

Mettlach, Germany (Km 37)
Mettlach is best known as the home of the ceramics manufacturer Villeroy & Boch, whose offices are housed in the former Benedictine Abbey of St Peter. The abbey was completely rebuilt from 1728 onwards, but earlier excavations at the site revealed buildings that date from AD 700. Some of the scenery along the river around the town is spectacular, notably adjacent to Cloef (see page 67).

Saarbrücken, Germany (Km 90.6)
Saarbrücken, the capital of the Saarland, lies on the River Saar at the mouth of the River Sulz. Dating back to Celtic and Roman times, it was first mentioned in the record books in AD 999. The city is the centre of the Saar coal-mining region, and iron- and steel-making are important industries, as are food processing and brewing and other industries. Architectural highlights include the Protestant Baroque-style Ludwigskirche, built in yellow and red sandstone from the region, and the grand, harmonious Ludwigsplatz on which it stands.

River Elbe

From the Czech Republic to Germany's sandy North Sea coast, an Elbe cruise offers a range of landscapes and some fascinating cities, most notably Prague, Dresden and Berlin.

The Elbe runs for 1,165km (724 miles) from its source in the Czech Republic to the North Sea coast of Germany, passing through a wide range of scenery en route. From the highlands of Bohemia it curves west then north to the dramatic sandstone massif south of Dresden, continuing through the hills and vineyards of Saxony to reach the marshy woodlands of the Lüneburg Heath and the flatlands of the North European Plain. The history of the river is inextricably linked with division. In earlier days, it divided the Slavs and the Germans; later, a stretch of the river separated the former East and West Germany. From the Czech border to beyond Wittenberg the Elbe flows through the heart of the erstwhile German Democratic Republic (East Germany), its towns and villages still perceptibly less prosperous than those ones further west.

Great cities have grown up along its banks, including beautiful, Baroque Dresden, and Hamburg, Germany's most important sea and river port. An Elbe cruise also travels a short distance along the Vltava

A Viking rivership on the Elbe.

River to the fairytale Czech capital, Prague, and much further north, along the Havel tributary to Berlin, until 1990 the city divided between East and West and now the united country's cosmopolitan capital. Fascinating historic towns along the river's course include Wittenberg, where Dr Martin Luther began the Protestant Reformation, Dessau, heart of the Bauhaus movement, and Meissen, world-famous for its fine porcelain.

Elbe cruises are available in a variety of permutations, usually between Berlin and Prague. Some continue north all the way to Hamburg; some even take in the coast and islands of the North Sea. All offer an opportunity to spend a couple of days in both Berlin and Prague, which are highly recommended.

Kiel Canal

At Brunsbüttel, near the estuary, the Elbe passes the mouth of the Kiel Canal (also known as the Kaiser Wilhelm Canal), a 98km (60-mile) man-made waterway connecting the North and Baltic seas. It was constructed by the German government in the late 19th century across the northwest of the state of Schleswig-Holstein, from Brunsbüttelkoog to Holenau, on the Kieler Bucht of the Baltic Sea, and became an international waterway following the signing of the Treaty of Versailles in 1919.

Did you know...?

...that the longest inland beach is on the River Elbe? Well, sort of. On 14 July 2002, between 80,000 and 100,000 people took part in the first International Elbe Swimming Day. The celebration was organised in 52 towns from the source of the Elbe in the Czech Giant Mountains to the mouth of the river in the North Sea. It was run by 'Project Living Elbe', together with the German organisation Deutsche Umwelthilfe, among other partners. The event, a swimming success, was designed to bring people's attention to the river, which, only a few years previously, had been extremely polluted. What was a sewer has been turned into a river in which one can swim, with the addition of more than 200 water treatment plants along its length.
...that in 2002 the Elbe reached its highest level since 1845?
...that the Rhein Falls at Schaffhausen are the widest in Europe?
...that both the Czech and German names for Elbe derive from Indo-Germanic *albi* or the Latin *albus*, meaning 'shining' or 'white'?

Major tributaries

The 440km (273-mile) -long Vltava (known to the Germans as the Moldau) is a Czech tributary of the Elbe, although its source lies in the Bohemian Forest in Germany. It joins the Elbe at Melnik, a short distance north of Prague, the Czech Republic's capital and the most important city along its shores.

Another tributary is the 343km (213-mile) -long Havel, which originates in the Mecklenburg lakes in northern Germany. It flows through Berlin to Potsdam and Brandenburg and enters the Elbe near Havelberg.

The Oder–Havel Canal is reached via the Berlin Lakes. Because the lakes and the Oder have a height difference of 36m (118ft), in 1934 a special vessel lift (Niederfinow) was completed in order to raise a rivership the required height in under five minutes.

Highlights on the Elbe from Hamburg (Germany) to Prague (Czech Republic)

On a river cruise between Hamburg (on the River Elbe) and Prague (on the River Vltava, a tributary of the Elbe), you are likely to visit some of the following towns and cities:

Hamburg, Germany (Km 623)

Best-known, somewhat unfairly, for its raunchy nightlife, Hamburg is actually a very dignified and elegant city, the notorious Reeperbahn red-light district aside. It is Germany's main seaport, despite the fact that it is some 110km (70 miles) inland, on the right bank of the Elbe where it meets the River Alster.

The city is crisscrossed by canals and has numerous green squares and corners, with lively street cafés. Exploring the canals and waterfront on a boat tour is one of the most restful ways to get around. Otherwise, things to see include the Rathaus (Town Hall), built in neo-Renaissance style in 1887 and set in one corner of the Binnenalster, an inland lake. On Sunday mornings, head for the Fischmarkt, a noisy, atmospheric marketplace where everything from fish to household clutter is sold. The city has numerous museums, including the Kunsthalle, which houses one of Germany's finest collections of art, with exhibits from the 13th to the 20th centuries. Hamburg is also good for shopping; there are a lot of high-quality boutique shops, while the major department stores are located in Jungfernstieg, Mönckebergstrasse and Spitalerstrasse.

Berlin, Germany (River Havel, no km marker)

Germany's capital actually lies on the River Havel, which passes through a complex system of lakes and locks, so river cruisers usually moor up at Potsdam and passengers are brought by coach to the city centre. Berlin has metamorphosed since the fall of the Wall in 1990 into a buzzing, thriving metropolis, drawing artists and entrepreneurs, movers and shakers into its midst. Innovative architecture, ultra-chic shopping along the Kurfürstendamm, grand boulevards and lavish monuments collectively create one of Europe's most exciting capitals – and the nightlife is legendary, too.

Most cruise itineraries allow a couple of days in Berlin, to take in the beautiful neoclassical buildings along Unter den Linden, the Brandenburg Gate and the Reichstag, the Museuminsel (Museum Island), now a Unesco World Heritage Site. Slightly more off the beaten track are some of the multicultural suburbs such as Kreuzberg, arty and newly gentrified Prenzlauer Berg or the patrician Charlottenburg, or the nearby lakes and forests.

Brandenburger Tor: The Brandenburg Gate has played varying roles in the history of Berlin. Napoleon marched through here on his triumphant way to Russia, and when the Berlin Wall fell in 1990, the gates came to symbolise freedom and unity. The sandstone structure is based on the gateway to the Acropolis in Athens.

The Reichstag: The Reichstag, restored to prominence with the return of the goverment to Berlin in 1999 and crowned by a spectacular glass dome designed by Sir Norman Foster, was originally built in the late 19th century in Italian Renaissance style. A broad spiral ramp enables visitors to watch parliamentary proceedings from above.

Elbe

Museuminsel: Between the River Spree and Kupfergraben lies Museum Island, which ranks as one of the world's finest museum complexes. The stunning diversity of displays includes everything from ancient archaeological artefacts to early 20th-century German and European art.

Kurfürstendamm: Inspired by the Champs-Elysées in Paris, Ku'damm (as it's usually known) is the most popular boulevard in Berlin, and is flanked by a series of exclusive hotels, department stores and cafés. In the 1920s it became the meeting-place for Berlin's intellectuals.

Checkpoint Charlie: From 1961 until 1989, Checkpoint Charlie was the only crossing point between East and West Berlin. Today, the former border crossing has become a shrine to the Berlin Wall's memory. Nothing remains of the actual military installation today, although a small guardhouse was rebuilt in the middle of the street. For more information on the general history of the Wall, visit the nearby Museum Haus am Checkpoint Charlie 5 at Friedrichstrasse 44.

Tangermünde, Germany (Km 388)

Tangermünde is a former Hanseatic League town with many fine examples remaining of Gothic brick architecture and half-timbered houses.

Magdeburg, Germany (Km 326–333)

Magdeburg is located about mid-way on the Elbe, southwest of Berlin, positioned at a natural crossroads on the Elbe at the junction of six railway lines and seven arterial roads. The city is linked with Berlin and the lower River Oder by a system of canals, and to the River Rhein by the Mittelland Canal. It was almost destroyed in 1945, but is now a superb example of a traditional German town, albeit reconstructed. The town's museum houses the *Magdeburg Rider*, Germany's oldest equestrian statue, created in 1240. There is a replica of it in front of the town hall. Other notable city sights include the world's third-tallest wooden structure, a 60m (197ft) -high 'Millennium Tower' (Jahrtausendturm), constructed as an exhibition centre in time for the turn of the century. Famous former residents of Magdeburg include the composer Georg Philip Telemann.

Wittenberg, Germany (Km 215)

Not to be confused with another town with almost the same name (Wittenberge – located further along the Elbe), Wittenberg is a sleepy town, brought to life by hordes of visitors who come here to see where the Protestant Reformation began. The mooring is some distance from the town, so it's best to take a coach tour.

Dr Martin Luther, an Augustine monk and university lecturer, famously nailed 95 theses to the door of the Palace Church on 31 October 1517, an act which is defined by historians as beginning the Reformation. Three years later, Luther was excommunicated by the Pope. Luther's house can also be visited, as can St Marien's Church, where he preached. An oak tree marks the spot where he burnt the papal bull condemning his doctrines. Nearby is Luther Hall, a museum dedicated to the Reformation.

Meissen, Germany (Km 80–83)

Meissen is a lovely old town, dominated by the slender Gothic spires of its cathedral and the hulking Albrechtsburg Castle, built in 1525. There has been a settlement since AD 968, but the town really rose to fame in 1710 with the advent of porcelain manufacture.

Augustus the Strong, Elector of Saxony (where he was known as Frederick Augustus I) from 1694 to 1733, had earlier employed the renegade alchemist Friedrich Böttger to make gold, partly in order to raise much-needed funds for the state, and partly (of course) out of personal greed. Not surprisingly, this scheme had failed, but in 1709 Böttger realised that valuable white porcelain could be made from nacrite, of which there were large deposits nearby, and the castle was quickly turned into a factory. The famous blue-glaze technique was discovered in 1740, and the porcelain soon became known all over the world. The castle houses an art collection today, with a number of early Meissen pieces.

Pillnitz, Germany (Km 50)

One of Saxony's architectural treasures, Pillnitz Palace – built to rival Buckingham Palace and Versailles – houses an impressive collection of fine jewellery and porcelain.

Dresden, Germany (Km 50–61)

The Elbe runs for 25km (15 miles) right through the middle of this venerable German city, the capital of Saxony once again since 1990 and world-renowned for its fabulous art treasures, which have given it the epithet 'Florence on the Elbe.' There are water

---

The Oder

Renowned as a sanctuary for birdlife, the Oder is a little-cruised river that forms the border between Poland and Germany for a distance of 186km (116 miles). This isolated river valley is green and lush, lined with meadows and ancient forests, as well as expanses of grass and moorland. Apart from the occasional sleepy hamlet, the only signs of human life are cyclists and hikers. But this was also the region in which the Russians broke through the German lines in World War II to commence their final assault on Berlin, and it is rich in history.

When cruises operate on the Oder, they usually start in Berlin, travel east along the Havel to join the Oder, and then sail either south to Wroclaw (Breslau) or north to Szczecin, close to the river's mouth on the Baltic Sea.

Meissen at night.

meadows and green parks close to the centre giving a marvellous feeling of open space. The river cruise landing stage is right in the centre of the city, and most boats spend the night here, a good opportunity to see the beautiful sandstone buildings illuminated by dramatic floodlights.

Dresden will always be remembered for the devastating bombing in 1945, which flattened the city centre and cost some 35,000 people their lives. For years, the Frauenkirche (Church of Our Lady) was left ruined, as a reminder of the destruction, but it has now been rebuilt as an exact replica of its former self. The city centre is now a protected Unesco site and has almost been fully restored, thanks to a 50-year rebuilding project.

Dresden is a very attractive city and, for many, is a highlight of an Elbe cruise. The Town Hall Tower, standing at 100m (330ft), will always by law be the tallest building. The 13th-century Kreuzkirche, meanwhile, rebuilt in 1764 after the Seven Years War, is said to contain a fragment of the Holy Cross, and is a wonderful example of Baroque architecture.

Another beautiful Baroque building is the meticulously restored 18th-century Zwinger Palace, a superb collection of graceful pavilions on the south bank of the Elbe, known for its superb art collection of Old Masters, including pieces by Raphael and Rembrandt.

Music-lovers should see the incredible Semper Opera House, in which performances are given from September to May. On the opposite side of the river (the left bank) is the quadrilateral Japanese Palace, built to display Augustus the Strong's superb collection of Meissen porcelain and tableware.

The River Moldau starts at Km 0.

Königstein, Germany (Km 17)

Once you've passed the spa town of Rathen, set against a natural amphitheatre of cliffs, the dramatic medieval Königstein Fortress comes into view, 360m (1,180ft) above the river. Cruise ships usually stop here for a brief visit, taking passengers by coach to the fortress. Königstein has been rebuilt and strengthened several times, and in its day was considered impregnable; a well was dug 150m (490ft) into the rock in case of siege. Inside, you can see the living quarters and workshop of Friedrich Böttger, the alchemist who discovered the secret of making true porcelain in 1709. Prior to this, Böttger was incarcerated here from 1706 to 1707 when the castle served as a jail – the Elector of Saxony, Augustus the Strong, had held him in 'protective custody' in order to be the beneficiary of the alchemist's quest to manufacture gold. Other prominent prisoners included the social democrat August Bebel and the poet Frank Wedekind.

Prague, Czech Republic (Km 45–55)

Starting or finishing point for most Elbe/Vltava cruises (although the vessel actually docks at Ústí, 70km/43 miles to the north), the romantic city of Prague is located on a curve of the winding Vltava River, a tributary of the Elbe, and known to Germans as the Moldau. Graceful bridges span the river, including the famous Charles Bridge, the Lesser Quarter clinging to one side and the Old Town to the other, surveyed from above by the 10th-century Hradčany (Prague Castle). The city has inspired composers including Mozart, Smetana and Dvořák, as well as poets, writers, revolutionaries and intellectuals. It's still a great university city and seat of learning, with nightlife to match in the legendary bars and pubs.

If your river cruise ends in Prague, try to stay for at least a couple of days, so that you have plenty of time to visit the highlights, which include the following:

Charles Bridge (Karlův most): Slightly curved and spanning the Vltava between the Old Town and the hill leading up to the castle, Charles Bridge is a Gothic masterpiece, with the added impact of some fine Baroque sculpture. The first stone bridge was constructed here during the second half of the 12th century, in place of the wooden structure that was situated further to the north. The 30 statues adorning the bridge were added over a period of 250 years. The oldest and most significant statue is that of St John of Nepomuk, which was installed in 1683. Many are now replicas and the valuable originals can be seen in the Lapidarium of the National Museum. The bridge is usually very crowded with sightseers; for a more atmospheric experience visit early in the morning or late at night.

Prague Castle (Hrad): With its commanding position high above the river, the castle has been key to every epoch in the city's history. It is the most extensive complex of buildings in the city, containing St Vitus Cathedral, the Royal Palace and many other monuments. It also serves as the seat of the president of the republic.

St Vitus Cathedral (Katedrála sv. Víta): Prague's magnificent Gothic cathedral contains not only chapels and tombs, but also some fine stained glass, including the window designed by Art Nouveau artist Alphonse Mucha. The main attraction inside the cathedral is St Wenceslas's Chapel, built by Peter Parler in which the national saint Wenceslas was interred.

The saint's sacred place is exceptionally ornate; walls are decorated with polished jasper, amethysts, agate and emeralds, as well as fine gilding and frescoes.

Jewish Quarter (Josefov): The Jews of Prague suffered persecution from the Middle Ages, but found some freedom in their ghetto, now preserved as the Jewish Quarter and a memorial to their tenacity. The earliest mention of Prague's Jewish community comes from a document by the Jewish merchant Abraham ben Jakob, dated 965. The ghetto, built in about 1100 and surrounded by a wall, soon became one of the largest Jewish communities in Europe. Major sites include the Old-New Synagogue, the oldest remaining synagogue in Europe in which services are still held. Nearby, the Old Jewish Cemetery is both a moving and fascinating place and was the last resting place for Jews between the 15th and 18th centuries. The number of graves is much greater than the 12,000 gravestones would suggest – this was the only place where Jews could be buried, so graves were layered one above the other. The Jewish community was destroyed in World War II, when thousands were sent to their deaths. Today there are around 1,500 people of Jewish descent in Prague.

Loreto Church: The Loreto Church is dedicated to the Virgin Mary and is the most famous pilgrimage church in Prague. The ornate facade and frescoes in the cloister date from the 18th century. In the tower is a glockenspiel of 27 bells, which play a Czech hymn to the Virgin Mary every hour. The highlight is the Treasure Chamber, which contains the remarkable Diamond Monstrance, a gift from a Bohemian nobleman. It was made in 1699 by Baptist Kanisch-

Prague and its bridges.

bauer and Matthias Stegner of Vienna and is studded with over 6,000 diamonds.

Old Town Square (Staroměstské náměstí): Prague's picturesque Old Town Square is the natural midpoint of the Old Town, and the heart of Prague. Memorial tablets on the Town Hall Tower are reminders of various important events that have taken place here over the centuries. In the 12th century the Old Town Square was a central market place and a major crossroads on central European merchant routes. Over the next few centuries many buildings of Romanesque, Baroque and Gothic styles were erected. The Jan Hus monument in the centre of the square is in honour of the 15th-century reformer who stood up against the corrupt practices of the Catholic Church.

Astronomical Clock: The astronomical clock on the Town Hall Tower dates from 1410. It consists of three parts. In the middle is the actual clock, which also shows the movement of the sun and moon through the zodiac. Underneath is the calendar, with scenes from country life symbolising the 12 months of the year, painted by Josef Manés (these have now been replaced with replicas). The performance of the upper part of the clock is what draws the hordes of tourists. On the hour the figures play the same scene: Death rings the death knell and turns an hourglass upside down. The 12 Apostles proceed along the little windows that open before the chimes, and a cockerel flaps its wings and crows.

Týn Church: The landmark pointed towers of the Týn are one of the icons of Prague, looming 80m (260ft) above the Old Town. The building was erected between 1365 and 1511, and features many noteworthy Bohemian Baroque works of art and the oldest baptismal font (1414) in Prague. To the right of the high altar is the tombstone of the famous Danish astronomer Tycho Brahe, who worked at the court of Rudolf ll. The church is a source of great national pride, and the facade, particularly when floodlit at night, is one of the finest sights in the Old Town.

National Gallery (Národní galerie): In Sternberg Palace, within the castle complex, is the National Gallery, which houses a fine collection of European art. There are three levels; the ground floor houses German and Austrian art from the 15th to the 18th centuries; the first floor comprises the art of antiquity, icons and the art of the Netherlands and Italy of the 14th to the 16th centuries; the second floor has Italian, Spanish, French, Dutch and Flemish art of the 16th to the 18th centuries. Albrecht Dürer's large-scale *Feast of the Rosary* is perhaps the most famous exhibit.

Wenceslas Square (Václavské náměstí): Nearly a kilometre (two-thirds of a mile) long, Wenceslas Square is not really a square at all, but a wide boulevard. Nowadays, the former horse market is dominated by hotels, bars, restaurants, cafés, banks and department stores. It is a busy area, along which half of Prague seems to stroll. The historic square is crowned by the giant

equestrian statue of St Wenceslas, erected by Josef Myslbek in 1912 after taking 30 years to plan and design.

National Theatre (Národní divadlo): This is the city's main cultural venue and a potent symbol of the Czech spirit. In 1845 the ruling Habsburgs turned down the request for a Czech theatre. In response, money was collected on a voluntary basis, and the building of the theatre was declared a national duty. Built in an Italian Renaissance style in 1881, the theatre was destroyed in a fire just before it was due to open. Under Josef Schulz's direction, using many notable artists including Vojtěch Hynais, it was quickly rebuilt with the aid of endowments and donations and opened in 1883. The auditorium is only open to the public during performances.

North German port cities

Some river cruises also visit sea ports that lie within protected areas of the coastline. In the 19th century, wealthy Berliners came to the region to recuperate in fashionable coastal bathing resorts.

Cuxhaven (Km 730): The citizens of Cuxhaven in Lower Saxony once controlled all shipping in and out of the River Elbe. Today, however, it is one of the largest fishing ports in Germany and the centre of its fish processing industry. It is also home to Germany's oldest lighthouse, built in the 14th century on the island of Neuwerk.

Lauterbach, Isle of Rügen, Germany: Although few people think of islands when you mention Germany, Rügen is, at 926 sq km (357.5 sq miles), Germany's largest island, separated from the mainland by a narrow channel, although joined to the mainland by a 2.5km (1.5-mile) -long bridge. It is the port for Lutbus, an elegant, all-white city that formerly had a royal residence, although its castle was demolished in 1960. Today, you can stroll around the castle gardens. The popular bathing resorts of Baabe, Binz, Göhren and Sellin are located on the southwest of the island.

Wolgast, Isle of Usedom, Germany: Another 'island,' Germany's second largest and its easternmost, lies near the mouth of the River Oder, and the border with Poland. It is a mix of old established verdant forests (part of the national park) and white sandy beaches. Wolgast itself lies on the mainland at the point where a road bridge connects it with the island.

Stralsund, Germany: Located on the Baltic Sea coast and surrounded by three lakes, this port city, founded in 1209, features some fine architecture of Gothic red brick buildings, similar to those of nearby Lübeck. Although it has been the subject of many battles in the past, this important centre of maritime navigation has today been restored to its former glory.

Zingst, Germany: Sitting on a small peninsula, much of which is a national park (Vorpommersche Boddenlandschaft), the town has the character and charm of a typical German village untouched by time. Nearby, there are long sandy beaches and forests.

River Rhône

A trip along the Rhône incorporates the gastronomy of Burgundy and Lyon, the Roman ruins of Vienne and Arles, the magnificent historic papal city of Avignon and modern-day cowboys in the Camargue.

The evocative names of Burgundy, Avignon, Lyon and Mâcon conjure up all kinds of delicious images, from fields of yellow sunflowers and purple lavender to ruby-red wines, truffles, rich cheeses and plates of charcuterie, not to mention magnificent Roman antiquities and colourful market towns. The Rhône flows through the gastronomic heart of France, carving its way across some of the most beautiful wine-growing country, as well as handsome, historic cities such as Avignon and Arles.

The Rhône has always been an important trade route, linking northern Europe to the Mediterranean and forming a means for armies from the south to move north through the continent. It is 813km (505 miles) long, and starts its journey in the Swiss Alps, just upstream from Lake Geneva. It descends westward through a long valley between the Alps and the Jura Mountains to Lake Geneva, and then enters France. The final section is from Lyon to the Golfe du Lion and the Mediterranean, which it enters through a two-armed delta that begins at Arles

River Royale on the Rhône.

and extends for approximately 40km (25 miles) to the sea. The arms are known as the Great Rhône and the Little Rhône, with the unnavigable salt marshes and lagoon of the Camargue between them.

A Rhône river cruise starts either from Lyon, the country's gastronomic capital, located in the heart of the country between the Saône and Rhône rivers, or from Chalon-sur-Saône. In the reverse direction your journey will start from from Arles or Avignon in Provence. If you are a devotee of French cuisine, it is worthwhile considering a stay of at least an extra day or two in Lyon. A visit on the third Thursday of November is always lively, since that's the date that Beaujolais Nouveau, cultivated near Lyon, is released for sale each year.

Highlights from Chalon-sur-Saône to the Camargue

Chalon-sur-Saône

This important inland port in the heart of Burgundy is located at the confluence of the River Saône and the Canal du Centre. Chalon is often the start for excursions to Dijon, considered by many to be the underrated capital of Burgundy (Dijon has a fine range of restaurants, excellent city museum and attractive Flemish-influenced architecture). Chalon's town's heart is the place St Vincent, with its colourful half-timbered houses and cathedral, the oldest parts of which date from the 11th century. It was also the birthplace of photography in 1822 – Kodak still has a presence here.

Mâcon

Nestled neatly into the west bank of the River Saône at the end of a 14th-century bridge (Pont St-Laurent), Mâcon is located at the southern end of the Burgundy wine region and plays an important part in its wine trade. May is the month when Mâcon hosts the Burgundy wine sales. The Unesco-protected Ben-

Did you know...?

…that the River Rhône is the only major river that flows directly into the Mediterranean?
…that the river has famously fierce currents? Climatic conditions (eg the mistral) and seasonal changes (eg bringing meltwater from the Alps) create extra navigational difficulties.
…that the French for 'lock' is *écluse*?

View of Lyon from Fourvière Hill.

edictine Abbey of Cluny, 25km (15 miles) northwest of Mâcon, is the highlight of a visit to this area, although wine lovers could travel to the region to taste the local wines.

Lyon

Lyon, the gastronomic capital of France, actually lies on a little peninsula between the Rhône and Saône

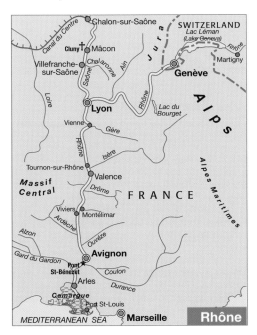

rivers. It was founded more than 2,000 years ago and is today the second-largest city in the country, and its most important educational centre outside Paris. The city's reputation for wonderful food is completely deserved and there are countless local specialities to try, among them *quenelles de brochet* (mousse of pike) and a huge array of magnificent charcuterie. Notable Michelin-starred chefs connected with the city include Paul Bocuse, Guy Lassausaie and Philippe Gavreau.

There's also an eclectic collection of museums in the city, including the Musée Historique des Tissus et des Arts Décoratifs – a wonderful textile museum with some rare exhibits, and the Musée des Beaux Arts, its collection ranked second in France only to that of the Louvre.

A visit to Lyon also usually includes a trip up Fourvière Hill, either a clamber up steep steps or a funicular ride. At the top, you can visit the Basilique de Notre-Dame and gaze out over the city's rooftops, past the two rivers to the vineyards beyond.

Vienne

This town's position, between the Beaujolais and Burgundy wine regions, makes it the gateway to the countryside around Lyon. Most notable, however, is the town's amazing Roman heritage: Vienne has one of the best-preserved Roman amphitheatres in France, on the slopes of nearby Mt Pipet, seating 13,000 and still used for theatrical performances. The Temple d'Auguste et de Livie in the town itself is also an arresting example of 1st-century Roman architecture. Vienne is well known for its jazz festival, which normally takes place in July.

Pont St-Bénezet and Palais des Papes, Avignon.

Tournon-sur-Rhône

The scenery as the river carves its way south is rugged and mountainous, dotted with castles and jagged rock outcrops, although vineyards are still the main feature along the banks. Tournon is one of the region's most attractive cities, nestling on the bank of the river and overlooked by its 10th-century castle, built into a rock. An excursion from here enjoyed by many river cruise passengers is a ride on a nostalgic steam-hauled train to the Ardèche region (between Tournon and Lamastre), a wild, limestone upland of craggy cliffs, gorges and caves, with red wine and lavender its main products. There are also excursions by coach to the Gorge de l'Ardèche: a road runs along the top of the red-rock gorge, the river a silvery ribbon hundreds of feet below, and there are various lookout points and peculiar rock formations.

Between Tournon and the city of Valence, the Rhône is reinforced by the turbulent waters of the Isère, flowing in from the Alps to the northeast.

Viviers

This quiet town dates back to the 5th century, when it was an episcopal seat. It still retains its old-world charm today, with medieval houses and an impressive cathedral.

Avignon

The river is broadening out now as it enters Provence and nears the Mediterranean, although the scenery is still undulating and rich with colour – yellow sunflowers all summer long, and ranks of purple lavender spread across the hilltops, scenting the air.

The beautiful university city of Avignon is totally encircled by medieval walls and known as the 'City of Popes'; in the 14th century, this was the residence of the papacy for 70 years. The ravishingly handsome medieval Palais des Papes at the centre is one of the great wonders of France, and was once considered to be the heart of the Christian world.

Nearby are the remains of the famous Pont St-Bénezet, which juts out across a branch of the river, and is the subject of one of the most famous French nursery rhymes, *Sur le Pont d'Avignon*. The city has a terrific buzz on warm summer nights, with outdoor cafés and bars lining the streets and free entertainment provided by buskers and street artists, especially during the Theatre Festival in July.

Arles and the Camargue

This small town, located on the banks of the River Rhône, boasts many Gallo-Roman ruins, including an amphitheatre that can hold 20,000 called Les Arènes that is still used for bullfights and plays today. A visit to the animated place du Forum, in the very heart of town, is a must. Vincent van Gogh, who lived here for a while, immortalised in vibrant colours many of this city's highlights.

From Arles, you can take an excursion (typically included in the cost of your holiday) to the Camargue, the delta of the River Rhône and one of Europe's finest nature reserves, with its unspoiled landscape and wildlife (renowned for its wild, pink flamingos, black bulls and white horses). You may be lucky enough to watch the *gardians*, the modern-day Camargue cowboys who still tend their bulls on horseback.

River Seine

A voyage along the Seine offers beautiful scenery, from romantic Paris to bucolic Normandy and historic Rouen to the pretty port of Honfleur. Gastronomic delights and wine tours add to the appeal.

From the iconic French capital to Honfleur, one of the most picturesque of all French ports, the Seine has been witness to some of the most remarkable characters throughout history: Joan of Arc, Van Gogh, Seurat and Claude Monet. A cruise along this slow-flowing river is a gentle voyage through some of France's most mellow countryside, of farmland and meadows, historic towns and sleepy villages. It is also a gastronomic adventure, in the land of brie and camembert cheeses, Calvados liqueur and Normandy cider.

The Seine is is 780km (485 miles) long, and its source is 471m (1,545.2ft) above sea level on Mont Tasselot in the Côte d'Or region of Burgundy. It is the longest navigable waterway in France, and carries more commercial traffic and freight than any other river or canal in the country. It flows northwest of Dijon, Burgundy, through the dry chalk plateau of Champagne then through Paris, Giverny, Rouen and across Normandy before emptying into the English Channel not far from Le Havre. The estuary is wide and extends for 26km (16 miles) between Tancarville and Le Havre. The relatively flat Seine is slow-flowing and hence eminently navigable. On its journey, it is joined by the Aube, near Romilly, the Yonne, near Montereau, and the Marne, its greatest tributary, near Paris.

Riverships can go all the way to Paris all year round – the reason why the port of Paris trans-ships more than 20 million tons of cargo each year.

Highlights from Paris to Honfleur

Paris (Km 0)

The major highlight is, of course, Paris, perhaps the most romantic city in Europe.

It is cut through the middle by the slowly meandering River Seine and edged with gentle hills. The Seine is the capital's widest avenue; it is spanned by a total of 37 bridges, which provide some of the loveliest views of Paris. The fascination of the French capital is eternal and has long been a magnet to artists, writers, philosophers and composers. Its grand architecture, fine cuisine and haute couture combine to make Paris one of the most glamorous European capitals. Île St-Louis, in the middle of the River Seine and at the heart of the city, is the official start of kilometre markings along the River Seine.

There are too many city highlights to cover here in full, so what follows is a classic top-10 big sights. If you know the city already, less obvious delights include the Marais area, with its show-stopping place des Vosges, or the adjacent, more edgy, Bastille. Otherwise, head to the literary St-Germain, explore the city's other key waterway, the Canal St-Martin, or, if shopping appeals, the so-called 'grands magasins' (department stores), including Galeries Lafayette and Printemps. Alternatively, if the weather allows, simply relax in the elegant Parisian parks, such as the Jardin du Luxembourg or the Tuileries or else just along the arty banks of the Seine itself.

Key sights include:

Musée du Louvre: One of the largest palaces in Europe has assembled an incomparable collection of Old Masters, sculptures and antiquities, housing 35,000 works. It has three wings, and the superb collections are divided up into seven different sections, each assigned its own colour to help you find your way around. Highlights include Leonardo da Vinci's Mona Lisa.

Tour Eiffel: No visit to Paris would be complete without a trip to the Eiffel Tower, symbol of the city and of France herself. The metal giant looms over the

River Baroness cruising along the Seine.

Monet's house and garden at Giverny.

area southwest of the centre. This icon of iron girders was chosen as the centrepiece to the World Fair of 1889. The first two floors are negotiated on foot or by lift, and then another lift goes up to the top. From here you will see a spectacular city panorama, best viewed one hour before sunset.

Notre-Dame: The cathedral's position on the banks of the Seine is an unforgettable setting. Just as Gothic cathedrals were considered symbols of paradise, so the entrance facade, with its series of sculptures, was considered to be the gateway to heaven. The stories of the Bible are depicted in the portals, paintings and stained glass of the cathedral. The scale exceeded all earlier churches – Paris became the capital only a few years before the foundation stone was laid, and the building was designed to reflect the power of the state and its church. Construction work on the cathedral began in 1163 and was finished around 1240. The exquisite 13th-century north and south rose windows are star attractions.

Arc de Triomphe: Built between 1806 and 1836, this triumphal arch is the epitome of French grandeur. The many statues on the main facade glorify the insurrection of 1792 and Napoleon's major victories.

Centre Georges Pompidou: Made entirely of glass and surrounded by a white steel grid, the Pompidou Centre is the main showcase for modern and contemporary art in Paris. Now a much-loved city icon, Richard Rogers and Renzo Piano's 'inside-out' design was controversial when it was unveiled in 1977.

Sacré-Cœur: Set in Montmartre is the virginal-white Basilique du Sacré-Cœur. Perched on a hill, its Byzantine cupolas are as much a part of the city skyline as the Eiffel Tower; when the lights are turned on at night, the Sacré-Cœur resembles a lit wedding cake. It can be reached by walking up 250 steps or by taking a funicular cable car.

Musée D'Orsay: France's national museum of 19th-century art is housed in the former Gare d'Orsay, an ornate Beaux-Arts train station, opened in 1900 to serve passengers to the World Fair. It's an immensely dramatic setting, worth visiting for its own sake. But the museum's contents are unmissable too: there is a major collection of paintings by the Impressionists, plus works by Delacroix and Ingres.

Musée Rodin: Housed in the Hotel Biron is the Rodin Museum. Auguste Rodin came to live here in 1908 and stayed until his death in 1917. Here you can admire Rodin's famous works, *The Kiss* and *The Thinker*, reputedly based on Dante contemplating the Inferno.

Sainte-Chapelle: This is a masterpiece of Parisian Gothic Rayonnant architecture on the Île de la Cité. The beautiful 13th-century stained glass, magnificently displayed in 85 major panels, is without equal anywhere in Paris.

Versailles: Located southwest of Paris lies the grand Palace of Versailles. Take the RER line C5, which will drop you a short distance away. Allow a full day to visit the chateau and its magnificent formal gardens.

Conflans–Ste-Honorine (Km 68)

Situated on the confluence of the Oise and the Seine, Conflans was an important shipping centre from 1855 onwards, when a chain was laid along the bed of the Seine allowing barges to be hauled upstream to the capital. Highlights of the town include the Montjoie Tower and St-Maciou church. A religious festival is held here for three days each June, and riverships flock to attend. Many riverships also moor here overnight.

Melun (Km 110)

About 45km (28 miles) from Paris, Melun (the Romans called it Melodunum) is, like Paris, located on

---

Did you know…?

…that the name Seine comes from the Latin name 'Sequana', the goddess of the river?

…that the Seine is the third-longest river in France, after the Loire and the Rhône?

…that Joan of Arc's ashes were supposedly scattered in the Seine at Rouen?

…that the first steamboat on the River Seine was in 1816? However, it actually frightened the people along the river banks because the vessel's steam engine sprayed out smoke and sparks.

…that the composer Puccini set his 1918 opera *Il Tabarro* (The Cloak) aboard a barge on the Seine?

…that in 1991 the banks of the Seine in Paris were declared World Heritage sites? Unesco calls the French capital 'a river town', with banks 'studded with a succession of masterpieces'.

both banks of the Seine, on the northern edge of the forest of Fontainebleau. Its ancient church of Notre-Dame stands on an island between two branches of the river. The town is a centre of commerce for the agricultural district of southern Brie. The famous brie de Melun is made here – quite different in texture and taste to the bries of Coulommiers, Meaux and Montereau.

Located about 6km (4 miles) from Melun is the 17th-century royal Château de Fontainebleau, home of French kings and emperors from François I to Napoleon and well worth a visit, if time allows.

Giverny (Km 147)
World-famous as the setting for the water-lily pond and graceful arched bridge immortalised by the painter Claude Monet, who lived here for 43 years, Giverny is one of France's most-visited sights, receiving 500,000 tourists a year, some of them clutching easels and paint, hoping to recreate the master's work. You can visit the house and, of course, the garden, which is especially glorious, even if the throng of tourists does take a little of the shine off it. The Musée d'Art Americain Giverny, located just along the main road in the village and showcasing the works of US-born Impressionists who were inspired by Monet, is also worth a visit.

Rouen (Km 238–245)
Rouen is known as the 'City of 100 Spires,' and you can see its graceful skyline as you approach along the river. Until the 17th century, it was the second-largest city in France, and is still important today as France's fourth-largest port. Although badly damaged during World War II, the city has been extensively restored – in particular the 700 or so half-timber-framed buildings on the right bank of the river in the old quarter. The spot everybody wants to see, though, is the marker on the pavement in the place du Vieux Marché, where Joan of Arc was burnt at the stake as a witch in 1431.

Other sights include the magnificent Cathédrale Notre Dame, the western facade of which was painted by Monet (the work is housed in the city's Musée des Beaux Arts), and the medieval Église St-Maclou,

which contains some superb wood carvings. Also look out for the Gros Horloge, a splendid, gold-faced clock mounted on a building which creates a bridge across one of the narrow streets.

Caudebec-en-Caux (Km 309.5)
The medieval town of Caudebec-en-Caux is only a short cruise downstream from Rouen, through pretty Normandy scenery of woods, orchards and fields. The main attraction is the Église Notre Dame, the construction of which was started by the English when they had conquered the town in the 14th century, but completed by the French in 1439 after they had won the town back. The church is in Flamboyant Gothic style, with intricate stone carvings, flying buttresses and graceful spires. Tours of the town also include a visit to Jumièges Abbey, which was consecrated in 1067 in the presence of William the Conqueror.

Honfleur (Km 355)
The Seine broadens out into a wide estuary as it approaches the coast, and is busy with commercial traffic. Honfleur is a charming old port city on the southern shore of the Seine Estuary, opposite the port of Le Havre; most cruises turn around here and head back to Paris. It was from Honfleur that French settlers set out for the new lands of Canada in the 16th century. The town really is the stuff of picture postcards, particularly around the inner harbour, the Vieux Bassin, where narrow medieval houses overlook a colourful yacht and fishing harbour.

It's no surprise that the light, the space, the old coloured buildings and the boats have attracted artists for years, including Boudin and many of the Impressionists. You can see their work in the Musée Eugène Boudin, which has an ethnographic section detailing the history of the town as well as several rooms containing paintings, mainly from the 19th century, of the town, including some work by Monet. Buying French bread and cheese or duck pâté and having a picnic on a bench beside the river is highly recommended here.

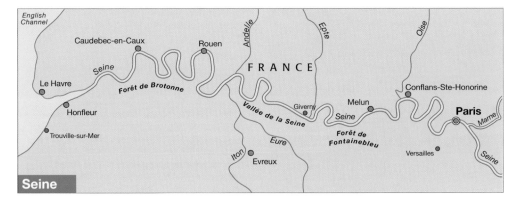

River Po

A cruise on the Po is a great way to see some of Italy's most breathtaking cities and sample the regional cuisine. Few towns are on the river itself, so most excursions involve a bus trip.

The River Po is, at 670km (416 miles) long, the longest river in Italy. It starts in the northwest near the border with France, rising on Monte Viso near the southern end of the Cottian Alps. It then flows eastward through Italy's heartland and empties into the Adriatic Sea to the south of Venice. It is fed from numerous small rivers from the Alps, including the Adda, Mincio, Oglio and the Ticino. Today, it runs through the north Italian provinces of Lombardy, Emilia-Romagna and the Veneto.

After the fall of the Roman rulers in the 8th century, many people moved inland, away from the River Po delta. The dykes fell into disrepair, and the river formed its own course. It was approximately 400 years ago that the Po Delta shaped itself into a sort of triangle. The longest arm of the triangle was formed by the coastal dunes. As the lagoons silted up, the coastline moved at the rate of 500 yards every 100 years towards the sea, which created the river's ever increasing delta.

River Countess in Venice.

Although the plain was mostly marshland, the canalisation of the area was started as long ago as the 12th century, although it was only between 1604 and 1660 that a canal was dug to divert the river, so that it flows directly into the sea; the mouth of the main arm was blocked off and all river traffic was halted. So much silt is brought by the river and deposited in the fertile deltas at its mouth that it is reported to be advancing into the Adriatic Sea at a rate of 60m (196ft) per year.

Today, the shallow, slowly meandering River Po is navigable from Nizza Monferrato, a city in northern Italy's Piedmont region, to the Adriatic Sea, through some of Italy's loveliest unspoiled land.

Po floods

However, all is not always serene and calm. In 2000, some 43,000 persons were evacuated in Italy following flooding from heavy rains in the western and central plains of the River Po. The floodwaters moved eastwards along the river, closing factories and schools and disrupting telecommunications, and a state of emergency was declared by the Italian government. The floods affected Cremona and Mantua, both of which were highlights of River Po cruises.

Cruising the Po

Given the historical riches of the region, it may seem surprising that there aren't more river cruises on the Po. There are reasons for this, however: the Po is not an easy river for larger ships to navigate, as its depth changes constantly; capacity is therefore limited to smaller vessels. Indeed, riverships that draw very little water have been specially constructed to navigate this scenic route.

Did you know?

…that the Latin name for this river was Padus?
…at its widest point, the river measures 503m (1,650ft)?
…that in 2005 the Po hit global headlines when it was found to be carrying the equivalent of almost 4kg (8.8lbs) of cocaine daily, way above official estimates for cocaine consumed? (This figure indicates around 40,000 doses of cocaine daily for the region, whereas the official statistics are about 15,000 doses per month for young adults in the region.)

Mantua's Piazza dell' Erbe.

Cruising along the Po River is centred around Venice and its lagoon, which was created by the estuaries of three rivers, the Adige, Brenta and Po, and is separated from the Adriatic Sea by a row of sand bars. It is about 51km (32 miles) long. Most Po cruises operate a long summer season, from late March to early November. Spring is a wonderful time to visit, before the cities get too crowded and Venice becomes clogged with tourists and, more to the point, its canals begin to smell less than fragrant. October is also a good month, as the trees begin to turn, a gentle mist hangs over the fields at sunrise, the searing heat of the days lessens and the long lines of tour buses thin out.

In February, it's Carnival in Venice, a glamorous and frenetic annual festivity that typically lasts for about two weeks. River cruise companies usually operate special Venice and lagoon cruises during this period.

Note

At the time this book was produced and published, cruises along the River Po had been put on hold. In the aftermath of the capsizing of *Costa Concordia* in 2012 the Italian authorities implemented new safety regulations in April 2012. Both *Bellissima* of Nicko Tours and *Michelangelo* of CroisiEurope are presently restricted to cruising the Venice Lagoon, as the authorities require additional certification for the open water stretch between Chioggia and the mouth of the Po, which leads to the Adriatic Sea. (Italian authorities require the river vessels to comply with several mandates that normally apply only to ocean-going cruise ships, as they transit the open sea, although for just a few kilometres. This requires substantial modification to the riverships in order to comply.)

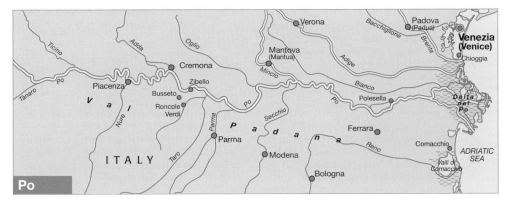

Juliet's House, Verona.

Highlights from Mantua to Venice

There are no kilometre markers along the Po. Cruising distances are short, and most of the time is spent sightseeing away from the boat.

Mantua (Mantova)

Mantua, hometown of the poet Virgil, is fortunate to be located close to three lakes. The old centre perches serenely on a peninsula that juts out into the lakes. Sadly, the nearby petrochemical plants have brought pollution, but the setting is nonetheless picturesque. The city itself has ancient stone churches, small shops, lovely squares and pavement cafés. The most impressive squares are the Piazza dell'Erbe with its marketplace, the medieval Piazza del Broletto, and the attractive, cobbled Piazza Sordello.

Mantua was the seat of the powerful Gonzaga dynasty in the 14th century, when this was a flourishing centre for the arts. The 500-room Palazzo Ducale compound is testament to the family's great wealth, with a huge collection of Renaissance art and frescoes. The Palazzo's most important fresco cycle is in the Camera degli Sposi, in which Andrea Mantegna's frescoes depict the court life of Ludovico Gonzaga in intricate detail, right down to his favourite dog and the court dwarf.

The Palazzo Te, built by Federigo Gonzaga for his mistress, stands outside the walled part of the city and, with its sweeping gardens, is located opposite the cathedral; this elegant country palace served as an inspiration for Versailles, the Nymphenburg (Munich) and Schönbrunn (Vienna).

Cremona

Cremona is indisputably the world's violin capital, its fame dating back to the period between the 16th and 18th centuries, when great names such as Nicolò and Hieronymus Amati, Giuseppe Guarneri and, most famous of all, Antonio Stradivari, who was born here in 1644, set out to create the perfect stringed instrument. An excursion will probably take you to one of the workshops of a present-day violin maker as well as to the Museo Stradivariano. Cremona is also famous for its 12th-century cathedral and square, as well as for having Italy's tallest bell tower.

Ferrara

During the Renaissance period, Ferrara was the seat of many patrons of the arts. Impressive monuments include the 13th- to 15th-century cathedral, the Palazza Schifonoia (which contains frescoes from the 15th century), and the Castello Estense. The centre of the city has been designated a World Heritage site. Typically, there may be an excursion from Ferrara to visit Bologna, depending on itinerary and operator.

Piacenza

The streets of the city of Piacenza were originally laid out in a rectangular grid by the Romans but, sadly, no Roman monuments have survived. The cathedral, built in the Lombardy-Romanesque style between 1122 and 1253, is a splendid example of the period. Cereal growing and viniculture form most of the economy of this city, which is also a major transportation centre on the road between Milan and Bologna.

Bologna

Although some distance from the river (around 45km/28 miles south), the city of Bologna is well worth a visit, if offered as an excursion. The city is of great historical interest and has excellent shopping, particularly for food.

Located to the north of Florence, Bologna is the principal city of the Emilia-Romagna region and lies at the foot of the northern Apennine mountain range, some 55m (180ft) above sea level. In 1088, the first university in Europe was established here; by the 12th century, many wealthy families were resident in the city. In the competitive spirit of the age, each family attempted to outdo their neighbours by building a large tower on their properties – needless to say, the bigger the tower, the more important the family. At one point there were 180 of these medieval skyscrapers looming over the city, 15 of which still stand.

Parmesan

True parmesan cheese (parmigiano-reggiano) is manufactured from 15 April to 11 November in Parma (also in the provinces of Bologna and Mantua). It is made from skimmed cow's milk (32 percent butterfat), which is mixed with rennet and cooked for 30 minutes. After going through several rounds of draining and drying, it is coated and formed into cylindrical shapes weighing about 30kg (67.5lbs), with slightly convex sides. It takes about one year to mature and has a yellow, crumbly consistency.

Highlights include the Piazza Maggiore and the neighbouring Piazza Nettuno, both in the heart of the city, surrounded by graceful Renaissance and medieval buildings. Both piazzas are great gathering-places, full of outdoor cafés and street artists, and buzzing with life. Between the two squares is a huge bronze of *Neptune* by the French sculptor Giambologna.

Bologna's beautiful Basilica di San Petronio is one of the largest churches in the world. Look out for the carvings depicting scenes from the New Testament by Jacopo della Quercia, and frescoes by Giovanni da Modena. Within walking distance from here is the Pinacoteca Nazionale, in the old university quarter, with works by Giotto, Raphael's *Ecstasy of St Cecilia* and some minor El Grecos and Titians.

Verona

Another highlight along the Po is the Romanesque city that inspired Shakespeare's *Romeo and Juliet* (and *The Two Gentlemen of Verona*), offered as a half- or full-day tour and, during the Opera Festival season of July and August, as an evening event.

Verona lies on the winding Adige River, which descends from the Italian Alps to run parallel with the Po before emptying into the Adriatic just to the north of the Po Delta, on a plain at the foot of the Lessini Mountains, approximately 105km (65 miles) west of Venice. The compact medieval centre lends itself to slow wandering, its shopping streets lavishly paved with smooth marble, and some of the 600-year-old facades decorated with intricate frescoes.

The city was the seat of the Scaligeri family, one of northern Italy's most important dynasties, throughout the medieval period. Towards the end of their rule, the family built Castelvecchio, a solid-looking fortress, damaged in World War II but subsequently restored.

The Roman Arena, a stunning creation in rose-coloured marble on the Piazza Bra, dates to the 1st century AD and is the third-largest Roman amphitheatre in existence. If you get a chance to go to the opera, take it; the atmosphere inside is amazing and the evening really is a special occasion, with well-known Italian operas performed under the stars and fans flocking from all over the world.

An even bigger lure for most, though, is Casa di Giulietta (Juliet's House) on Via Cappello, just off Via Mazzini, the main shopping street. The star-crossed lovers are fictional, although they are based on real families, the Cappello and the Montecchi. Whether these families were actually feuding, however, is questionable. You can see the famous balcony and recite the immortal lines, but the chances of photographing the old house without a coach party in front of it are slim.

Verona is also known for its regional wines, Bardolino, Recioto, Soave and Valpolicella, and has a good supply of outdoor cafés where you can sit with a chilled Soave and a plate of antipasti, read the paper and watch the world go by.

Padua (Padova)

An historic university town (Galileo was professor of mathematics here in 1592), Padua lies on the River Bacchiglione, west of Venice. Highlights include its great basilica, St Andrew's, built to house the body of the saint after which it is named (the town's patron saint) and completed in the 14th century. The high altar is decorated with magnificent

Old wooden boats in a Chioggia canal.

bronzes by Donatello. Padua is home to the oldest botanical garden in the world, founded in 1545. It's also worth paying a visit to the food market, the Mercato Sotto il Salone, for its wonderful variety of produce.

Parma

Set in wooded, gently hilly countryside south of the Po on the Torrente Parma tributary, Parma is famed for its hams and cheeses. Parma itself deserves recognition for more than gastronomy; Verdi and Toscanini composed many great works here, and the cathedral is famous for Correggio's *Assumption of the Virgin* in the cupola, which took six years to paint. The other important sight is the Galleria Nazionale in the Palazzo della Pilotta, the 17th-century home of the wealthy Farnese family. The gallery contains work by Correggio, Francesco Parmigianino, Fra Angelico, Leonardo, Canaletto and Van Dyck.

The cobbled lanes around the old centre are lined with delicatessens selling Parma ham and parmesan cheese. There's also a colourful produce market in Piazza Ghiaia, south of Palazzo della Pilotta. Genuine parmesan cheese comes from two towns, Parma and Reggio Emilia, which between them have an official logo that should be embossed on the side of the cheese. The unique qualities of both the cheese and Parma ham are attributed to the humid microclimate of the immediate area around Parma. The salty chunks of meat are actually taken to cure in Zibello, on the banks of the River Po.

Chioggia

Chioggia is located on an island at the southern end of the Venice Lagoon, about 24km (15 miles) south of Venice. It is Italy's largest fishing port, and will instantly remind you of Venice itself, with its winding, narrow streets and canals, and old-world charm. The most notable buildings are the 11th-century cathedral and the churches of San Martino (1392) and San Domenico (14th century), both of which house valuable paintings.

Venice (Venezia)

Beautiful, dreamy, romantic Venice, straddling 118 islands on the edge of the Venice Lagoon, has inspired poets, artists, musicians and lovers, and brings endless superlatives to the lips of visitors today. No matter that is it sinking at an alarming rate, floods frequently, smells of drains in the hot summer months and the canals are as clogged with traffic, albeit waterborne, as the streets of Rome. Venice is on every river cruise passenger's must-see list

River cruise vessels moor along the Giudecca Canal, between the ocean cruise terminal and the entrance of the Grand Canal. You can walk from the mooring points to St Mark's Square in 20 minutes. Our key highlights are listed below:

Rialto Bridge (Ponte de Rialto): This famous bridge crosses the Grand Canal at what used to be the busiest trading centre in the city – the Rialto market district. Two rows of shops lie within the solid, closed arches – the feature which gives it its unique appearance. This is a great place to pause and watch the river traffic, and admire the majestic sweep of palaces and warehouses swinging away to La Volta del Canal, the great elbow-like bend in the canal.

St Mark's Basilica and Museum (Basilica & Museo di San Marco): The basilica is the centrepiece of St Mark's Square and is the most famous of the churches in Venice – a place the aesthete John Ruskin called 'a treasure heap, a confusion of delight.' Best visited in the morning, the basilica, which was modelled on Byzantine churches in Constantinople, remains a glorious confusion. Despite the sloping irregular floors, an eclectic mix of styles both inside and out, the five low domes of unequal proportions and some 500 non-matching columns, St Mark's still manages to convey a sense of grandeur as well as jewel-like delicacy.

Attached to the basilica is a museum housing some of St Mark's finest treasures. The star attraction is the world's only surviving ancient *quadriga* (four horses abreast), known as the *Cavalli di San Marco* (The Horses of St Mark). These are the gilded bronze originals believed to have crowned Trajan's Arch in Rome, but later moved to Constantinople, where Doge Dan-

---

Prosciutto

Langhirano is a town about 20km (12.5 miles) to the east of Parma, known as the place where Pio Tosini (who died in 2002 aged 95) argued that the silky air-cured ham produced in the town, and refined for the last century, should be known as *prosciutto di Langhirano*. He lost, and the speciality became known by its present tag, *prosciutto di Parma* (Parma ham).

Langhirano is located between a small mountain range and plains with a small stream to the north – ideal conditions for nature to provide the cure.

After being salted twice, hams then rest for 24 days at 1–4° Celsius (34–39° Fahrenheit), before being passed through a pummelling tunnel to take away any excess salt

and relax the tissue to allow the remaining salt to penetrate evenly. The last drop of blood is removed by a 'squeezer' – a person who literally squeezes the hams, before they are sent to rest for 70 days.

The hams are then hung and pre-cured for three months. Each prosciutto is then serially stamped, starting with the number of the farmer who bred the pigs, the number of the abattoir, and the curer. When the ham has cured for one year, the Consorzio di Prosciutto inspects it using a pointed piece of porous horse bone from the femur to decide whether it is good enough. When the inspector has given his approval, the ham receives its Ducal stamp before being dispatched.

Venice, the highlight of any river cruise on the Po.

dolo claimed them as spoils of war, bringing them back to Venice. Replicas adorn the facade in order to protect the originals from corrosion.

Doge's Palace (Palazzo Ducale): For nine centuries, the magnificent Doge's Palace was the seat of the Republic, serving as a council chamber, law court and prison, as well as the residence of most of Venice's doges. The architects of this massive structure, with peach-and-white patternings in its distinctive brick facade, achieved an incredible delicacy by balancing the bulk of the building above two floors of Istrian stone arcades.

Grand Canal (Canal Grande): A trip along the Grand Canal, Venice's fabulous highway, is an unforgettable experience. Along certain sections of the canal the gondolas still function as *traghetti* (ferries) and, from the station to St Mark's Square, the banks are lined with ornate palaces and grand houses, mostly built between the 14th and 18th centuries. While some have been restored, others have a neglected air, awaiting their turn for renovation. Must-sees include the Ca'Grande, the Ca'Foscari, the Ca'd'Oro and the Guggenheim. As well as providing a cavalcade of pageantry, the canal offers a slice of local daily life, welcoming simpler craft such as gondolas and rubbish barges.

The Accademia: Housed in a former convent since 1807, the Accademia gallery displays the most complete collection of 14th- to 18th-century Venetian painting in existence. This outstanding gallery is arranged chronologically in 24 rooms, and includes works by Titian, Canaletto, Bellini and Carpaccio. Jacopo Tintoretto's dazzling St Mark's paintings, notably the haunting *Transport of the Body of St Mark*, are also here.

San Rocco: The area of San Polo that lies within the

bend of the Grand Canal is home to the Scuola Grande di San Rocco, famous for its paintings by Jacopo Tintoretto. His magnificent works adorn every surface: the images are larger than life, full of chiaroscuro effects and floating, plunging figures in dramatic poses. One of the best-known is *The Glorification of St Roch*.

Scala del Bovolo: The Palazzo Contarini has an outstanding external spiral staircase in its interior courtyard, the Scala Contarini del Bovolo, a Lombardesque work dating from 1499. Bovolo translates as 'snailshell' in Venetian dialect.

Ca D'Oro: The 15th-century Ca D'Oro is the city's most magnificent Gothic palace. On the facade, the friezes of interlaced foliage and mythological beasts were originally picked out in gold. The restored and modernised interior now features the Galleria Franchetti, which houses numerous Renaissance bronzes and sculptures.

The Frari: Officially known as Santa Maria Gloriosa dei Frari, this austere Franciscan centre is the largest and greatest of all the Venetian Gothic churches, founded in the 13th century and rebuilt in the 14th and 15th centuries. The adjoining cloisters house the state archives. The church's greatest treasure is Titian's *Assumption*, his masterpiece, hanging above the high altar. The great painter is buried here.

St Mark's lion

The winged lion represents St Mark, the patron saint of Venice, and adorns buildings, bridges and doorways. Whereas the seated lion represents the majesty of state, the walking lion symbolises sovereignty over its dominions. A golden winged lion of St Mark still adorns the city standard, and remains the symbol of the Veneto.

River Douro

The picturesque scenery of the Douro Valley in the north of Portugal makes it a glorious cruise destination. The journey is usually a round trip from Porto, taking in country estates and port wine institutes.

The Phoenicians and Romans mined gold in the Baixo Douro region and used the river to transport the ore to the coast – hence the name, which means 'of gold', although some poetically say that the name also derives from the golden sheen of the river as it reflects the sunlight, and the sand-coloured hills through which it flows.

The Douro region itself lies north of the river, while to its south is Biero Alto. The river starts with small beginnings in the high hills of the Picos de Urbion, in Spain's Soria Province, to the north of Madrid (the river is called 'Duero' by the Spanish). It then flows west across to the border with Portugal, before turning southwest and delineating the border for approximately 97km (60 miles). It then flows west again, meandering though some enchanting countryside en route, including sleepy villages, castles and vineyards that have remained remarkably unchanged and pastoral for hundreds of years, before hitting the Atlantic at Portugal's second city, Porto (Oporto).

Sailing through Porto.

The river serves as a transportation route for wine products of Portugal's Paiz do Vinho region, and also supports a fishing industry. The river is navigable within Portugal, although there are rapids and occasional flooding in its lower reaches. Only vessels with a very shallow draft can enter the river due to sandbars at its mouth.

From Porto, you cruise 'upstream' and cross several dams, including the Crestuma-Lever and the Pachino. Excursions are made by motor coach to various *quintas* (country estates) and establishments that produce the region's favourite tipple – port.

A series of dams were constructed along the Douro in the 1980s for flood control and for the generation of electricity and hydroelectric power. Fortunately, the planners had the foresight to include locks within the dams, and these have enabled navigation right through Portugal and into Spain. The once fast-flowing river is now like a series of connected tranquil lakes with spectacular scenery.

In addition to the city highlights en route, the other attractions of a Douro cruise include the Portuguese cuisine, which is simple but full of taste. Fresh fish and seafood play an important part, as do ham and chicken, and fresh vegetables that are typically grown by small farms that do not use pesticides. Locally produced wines are plentiful, of good quality, and usually enjoyed with lunch and dinner. Events might include a *fado* (literally, fate) evening, a great chance to sample this unique Portuguese form of music that always tells a sad story.

Did you know?

…that the best time to visit the Douro Valley is during the *vindima*, in late September and early October, when the grapes are being collected?
…that wine has been produced in the Douro Valley for around 2,000 years? It is also one of the world's oldest designated wine-producing regions – its demarcation dates to the mid-18th century.
…that the Douro is the third-longest river on the Iberian Peninsula, after the Tagus and the Ebro?
…that the *Spirit of Chartwell*, which cruises on the River Douro, was chosen by Queen Elizabeth II as the royal barge to lead the 1,000-strong flotilla during the celebrations and Diamond Jubilee Pageant in London on 3 June 2012?
… that nine dams have been built along the Douro's length?

Note that cruises along the Douro often offer a bus excursion from the border town of Vega de Terrón to the historic Spanish university city of Salamanca.

Highlights on a round trip from Porto

Only a handful of cruise companies operate on the Douro, usually offering seven-night itineraries starting and finishing in Porto. Typical stops include Peso da Régua, Pinhão, Ferradosa (for São João) and Vega de Terrón (a jumping-off point for Salamanca, across the border in Spain). Apart from the joy of cruising the river as it carves its way through the steep hills, most of the excursions are a coach journey away from the various stops. Each itinerary crosses several dams, including the Crestuma-Lever and the Pachino. Cruises can be combined with a stay in Lisbon and Coimbra, Portugal's former medieval capital and still an important university town, using local trains for transport.

Porto

Located on the Douro, Porto (Oporto) is Portugal's second largest city, the heart of the port-wine trade and one of the most attractive cities on the Iberian Peninsula. It dominates the hillsides above the Douro, tumbling down the side of a gorge carved from granite by the fast-flowing water. The gorge is spanned by several graceful bridges, leading to Vila Nova de Gaia on the opposite bank, where all the great port lodges are located, including Cockburns and Sandeman – their English names reminders of the fact that British merchants controlled the industry from its inception. Cruise boats moor up in the heart of the city on the Vila Nova side, within easy reach on foot of the medieval town, the Ribeira district. On the banks of the river you'll see the colourful *rabelo* boats that were once used to transport port down from the vineyards.

The historic city has Unesco World Heritage status and was designated a European City of Culture

Rabelo boats once transported port down from the vineyards.

in 2001. The city centre is a chaotic mix of medieval alleys, the old fisherman's quarter and a skyline of ornate Baroque towers, all crowned by a magnificent cathedral. Highlights include the Ponte Dom Luis I (the iron bridge), an impressive steel railway bridge that looms over the vividly painted houses of the Ribeira district and spans the river to the south bank. Built in 1886, the bridge has two decks, the upper one for the metro, and leads directly to port cellars in Vila Nova de Gaia.

There's also the cathedral, Sé, which crowns the highest point of the granite rock on which much of the old town stands. It was built as a defensive fortification in the 12th century, and despite extensive alterations it has retained its fortress-like appearance. The 18th-century Torre dos Clérigos is the tallest granite tower in Portugal and has become the emblem of Porto. Unless you really have no head for heights it is worth climbing the endless spiral staircase with 225 or so steps for the dazzling view over the city, the river Douro and its estuary. Another notable church is Santo Ildefonso,

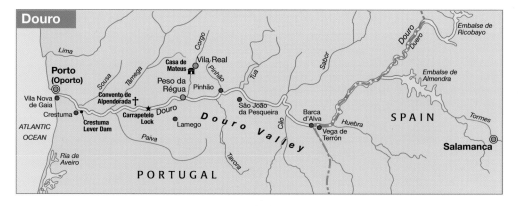

Casa de Mateus.

built in the 18th century and decorated with *azulejos* (glazed tiles) depicting scenes from the life of St Ildefonso and allegories of the Eucharist. Look out, too, for the Stock Exchange, built on the site of a convent, which burnt down in 1832. It is noted for its opulent neo-Moorish reception hall. Finally, across the Ponte Dom Luis I, are the port-wine lodges of Vila Nova de Gaia. Many of the larger ones welcome weekday visitors to tour the installations and taste their wines. Most prominent is Sandeman, whose distinctive silhouette rises on the skyline.

Peso da Régua

From Porto the Douro snakes eastwards to Peso da Régua past wooded valleys, fields of almond trees and quiet villages. Shortly after leaving Porto, the rivership passes through the floodgates of the Crestuma Lever Dam, one of several built over the last few decades to tame the river, which was previously difficult to navigate. Some cruises stop for the evening at Bitetos, with an excursion to the nearby 11th-century Convento de Alpendorada, which overlooks the river. The monastery hosts medieval-

style banquets and wine-tastings, and provides an atmospheric setting for dinner. The Carrapetelo Lock, with a maximum lift/drop of 35m (115ft), is also a highlight of this stretch of the river.

The port region proper begins at Peso da Régua. At this point, the river suddenly enters a region of steep hills covered with green vineyards, and the occasional lavish manor house set back from the river. Giant lettering on the hillsides denotes each grower's name. Peso da Régua is the home of the Port Wine Institute, and almost all its inhabitants have some connection with the port-wine trade; in the past, this was the starting point for the *rabelo* boats, laden with barrels, on their long and treacherous journey to Vila Nova de Gaia on the coast.

For river cruise passengers it's now a departure point for coach tours to Vila Real, 25km (15 miles) to the north, and noteworthy as home to the Casa de Mateus.

Pinhão

This small, rustic Douro town, located at the end of the wine trail, is known for its picturesque setting and its proximity to the *quintas*, the country seats of the big names in port production. The railway station has some beautiful *azulejos* on the walls, depicting local scenes and culture. The town also has a bridge by the French architect Gustave Eiffel (of tower fame). Riverships stop here to run excursions to the wine-growing estates, where visitors learn about grape crushing, fermentation and blending. Even if you don't drink port, it is worth the visit simply to admire the beauty of the estates, some of them with lavish gardens on the river banks.

Vila Real (Casa de Mateus)

The magnificent 18th-century Baroque house and gardens of Casa de Mateus (daily June–Sept 9am–7.30pm; Mar–May & Oct 9am–1pm, 2–6pm; Nov–Feb 10am–1pm, 2–5pm) lies 3km (2 miles) outside the busy town of Vila Real. It belonged to the counts of Vila Real, and was the birthplace of the navigator Diego Cão, who discovered the mouth of the Congo River in central Africa. The estate has beauti-

---

Portuguese cuisine

Food in Portugal conjures up images of empire, with influences from its erstwhile colonies Brazil, Angola, Mozambique, Goa and Macau much to the fore. The voyages of the explorer Vasco da Gama brought back cinnamon and curry powder, and both are still important flavourings in Portuguese cuisine. Common ingredients include fresh fish and seafood, ham, chicken, and fresh vegetables that are typically grown on small, organic farms. It is the quality of the produce that delights many visitors, whether the nutty, earthy potatoes or the juicy tomatoes that taste like an explosion of flavour to those accustomed to bland supermarket varieties. Pork is the

dominant meat, and the wonderful charcuterie features in many soups and stews.

Some local specialities in Porto include tripe of veal with beans. The story goes that altruistic locals donated all their meat to the ships departing to conquer the New World, leaving only the tripe for their own consumption. More palatable are the local salt cod *(bacalhau)*, succulent roast lamb and the famous *caldo verde* – a soup of potatoes, cabbage and olive oil. Between spring and early autumn, sardines can be found as street food, cooked on small terracotta braziers. Sweet, egg-based puddings are also popular and go well with a glass of port.

Lamego.

fully cool, shady formal gardens and a fine *allée* of cedar trees. The area is famous for its Mateus Rosé wine, and an image of the house appears on all Mateus Rosé bottles. Vila Real itself has little of interest, although it is the largest town in the region, and is on the edge of a dramatic gorge carved by the River Corgo (a tributary of the Douro).

Barca d'Alva

This is a gentle spot that was once the upper navigation limit on the Douro. It is the closest point to the Spanish border (less than 2km/1.2 miles away), and sits among almond and olive groves. The town itself, usually just a stopping-off place for the night, is only a few hundred yards from the Spanish border, inside the Douro International Natural Park.

São João da Pesqueira

São João, usually offered as an excursion from Ferradosa or Pinhão, is a sprawling wine-growing village famed for its town hall, which has stunning tiled murals depicting port-wine-making scenes. It is surrounded by port *quintas* on a plateau that overlooks the valleys and vineyards of the Douro in a delightful, picture-postcard setting.

Lamego

Lamego, 12km (7.5 miles) south of the river and usually offered as a half-day tour from Peso da Régua on the return journey to Porto, is an important pilgrimage site, overlooked by the the Sanctuary Church of Nossa Senhora dos Remédios (Our Lady of the Remedies). A superb Baroque-style staircase of some 600 steps reaches the church, by which point most visitors are in need of a blessing from the saint. The view from the top, though, is worth it – it is absolutely stunning. In September, thousands of pilgrims flock to the town.

Lamego was once the trading post of the Moors who journeyed across from Spain. They left their legacy in the 12th-century castle with an unusual vaulted cistern. The town's museum houses an impressive collection of furniture, paintings, 16th-century Flemish tapestries, sculpture and jewellery from the Bishop's Palace within which it is situated.

Vega de Terrón (for Salamanca, 128km/80 miles away)

Across the Spanish border, riverships berth for the day at Vega de Terrón while their passengers visit Salamanca, a university town since the 13th century. The Plaza Mayor, a huge, elegant square surrounded by gracious sandstone buildings, is one of the most impressive and beautiful in Europe. The twin cathedrals, Catedral Nueva (16th-century Gothic) and Catedral Vieja (12th-century Romanesque), the latter with its spectacular silver Byzantine dome, are also well worth seeing.

Barge cruising

A barge holiday offers a wonderful opportunity to sample life in the (very) slow lane in beautiful surroundings, both on board and off. This chapter covers all the essentials.

In this chapter, we answer some of the basic burning questions potential barge cruise customers might like to ask.

Why go barge cruising?

Quite simply because barges let you de-stress completely. They provide an antidote to the pressures of life in a fast-paced world, with their calming, slow speed. They allow you to holiday in surroundings that are quite comfortable without being pretentious, plus you can expect fine food and, hopefully, enjoyable company. Barges are like little bed-and-breakfast places tucked away in some forgotten corner. There are typically no computers and no telephones, which should also help you to disconnect from all the usual concerns of everyday life.

In addition, of course, they provide a wonderful way to experience and explore new surroundings – effortless discovery, if you like.

Cruising on the Canal du Midi, southern France.

Tell me more

As with riverships, there are no casinos, no bingo or horse racing or other potentially objectionable parlour games, nor are there art auctions or other revenue-generating events that are for many a negative aspect of the ocean-cruise experience. And once on board, you only have to unpack once, which is hugely convenient compared with touring by road or train and constantly having to pack and unpack, as you change hotels.

What's the difference between a river cruise and a barge cruise?

The main difference is that cruise barges travel much more slowly (up to 6kph/3.75mph) than riverships (up to 18kph/11mph). They are also smaller and typically cater to a maximum of 12 persons, as opposed to riverships, which can carry as many as 300 passengers (although usually a maximum of around 200).

Are meals included?

They certainly are, as are wonderful cooks. Full board is included in the cruise fare, and everything is cooked to order. The chef purchases his/her own food in local shops and markets, so it's really fresh.

What about drinks?

All drinks (both alcoholic and non-alcoholic), including champagne and wines with dinner, are typically included.

Won't I get bored?

Hardly! There is always something to see on the canals – it's like live armchair travel.

Did you know...?

...that the Canal du Midi in the South of France was the incredible work of one man? It was the work of 17th-century engineer Pierre-Paul Riquet, who sacrificed a fortune to finance his dream of creating a waterway linking the Atlantic with the Mediterranean. The mammoth project took 14 years to complete, using 12,000 workers; it was finally finished in in 1681. There have been relatively few modifications since the canal was constructed, although the original wooden lock gates have been replaced with steel ones. The canal offers 386km (240 miles) of navigable waterway, skirting the sun-bathed shores of the Mediterranean and winding its way up towards the wine regions of Bordeaux.

Apart from totally unwinding, you can also be active if you wish. There are always lots of excursions and activities on offer. You can walk (probably faster than the barge can chug along), go bicycling (almost all barges have bicycles), hill climb, go hot-air ballooning, go horse riding or play golf or tennis. You can also go food shopping with the chef or learn some cooking tips from him or her. Or you could simply head into the nearest village for a baguette or two, or sample some local cheese or charcuterie.

How about dining?
It's casual. With so few passengers, everyone eats at the same time. There are no assigned tables, which hopefully provides an opportunity to make new friends.

How about special diets?
If you are on a special diet, let your travel provider know when you book your holiday. The chef will usually be pleased to accommodate you if possible. Some fresh foods will be purchased daily, which should mean that any special diets can be taken into account. Note that the galley on a barge is extremely compact, with little storage space for seldom-used items, so there won't be a big stash of unusual dietary items.

What's the best season for a barge cruise?
Late spring or early autumn (fall) are when you'll get the best weather for a cruise of this kind, although each season brings its own attractions. Note that cruise barges do not operate in winter.

Is barge cruising for singles?
The world of cruising is made for couples. Singles are an expensive afterthought, and few barges have dedicated cabins for singles. You can occupy a double cabin on your own, of course, but you will have to pay higher fares.

Are barge cruises for honeymooners?
Possibly! Barge cruises in France provide an utterly romantic setting. Most arrangements will have been taken care of before you sail, so all you have to do is show up. Some cruise barges have accommodation in double-, or queen-sized beds but, in general, cabins are small when compared to those in a typical hotel room.

If the budget is not a problem, the ultimate experience would be to charter a whole cruise barge (perhaps one of the smaller ones, for 4 to 6 passengers). You could sleep in different cabins each night and have a wonderful, indulgent, exclusive honeymoon.

Is barge cruising for families with children?
More families are discovering the joys of chartering a whole barge – most of them accommodate between 4 and 12 people, which could cover one or two average-sized families, or one such family plus friends. Meals and excursions can also be tailored for

Cycling alongside the Canal du Midi.

all tastes and age ranges. Well-respected operators such as Abercrombie & Kent specialise in holidays of this kind. Parents will, of course, need to be extremely vigilant about young children falling overboard when clambering around the deck.

Are barge cruises suitable for disabled passengers?
Unfortunately they are not well equipped for passengers with disabilities. Cruise barge cabins are not the only problem, but getting from shore to vessel and vessel to shore can prove extremely difficult. My advice is to try a larger rivership, rather than a cruise barge, as these are much better equipped (more have lifts as well as larger cabins/suites that can better accommodate wheelchairs).

Are tips included?
In general, tips are not included. As a guideline, you should allow €8–10 (£6–8) per person, per day for gratuities. You give these to the barge master on the morning of disembarkation, and they will be shared among the crew.

Is airfare included?
Generally, airfare is not included, although it may be included in packages available through specialist operators. Check when purchasing.

Is insurance included?
No. To summarise briefly, for health cover, travellers from within the EU are covered to some degree with EHICs, but you are well advised to take out travel insurance with full medical cover (including repatriation by air ambulance) before travelling. Visitors from the US will need to take out full medical cover.

Is there a difference between cruise barges?
The appointments and interior decor range from rustic but comfortable to pure unabashed luxury, with prices to match.

What is the electric current?

Almost all cruise barge cabins have 220-volt electrical outlets. Take an adapter for any electrical appliance you use (hairdryers are usually provided).

Will I get seasick on a barge cruise?

No. The movement of water on the rivers and canals is so slight that it is extremely unlikely that anyone would suffer from motion sickness.

Are there medical facilities on board?

No. First-aid kits are carried, cruise barges are always close to land, and any necessary arrangements in the event of a medical problem can be made relatively quickly.

How pregnant can I be if I take a barge cruise?

Typically most barge cruise companies will not allow a mother-to-be on a cruise past her 28th week of pregnancy. You may be required to produce a doctor's certificate in order to be allowed to travel. Fortunately, you'll never be far from shore, where medical help can be summoned quickly, day or night.

Can I smoke on board?

Smoking on barges is usually restricted to the open deck area (as on riverships).

What about security?

Barges do not have key cards, generally speaking. Most have locking cabin doors, but the house-party atmosphere is supposed to engender an element of trust between passengers. The barge should always be locked if all passengers and crew are ashore.

What is a barge cruise?

It's about life in the very slow lane. Remember the 1960s song, 'Feelin' Groovy'? The lyrics 'Slow down, you move too fast' are perfectly apt here. There are just two speeds to a cruise barge: dead slow, and stop. So, slow down – way, way down – and simply pootle on your way. It called the 'CD' approach – chug and drift, as you wind your way through some of the most tranquil landscapes in Europe.

Although there are some variations, a 'standard' canal barge cruise is six days long, with each cruise barge operating on fixed itineraries. (The seventh day can then be spent in cleaning and preparing the vessel again for the next set of passengers.)

Every cruise starts in a civilised manner with a glass of champagne and moves gently through picture-postcard countryside. One of the first things to notice is the assortment of flowers and flower boxes that litter the uppermost deck – barge owners delight in trying to outdo each other.

There's nothing quite like pastoral countryside to take you back in time. Going more slowly than a person would on foot, cruise barges travel along the canal systems as well as the rivers. They cover very little in terms of distance but offer more time to get to know the countryside. You really can experience the colours of the blackberry bushes that overhang the path instead of speeding by them, as on a typical river cruise.

Auxerre is the centre of barging in France.

Taking a barge cruise is one of the very best ways to experience a country in small doses. In Europe, barge cruises can be taken in Belgium, France, Germany, the Netherlands and the UK, although the most popular country is undoubtedly France, where barge cruising has been carefully packaged and practised for many years.

Cruise barges (the French word for barge is *peniche*, although the French also call it *la maison qui marche* – 'the house that walks') chug along slowly in the daytime and moor early each evening, giving you time to pay a visit to a local village and get a restful night's sleep (no late nights or noisy overnight travelling).

The inland waterways of Europe all adhere to the CEVNI regulations (Code Européen des Voies de la Navigation Intérieure), which is a UN instrument with international authority and relevance.

French cruise barges have a reputation for excellent food and wine, and good conversation (no doubt the latter is to some degree the direct result of the former). As is typical in France, meals on cruise barges tend to be slow, sociable occasions. Locally grown fresh foods are usually purchased and prepared each day, allowing you to live well and feel like a houseguest. There is no mass dining here.

And you need to be as good at socialising as you are at eating when you join a barge cruise on your own (or as a couple), as you will be living in close quarters with a handful of others (most likely total strangers). A good sense of humour and an international outlook on life helps. Note, however, that most cruise barges can also be chartered exclusively, so you can just take your family and friends.

Design and layout

Many cruise barges have been skilfully converted from cargo- or munitions-carrying barges, most of which were built in either the Netherlands or Scotland (*L'Art du Vivre* is an example of a Scottish-built barge), while a handful of new ones have been constructed expressly for holidaying in the past few years. Most have the timeless appeal of a tiny country house.

Cruise barges are typically between 30 and 50m (100–166ft) in length, with a beam (maximum width) of between 5 and 7.3m (16.5–24ft), although their actual size depends on the area of operation and the ability to manoeuvre in the many locks that line the canals.

A cruise barge almost always has a steel hull, with a flat bottom, and will (with a few exceptions) have been converted from a cargo-carrying vessel. Their cruising speed is generally up to 6kph (3.75mph). Most carry a maximum of 12 passengers (although a few carry up to 24 passengers), and they tend to be beautifully fitted out with rich wood panelling, full carpeting, custom-built furniture and fine fabrics. Each barge has a dining salon/lounge-bar. Barge captains are often owner/operators, typically taking great pride in their vessel.

The cruise barge *Anjodi* in Languedoc.

Some have air conditioning, and most have some form of heating. Most also have some kind of canopied sun deck. Cruise barge interiors always have plenty of cosy cushions on lounge seats and armchairs. Most cruise barges carry bicycles for your use; others may have a minibus that tootles alongside, ready to take you on excursions, all of which are included in the cruise fare.

Many cruise barges that carry fewer than 12 passengers have their own idiosyncrasies and niceties. Most are immaculately kept by their very proud owners, who lavish time and money on a high level of maintenance.

Cabins and suites: Cabins tend to be rather small, but homely, although the overall look does tend to depend on the owner's preference in terms of decor. While most cruise barges are strictly for couples (with queen, double or twin beds), some barges also have single cabins. The size of cabins varies considerably – while there is no average cabin size, they measure from a tiny 6 sq m (64.5 sq ft) to a luxurious 24 sq m (258 sq ft). All cabins aboard *La Nouvelle Etoile* measure 18.5 sq m (200 sq ft).

Many cruise barges have suites measuring about 15 sq m (161.5 sq ft). The 'Monet Suite' aboard *L'Impressioniste* measures 15.77 sq m (169.8 sq ft), for example, and the 'Nuits-St-Georges' Suite aboard *La Belle Epoque* measures 15.36 sq m (165.3 sq ft). Further down the scale, the three twin-bedded cabins (often erroneously

Luxury cruise barge crossing the Loire on the aqueduct at Briare.

called 'staterooms' by enterprising marketeers) aboard *Nymphea* measure 6.25 sq m (67.2 sq ft).

If you want more space in your 'bedroom', you'll need to check the details carefully with your cruise barge booking agent or the owner, if you book direct (not recommended). The *Saint Louis* (available for whole vessel charter only) has cabins with a decent size of 11.7 sq m (127 sq ft).

Bathrooms: Cabins usually have en suites, with a toilet, basin and shower at least.

Design specifics: Let's look at some of the details that make cruise barges so distinctive. What makes one cruise barge more luxurious than the next – apart from the size of the cabins – is the use of space and the quality of its decor, cabinetry and furnishings (in addition to the specialised local knowledge of the captain and crew, plus the quality of the cuisine).

Anjodi has a hot tub and a skylight in the salon. *Anacolouthe* has a baby grand piano in its lounge, which has rich wood panelling and a red colour scheme. *Elisabeth* has a split-level dining room with oak beamed ceiling. *Fleur de Lys* has a grand piano in its lounge and some rare vintage wines in the cellar, while bathrooms have two washbasins, as well as romantic canopied beds.

Fleur de Lys is also the only cruise barge I know of with a lounge decorated with fine antiques and a grand piano, plus a heated (decent-sized) plunge pool on deck. *Horizon II* is a split-level design with beautifully panelled interiors. *L'Impressioniste* has an exercise room and spa tub. *La Belle Epoque* also has richly panelled interiors, a fitness studio, hot tub and even a sauna. *La Nouvelle Etoile* has internet access in all cabins, tiled bathrooms and a lift (the only cruise barge to have one). *Napoleon* has one bedroom with a large, marble-clad bathroom that is reminiscent of

some of the bathrooms in the legendary, deluxe Hotel Danieli in Venice, plus a sun deck measuring a spacious 75 sq m (800 sq ft).

Princess, built in 1973 by Daniel Ludwig, international shipping magnate and founder of Princess Hotels, has a canopied sun deck and cabin bathrooms with windows that open. *Quiétude* has an open fireplace. *Saroche* has a wood-burning stove in its split-level lounge, beautiful panelled interiors, satellite television and even its own washer/dryer (most unusual for a cruise barge). Meanwhile, *Sérenité* has lovely scrolled armrests on the dining room chairs, plus a very roomy dining room, with large, wood-trimmed picture windows.

Cuisine

The biggest event (indeed, it's the entertainment) of any barge cruise is the food. How you dine will depend on which cruise barge you choose. Dining ranges from homely cooking to outstanding nouvelle cuisine with all the trimmings. Tables are set with fine linen and china, and dinner is usually a leisurely candlelit affair, accompanied by rather good wines, some of which would be almost impossible to find outside the local producing region. Often, the owner of the barge, or his/her partner, is also the cook, and you can be assured that the ingredients are all fresh, and purchased almost daily.

Barge cruising in France

There are about 8,500km (5,280 miles) of navigable canals and waterways in France, and operators place their vessels in the best stretches, both for scenic beauty and architectural interest, as well as for ease of getting to and from your chosen cruise.

Locks

A barge cruise in France means going through a succession of locks, and nowhere is this more enjoyable and entertaining than on the Canal du Midi, with its 61 locks along the canal's 240km (149-mile) length or in Burgundy, where, between Dijon and Mâcon, a cruise barge can negotiate as many as 54 locks during a six-day journey. Lock hours of operation are civilised – between 8.30am and 6.30pm, with an hour off for lunch. If locks are of the hand-cranked type, you can lend a hand to open or close the lock gates – it's good exercise, and you get to talk to the lock keepers. Some lock keepers have a stock of vegetables to sell to the cruise barges.

Sights

Medieval walled towns, sleepy villages, towering cathedrals and cloistered abbeys, wine châteaux, chic shops, summer festivals and romantic hamlets all await you in France, dependent, of course, on the region in which you are cruising. In general, cruise barge companies split the country into several regions, and barges usually operate regular itineraries for the complete season (with few exceptions).

The key regions include Burgundy, home to the Canal de Bourgogne, Canal du Centre and the River Saône, and renowned for its fine wines and excellent cuisine. Highlights of the Canal de Bourgogne include the elegant historic city of Beaune, the vineyards of Meursault, Nuits-St-Georges, Santenay and Savigny, and the Unesco-protected Basilica of Vézelay and Abbey of Fontenay. Other attractions in the region include Auxerre, the centre of barging in France, and Chablis, another wine-tasting hotspot. Popular barge cruises include Dijon to Pont Royal (from big city to tiny hamlet) along the Canal de Bourgogne or from Dijon to Lyon along the Saône – a trip that is particularly good for wine lovers, who can visit all five appellations in one cruise.

Then there's the Loire Valley, also great wine country, where attractions along the Canal Latéral à la Loire include crossing Gustav Eiffel's 19th-century aqueduct at Briare (it crosses the River Loire, and so does your barge with you on board), the longest canal bridge in the world. Other highlights in the Loire include a visit to Montargis, often dubbed the 'Venice of France'.

An eastern France barge cruise would include Franche-Compté, east of Burgundy, as well as Alsace-Lorraine, which borders Germany, while southwestern France is another popular region, with Bordeaux and the Dordogne the highlights here. Provence is another great region for barge cruising in France, with a plethora of attractions including the great Roman cities of Avignon and Arles, the Roman aqueduct at the Pont du Gard and cowboys of the Camargue.

The cost

Rates typically range from €600 to more than €2,200 (£500–1,850) per person for a six-day cruise, varying according to the season, with those in the spring and autumn being the least expensive and those in the peak summer season the most expensive. I do not recommend taking children under the age of 16, unless you charter the whole barge exclusively for family and friends. Rates include a champagne reception, a cabin with private facilities, all meals, good wine with lunch and dinner, beverages (including an open bar), bicycles, side trips and airport/railway transfers. Other activities, such as horse riding, golf, tennis, or hot-air ballooning, can be arranged at extra cost.

At the beginning and end of the season (around April and November), the weather can be unreliable, so it's best to take clothing that can be layered, including sweaters, plus a waterproof windbreaker.

Arrival

If you are travelling by train, note that many European stations do not have porters, so travel light and use luggage with wheels. Note that not all stations have lifts, and at some you might have to cross a footbridge with lots of stairs to reach the exit, so make sure, too, that you can manage to carry your own luggage up the stairs.

Chartering a private cruise barge

Private 'whole barge' charters (often with special themes, such as a fine French 'dégustation' cuisine cruise) are the way to go if you want to travel with a few select friends or as a large family, although you'll certainly have to pay for the privilege. You can even arrange a 'tandem' cruise, with two barges on identical itineraries. The cost for a private charter of a six- or eight-person luxury cruise barge is between around €18,000 and €55,000 (£15,000–45,000) for one week.

French waterway terms
barge *un péniche*
beam *une largeur*
embankment *une digue*
distance marker *un point kilométrique*
dock *une darse*
downstream *aval*
(lock) gates *les portes*
length *la longueur*
lock *une écluse*
lock keeper *l'éclusier*
port (left side) *bâbord*
propeller *une hélice*
rudder *un gouvernail*
starboard (right side) *tribord*
towpath *un chemin de halage*
upstream *amont*
wheelhouse *une timonerie*

How we evaluate the riverships

To help you differentiate between riverships, we have rated each one according to the elements we consider key to providing a quality product. This section explains how the ratings and Berlitz star system work.

Just as I have been evaluating and rating ocean-going cruise ships professionally since 1980, I have also been travelling extensively aboard Europe's riverships in order to be able to draw up an independent Berlitz rating system for the 280-plus vessels in service. There is no official star rating system for riverships, so any star quoted in marketing material for a cruise is based purely on the opinion of the company selling that product. My aim has been to create an independent system, designed to work fairly across the entire spectrum of riverships in all segments of the marketplace, from budget to deluxe, and intended to enable the customer to make an informed decision as to which rivercruise to go for.

My rating system is explained in greater detail below, but, as an overview, I have rated each rivership out of a total of 500 points across five areas: the quality of its hardware/facilities, accommodation, cuisine, service/hospitality plus any 'other' components, with a maximum of 100 points in each category. In each area, the little things – the extra touches that improve

The retro-look *River Cloud II*.

the quality of the overall experience – mean the addition or deduction of points on the great scorecard.

I have then divided the total of 500 points up into ranges, to create my own independent Berlitz star ratings from 1 to 5. So any vessel awarded between 251 and 300 points is classed as a 3-star rivership; one gaining between 301 and 350 points is a 3-star plus rivership (I have quoted double categories for all except 5-star vessels to help differentiate within categories); and a rivership with a total of between 351 and 400 points is classed by Berlitz as 4-star, etc.

Ultimately, there really is no world's best river cruise line or river ship – despite what the brochures might claim – only the vessel and cruise that is right for you. Hopefully our ratings will go a long way towards helping you find your ideal match.

Criteria

The evaluations and ratings cover five principal areas, with a maximum possible score for each area of 100. **Hardware:** This includes the general profile and condition of the vessel, its age, maintenance, decking material, pools and hot tubs, deck furniture (such as deck lounge chairs – whether they are made of hardwood, stainless steel, or plastic, and are with or without cushioned pads). It also covers the cleanliness of the interior – eg the public bathrooms, lifts (elevators), floor and wall coverings, stairways, passageways and doorways.

This score also reflects the quality of the facilities, including the public rooms (typically including some or all of the main lounge, library and shop), the ceiling height, foyer, stairways, passenger hallways, lifts, wellness facilities, public restrooms, lighting, air conditioning and ventilation systems, floor coverings, plus the decor, and any artworks. It covers dining-room facilities including windows, chairs (with or without armrests), lighting and tableware including china, cutlery, linen and centrepieces (flowers). **Accommodation:** For suites/superior grades, this includes the design and layout of all suites, balconies, lighting, beds/berths, furniture (placement, and mattress quality), hanging space for clothes (including whether wooden or plastic hangers are provided), drawer space, bedside tables, vanity desks, lighting, mirrors, air conditioning and ventilation, audiovisual facilities, artworks, insulation and noise levels. It also covers soft furnishings, written information, tea- and coffee-making equipment, flowers, fruit, and bathrobes and slippers (if any).

It reflects the bathroom facilities, notably the shower unit, washbasin, cabinets, storage for toiletries, and the size and quality of the towels.

NB: suites should not be designated as such unless the sleeping room is completely separate from the living area.

For standard cabins this includes the design and layout of the space, furniture and fittings, clothes storage space, bedside tables, vanity unit, lighting, air conditioning and ventilation, artworks, plus bulkhead insulation and noise levels. It also covers soft furnishings and details such as the in-cabin information folder (list of services), flowers, fruit, slippers (if any), towels and bed linen, plus bathroom facilities, notably the shower unit, washbasin, cabinets, storage for toiletries and the towels.

Note that balconies can be described as 'full' (a full balcony, just enough to sit down) or 'French' (floor-to-ceiling glass doors opening onto railings, with just room enough to stick your toes out). Some vessels have both. Others have windows only, which may or may not open. Cabins on the lowest deck almost always have 'panoramic' windows instead (because they are too close to the water line). These can vary in size.

Cuisine: The score for this section covers the dining room, informal dining/buffets, the ingredients used and tea/coffee/bar snacks. Under 'dining room' we have included menus (variety and presentation), culinary creativity, the appeal, taste, texture, freshness, colour and balance of the food, plus garnishes, fresh fruit and wine list and wine prices.

Informal dining/buffets covers the hardware (eg hot and cold display units, sneeze guards, tongs and other serving utensils) plus presentation, food temperatures and food labelling.

Ingredients covers the quality of ingredients, plus their consistency and portion size.

Tea/coffee/bar snacks covers the quality and variety of tea and coffee provided. This includes afternoon tea, cakes and sandwiches, whether mugs or cups and saucers are provided, whether cream and milk is provided, and bar snacks.

Service: In the dining room this includes the restaurant waiting staff (serving, taking from the correct side, etc), wine waiters, communication skills, approach, uniform and finesse.

In bars and lounges, this covers the ambience, communication skills (between bartenders, service staff and passengers), attitude, personality, flair and finesse, plus the glasses used.

With relation to cabins it includes housekeeping, cleanliness, in-cabin food service, linen and bathrobe changes, and communication skills.

Miscellaneous: This category embraces a range of elements that do not easily fall into the ones above.

S.S. Antoinette bedroom.

It includes such miscellaneous areas as the accuracy of the information in the brochure/cruise provider's website, the quality of any information on the itinerary and on destinations visited en route, airport/train station transfers and the standard of any excursions. It also covers lecturers who come to speak on board, the quality of any entertainment provided and any in-cabin audio-visual equipment and channels.

The star ratings

Points are then converted into star ratings, as follows:

★★★★★ = 451–500 points
★★★★+ = 401–450 points
★★★★ = 351–400 points
★★★+ = 301–350 points
★★★ = 251–300 points
★★+ = 201–250 points
★★ = 151–200 points
★+ = 101–150 points
★ = 1–100 points

The five star categories are broken down below. Note that riverships that have a plus sign (+) next to their rating are a little better than the number of stars awarded.

5 Stars (★★★★★)

To reach this level, in terms of hardware, the vessel must have finely appointed, excellently designed interiors, all of which are spotlessly maintained. As for accommodation, suites (minimum size expected 25 sq m/270 sq ft) and large cabins (minimum 16 sq m/172 sq ft) should have the highest-quality fittings and furnishings. A choice of bed linen and pillows (regular goose down pillows or the non-allergenic type) should be provided, as should bathrobes for all passengers, plus high-quality personal toiletries. The cuisine must be the best dining available in a rivership, with at least three choices of main courses for dinner, plus pasta dishes for lunch. A full sit-down service must be provided by waiting staff schooled in the art of service and hospitality. All extras on a rivership of this kind (lectures, entertainment, audio-visual equipment, etc) would be expected to be of an extremely high standard. This is as good as it gets for a rivership.

4 Stars (★★★★)

To reach this level, a vessel must have well-appointed, well-fitted interiors and be very well maintained. In terms of accommodation, suites (minimum size expected 22 sq m/236 sq ft) and cabins (minimum 14 sq m/150 sq ft) must have fittings that are practical and made of high-quality materials. An excellent dining experience must be provided, and there must be at least two choices of main course (entrée) for dinner. Vegetarian options must be available for all meals. A full, sit-down service must be provided by waiting staff with a good knowledge of how to serve food and drinks professionally. Any components sitting within our 'other' category should be of a very high standard.

3 Stars (★★★)

To reach this level, in terms of hardware, a vessel must have nicely appointed interiors, although the style, finish or layout will be less elegant, refined or sophisticated than on riverships with a higher rating. The level of cleanliness throughout the vessel must be of a standard well above basic. As for accommodation, suites (minimum size expected 20 sq m/215 sq ft) and cabins (minimum 11 sq m/118 sq ft) must be of a good standard and very comfortable. Under cuisine, there will be a choice of main courses for dinner, and vegetarian options should be available for all meals. Service for meals should be provided by waiting staff with a good knowledge of how to serve food and drinks professionally. Any components relating to our 'other' category should be well above the minimum required.

2 Stars (★★)

To reach this level, a vessel (generally an unassigned rivership) must have interiors that are decent, although they may well be made from average-quality materials (more basic than those of a higher star rating). Overall levels of cleanliness on the ship will be above the basic. Suites (minimum size expected 18 sq m/193 sq ft) and cabins will be practical (minimum size 9 sq m/96 sq ft) but less luxurious and well equipped than on riverships of a higher rating. In terms of cuisine, there will typically be little or no choice of main courses for dinner. Breakfast and lunch will probably be self-service buffet-style meals. Waiters and waitresses will provide an acceptable level of service, although they may not have been as well-trained as staff on higher-rated vessels. Miscellaneous items covered under our 'other' category will likely be acceptable, although not sparkling.

1 Star (★)

At this level, the hardware on a rivership will include extremely utilitarian interiors that could do with improvement in terms of design, quality, functionality or perhaps how up to date they are. The accommodation will typically be small, not particularly well laid-out and simply equipped, and with poor sound insulation. The cuisine will be at the most basic end of the scale in terms of rivership food, with little choice and lower-quality produce used in its preparation than on higher-rated cruises. In terms of service, the waiting staff is unlikely to have been trained in the art of service. Miscellaneous 'other' category items may well be at the most basic level.

Queen Isabel dining room.

Alegria
★★★

A small, older rivership adapted for passengers with limited mobility.

Manager/operator	Shearings Holidays	
Entered service	1995	
Registry	Netherlands	
Identification number	ENI 02205451	
Length (m/yds)	89.9	

Number of decks (excluding sun deck)	2
Cabins (total)	50
Balcony cabins	No
Lift (elevator)	Yes (3)
Rivers sailed	Rhein

Plainly decorated, the *Alegria* has three lifts (elevators) serving all decks, wide hallways, 10 cabins designed for roll-in wheelchair access (with bathrooms with separate toilet), low-level service areas in bars plus restaurant tables designed for wheelchair users. The food is very basic but adequate for a buffet breakfast plus served lunch and dinner.

Berlitz's Ratings		
	Possible	Achieved
Hardware	100	68
Accommodation	100	48
Cuisine	100	54
Service	100	55
Miscellaneous	100	58
OVERALL SCORE		
283 points out of 500		

Alemannia
★★+

A rivership for the destinations; not the accommodation or food.

Manager/operator	Nicko Tours	
Entered service	1971	
Registry	Switzerland	
Identification number	ENI 07001703	
Length (m/yds)	110.0	

Number of decks (excluding sun deck)	3
Cabins (total)	92
Balcony cabins	No
Lift (elevator)	No
Rivers sailed	Rhein

Many people choose a river cruise for the itinerary and destinations. If you fall into this category, then *Alemannia*, with its small cabins, tiny bathrooms and limited storage space may be suitable. The restaurant is quite attractive, but don't expect fine food, because the galley is tiny and unable to turn out gourmet dishes.

Berlitz's Ratings		
	Possible	Achieved
Hardware	100	53
Accommodation	100	43
Cuisine	100	51
Service	100	48
Miscellaneous	100	50
OVERALL SCORE		
245 points out of 500		

Alina
★★★★

Choose this stylish rivership for a good-quality river cruise experience.

Manager/operator.......................... Phoenix Cruises
Entered service...2011
Registry ....Switzerland
Identification number ....ENI 07001934
Length (m/yds)...135.0

Number of decks (excluding sun deck) 3
Cabins (total) 110
Balcony cabins .... Yes (French)
Lift (elevator) ....No
Rivers sailed ....Danube

Alina is an extremely comfortable modern rivership with large cabins (most have French balconies), plenty of storage space and bathrooms that are practical and have large shower enclosures. The food is varied, good quality, extremely creatively prepared and well presented. Service is also good, from a well-trained crew.

Berlitz's Ratings		
	Possible	Achieved
Hardware	100	79
Accommodation	100	78
Cuisine	100	81
Service	100	68
Miscellaneous	100	76
OVERALL SCORE		
382 points out of 500		

Allegro
★★★

A rivership for a basic, but acceptable, no-frills river cruise.

Manager/operator..................................Kras Reizen
Entered service...1990
Registry ....Netherlands
Identification number ....ENI 02326758
Length (m/yds)...105.0

Number of decks (excluding sun deck) 2
Cabins (total) 73
Balcony cabins ....No
Lift (elevator) ....No
Rivers sailed ....Danube, Rhein

If you would be happy with a moderately comfortable but very small, plain cabin and compact bathroom, then *Allegro* may be suitable for you. The food is definitely not the high point, so choose it for the itinerary or the price point. The vessel is often used for group tours.

Berlitz's Ratings		
	Possible	Achieved
Hardware	100	48
Accommodation	100	52
Cuisine	100	56
Service	100	56
Miscellaneous	100	57
OVERALL SCORE		
269 points out of 500		

AmaBella
★★★★+

A tip-top contemporary rivership known for its high-quality cuisine.

Manager/operator .... AmaWaterways
Entered service 2010
Registry .... Switzerland
Identification number .... ENI 02332082
Length (m/yds) 110.0

Number of decks (excluding sun deck) 3
Cabins (total) 75
Balcony cabins .... Yes (French)
Lift (elevator) .... Yes
Rivers sailed .... Danube, Elbe, Rhein

AmaBella is a comfortable vessel with lovely decor. Most cabins have French balconies, ample storage space and large, nicely appointed bathrooms with large shower enclosures and more storage. The food and service is what most passengers remember after their cruise, because this company spends more on food and wine than most. This is for anyone seeking excellence.

Berlitz's Ratings		
	Possible	Achieved
Hardware	100	80
Accommodation	100	83
Cuisine	100	85
Service	100	80
Miscellaneous	100	85
OVERALL SCORE		
413 points out of 500		

AmaCello
★★★★+

Expect high standards and outstanding cuisine aboard this excellent rivership.

Manager/operator .... AmaWaterways
Entered service 2008
Registry .... Switzerland
Identification number .... ENI 07001862
Length (m/yds) 110.0

Number of decks (excluding sun deck) 3
Cabins (total) 75
Balcony cabins .... Yes (French)
Lift (elevator) .... Yes
Rivers sailed .... Danube, Elbe, Rhein

AmaCello is a high-quality, well-designed and spacious vessel with elegant interior decor. Most cabins have French balconies, and all are generously sized, well laid-out and very comfortable. Storage space is good, as is soundproofing. The marble-appointed bathrooms have large shower enclosures. Amenities include a fitness area with sauna. The cuisine is excellent, creative, varied and accompanied by good wines.

Berlitz's Ratings		
	Possible	Achieved
Hardware	100	79
Accommodation	100	83
Cuisine	100	85
Service	100	79
Miscellaneous	100	84
OVERALL SCORE		
410 points out of 500		

AmaCerto
★★★★+

This superb contemporary rivership is praised for its high-quality cuisine.

Manager/operator........................... AmaWaterways
Entered service...2012
Registry ....Switzerland
Identification number ....ENI 07001949
Length (m/yds)..135.0

Number of decks (excluding sun deck) 3
Cabins (total) 75
Balcony cabins .... Yes (French)
Lift (elevator) .... Yes
Rivers sailed .... Danube, Elbe, Rhein

This very stylish, contemporary rivership will provide you with a first-class river cruise. It includes an excellent variety of high-quality food and very good wines. With very roomy cabins (with French balconies) and bathrooms, good storage space, and a well-orchestrated excursion programme, *AmaCerto* is highly recommended for a fine river cruise experience.

Berlitz's Ratings		
	Possible	Achieved
Hardware	100	81
Accommodation	100	83
Cuisine	100	85
Service	100	80
Miscellaneous	100	85
OVERALL SCORE		
414 points out of 500		

AmaDagio
★★★★+

Outstanding cuisine and good service delivered in a contemporary rivership.

Manager/operator........................... AmaWaterways
Entered service...2006
Registry ....Switzerland
Identification number ....ENI 07001828
Length (m/yds)..110.0

Number of decks (excluding sun deck) 3
Cabins (total) 75
Balcony cabins .... Yes (French)
Lift (elevator) .... Yes
Rivers sailed ....French rivers

AmaDagio has very nicely appointed interior decor. The cabins, most of which have French balconies, good soundproofing, and ample storage space, are extremely comfortable. Bathrooms are generously sized, with good shower enclosures and large towels. You should have a particularly good river cruise, because AmaWaterways focuses its attention on the food and dining experience.

Berlitz's Ratings		
	Possible	Achieved
Hardware	100	79
Accommodation	100	83
Cuisine	100	85
Service	100	80
Miscellaneous	100	85
OVERALL SCORE		
412 points out of 500		

AmaDante
★★★★+

This very comfortable rivership delivers a high standard and excellent cuisine.

Manager/operator............................AmaWaterways	Number of decks (excluding sun deck) 3
Entered service...2008	Cabins (total) 75
Registry ....Switzerland	Balcony cabins ....Yes (French)
Identification number ....ENI 07001864	Lift (elevator) ....Yes
Length (m/yds)...110.0	Rivers sailed ....Danube, Elbe, Rhein

It's the food and service that most passengers remember after a cruise aboard this rivership because the company spends more on food and wine than most of its competitors. In addition, there's an excellent excursion programme. Overall, this rivership is a winner for anyone seeking the best-quality river cruise experience.

Berlitz's Ratings

	Possible	Achieved
Hardware	100	80
Accommodation	100	83
Cuisine	100	85
Service	100	81
Miscellaneous	100	85

OVERALL SCORE
414 points out of 500

AmaDolce
★★★★+

A rivership praised for its outstanding cuisine and high standards.

Manager/operator............................AmaWaterways	Number of decks (excluding sun deck) 3
Entered service...2009	Cabins (total) 74
Registry ....Switzerland	Balcony cabins ....Yes (French)
Identification number ....ENI 07001909	Lift (elevator) ....Yes
Length (m/yds)...110.0	Rivers sailed ....Various European rivers

AmaDolce is a very spacious, high-quality, well-designed vessel with elegant interior decor. Most cabins feature French balconies, not full ones, but all are very generously sized and well kitted out. Marble-appointed bathrooms have large shower enclosures. Amenities include a fitness area with sauna. The cuisine is excellent, creative and varied and accompanied by good wines.

Berlitz's Ratings

	Possible	Achieved
Hardware	100	80
Accommodation	100	82
Cuisine	100	84
Service	100	80
Miscellaneous	100	85

OVERALL SCORE
411 points out of 500

AmaDouro (Douro Cruiser)
★★★+

This smart-looking vessel delivers a well-rounded Douro cruise experience.

Manager/operator............................ AmaWaterways
Entered service...2005
Registry ....Portugal
Identification number ....IMO 329344
Length (m/yds)..78.1

Number of decks (excluding sun deck) 3
Cabins (total) 65
Balcony cabins ....Yes (full)
Lift (elevator) ....No
Rivers sailed ....Douro

Built for river cruises along the Douro, in Portugal, this vessel has small but practical cabins and bathrooms. The upper accommodation deck has cabins with balconies, while cabins on the lower deck have large windows. The interiors are fitted out with rich mahogany wood. Facilities include a small pool and hot tubs on deck. Good regional cuisine is the norm.

Berlitz's Ratings

	Possible	Achieved
Hardware	100	75
Accommodation	100	74
Cuisine	100	63
Service	100	66
Miscellaneous	100	70

OVERALL SCORE
348 points out of 500

AmaLegro
★★★★+

Choose this modern rivership for a top-notch river cruise experience.

Manager/operator............................ AmaWaterways
Entered service...2007
Registry ....Switzerland
Identification number ....ENI 07001837
Length (m/yds)..110.0

Number of decks (excluding sun deck) 3
Cabins (total) 74
Balcony cabins .... Yes (French and full)
Lift (elevator) ....Yes
Rivers sailed ....French rivers

The food and service are what most passengers remember after a cruise aboard this rivership, because the company spends more on food and wine than most of its competitors. Many cabins have balconies and large bathrooms, with good storage space, and the excursions are well organised. A good choice for a premium rivership experience.

Berlitz's Ratings

	Possible	Achieved
Hardware	100	79
Accommodation	100	82
Cuisine	100	85
Service	100	81
Miscellaneous	100	85

OVERALL SCORE
412 points out of 500

AmaLyra
★★★★+

Outstanding cuisine and good service on a contemporary rivership.

Manager/operator	AmaWaterways
Entered service	2009
Registry	Switzerland
Identification number	ENI 07001908
Length (m/yds)	110.0

Number of decks (excluding sun deck)	3
Cabins (total)	74
Balcony cabins	Yes (French)
Lift (elevator)	Yes
Rivers sailed	Various European rivers

AmaLyra is a spacious, high-quality vessel with elegant interior decor. Most cabins feature French (not full) balconies, but all are large and well appointed. Marble bathrooms have large shower enclosures. Facilities include a fitness area with sauna. The food is excellent, varied and plentiful. Service is very good. Bicycles are available for free.

Berlitz's Ratings

	Possible	Achieved
Hardware	100	80
Accommodation	100	82
Cuisine	100	85
Service	100	81
Miscellaneous	100	85

OVERALL SCORE
413 points out of 500

AmaPrima
★★★★+

Outstanding cuisine and high standards characterise this comfortable rivership.

Manager/operator	AmaWaterways
Entered service	2013
Registry	Switzerland
Identification number	ENI 07001958
Length (m/yds)	135.0

Number of decks (excluding sun deck)	3
Cabins (total)	82
Balcony cabins	Yes (French)
Lift (elevator)	Yes
Rivers sailed	Various European rivers

AmaPrima is an extremely comfortable vessel with warm interior decor, well-designed, practical cabins (some have twin French balconies) and elegant bathrooms with large shower enclosures. Features include a heated outdoor pool with 'swim-up' bar. Comfortable restaurant, impressive, tasty food and good wines. AmaWaterways knows how to do it right, and it shows.

Berlitz's Ratings

	Possible	Achieved
Hardware	100	85
Accommodation	100	83
Cuisine	100	86
Service	100	82
Miscellaneous	100	86

OVERALL SCORE
422 points out of 500

AmaReina
Not Yet Rated

Set to be a delightful rivership with extremely high standards and fine cuisine.

Manager/operator........................... AmaWaterways
Entered service..2014
Registry .... Switzerland
Identification number ....n/a
Length (m/yds)..135.0

Number of decks (excluding sun deck) 3
Cabins (total) 82
Balcony cabins .... Yes (French)
Lift (elevator) .... Yes
Rivers sailed .... Various European rivers

AmaReina should be stylish and contemporary with high-quality appointments and welcoming interior decor. Generously sized cabins (and double-sized suites) will feature French balconies (lowest deck cabins have fixed windows), ample storage space and elegant marble-clad bathrooms with large shower enclosures. The main restaurant should offer creative, well-crafted, varied cuisine and good wines. Erlebnis (a second restaurant) will feature a dégustation menu.

Berlitz's Ratings

	Possible	Achieved
Hardware	100	NYR
Accommodation	100	NYR
Cuisine	100	NYR
Service	100	NYR
Miscellaneous	100	NYR

OVERALL SCORE
NYR points out of 500

AmaSonata
Not Yet Rated

Excellent cuisine and good service in a stylish, contemporary rivership.

Manager/operator........................... AmaWaterways
Entered service..2014
Registry .... Switzerland
Identification number ....n/a
Length (m/yds)..135.0

Number of decks (excluding sun deck) 3
Cabins (total) 82
Balcony cabins .... Yes (French)
Lift (elevator) .... Yes
Rivers sailed .... Various European rivers

AmaSonata looks set to be chic, with high-quality appointments and delightful interior decor. Generously sized cabins (and double-sized suites) will feature French balconies (the lowest deck cabins have fixed windows), ample storage space and elegant marble-clad bathrooms with large shower enclosures. The cuisine should be excellent, varied and accompanied by good wines. Erlebnis (a second restaurant) will feature a dégustation menu.

Berlitz's Ratings

	Possible	Achieved
Hardware	100	NYR
Accommodation	100	NYR
Cuisine	100	NYR
Service	100	NYR
Miscellaneous	100	NYR

OVERALL SCORE
NYR points out of 500

AmaVerde
★★★★+

This excellent contemporary rivership is known for its high-quality cuisine.

Manager/operator............................ AmaWaterways
Entered service...2011
Registry .... Switzerland
Identification number ....ENI 07001725
Length (m/yds)...110.0

Number of decks (excluding sun deck) 3
Cabins (total) 76
Balcony cabins .... Yes (full)
Lift (elevator) .... Yes
Rivers sailed .... Various European rivers

AmaVerde has classy interior decor, fine furnishings and plenty of space. The cabins are well appointed and very comfortable; many have full balconies and good soundproofing. Bathrooms have large shower enclosures. However, it's the food (taste, creativity, variety) and service that most passengers remember. It's a winner for anyone seeking a high-quality cruise experience.

Berlitz's Ratings		
	Possible	Achieved
Hardware	100	84
Accommodation	100	82
Cuisine	100	86
Service	100	82
Miscellaneous	100	86

OVERALL SCORE
420 points out of 500

AmaVida
★★★★+

A rivership highly praised for its fine regional cuisine and top standards.

Manager/operator............................ AmaWaterways
Entered service...2013
Registry ....Portugal
Identification number ....n/a
Length (m/yds)..79.5

Number of decks (excluding sun deck) 3
Cabins (total) 53
Balcony cabins .... Yes (French)
Lift (elevator) .... Yes
Rivers sailed .... Douro

Specially designed for River Douro cruises, *AmaVida* features elegant interior decor. Two decks of very spacious cabins feature French balconies (cabins on the lowest deck have windows only) and ample storage space. The bathrooms are also well equipped. The restaurant is uninspiring but comfortable, and the food is noteworthy and nicely varied, featuring regional dishes.

Berlitz's Ratings		
	Possible	Achieved
Hardware	100	85
Accommodation	100	83
Cuisine	100	86
Service	100	81
Miscellaneous	100	86

OVERALL SCORE
421 points out of 500

Amadeus
★★★★

Choose this rivership for a very comfortable, well-planned cruise experience.

Manager/operator............... Various tour operators
Entered service................................1998
Registry ....Germany
Identification number ....ENI 08848003
Length (m/yds)..............................110.0

Number of decks (excluding sun deck) 3
Cabins (total) 73
Balcony cabins ....Yes (French)
Lift (elevator) ....No
Rivers sailed ....Danube, Rhein

This rivership is very comfortable, with very high-quality soft furnishings. The cabins are extremely spacious, with good-quality soft furnishings, twin beds that convert to a queen-sized bed, and even a writing desk. The bathrooms are smallish but still incorporate decent-sized shower enclosures. The cuisine could be better, although the galley is small.

Berlitz's Ratings	Possible	Achieved
Hardware	100	76
Accommodation	100	74
Cuisine	100	80
Service	100	77
Miscellaneous	100	77

OVERALL SCORE
384 points out of 500

Amadeus Brilliant
★★★★

A good choice for a first-rate cruise in comfortable surroundings.

Manager/operator......................... Evergreen Tours
Entered service................................2011
Registry ....Germany
Identification number ....ENI 04809350
Length (m/yds)..............................110.0

Number of decks (excluding sun deck) 3
Cabins (total) 67
Balcony cabins ....Yes (French)
Lift (elevator) .... Yes
Rivers sailed ....Danube, Rhein

The smart, finely decorated, contemporary *Amadeus Brilliant* should give you a very comfortable cruise experience. Except for two singles, all cabins are extremely spacious (especially the nine suites, with double the space) and have decent storage space and elegant bathrooms. Some have French balconies. Dinners are served at your table, with full tablecloth and cutlery setting.

Berlitz's Ratings	Possible	Achieved
Hardware	100	79
Accommodation	100	78
Cuisine	100	74
Service	100	74
Miscellaneous	100	76

OVERALL SCORE
381 points out of 500

Amadeus Classic
★★★★

A good-looking rivership but dated when compared to newer vessels.

Manager/operator.......................... Phoenix Cruises
Entered service..2001
Registry ....Germany
Identification number ....ENI 04801620
Length (m/yds)..110.0

Number of decks (excluding sun deck) 3
Cabins (total) 69
Balcony cabins ....No
Lift (elevator) ....No
Rivers sailed .... Danube, Rhein

This pleasant, very comfortable rivership features decor that is quite understated, almost refined, if a little dated. The cabins are comfy and practical, but small by today's standards, with no balconies and with windows that are not particularly large. Storage space is a little tight, too. The food is decent, but nothing is outstanding.

Berlitz's Ratings		
	Possible	Achieved
Hardware	100	73
Accommodation	100	73
Cuisine	100	72
Service	100	72
Miscellaneous	100	76
OVERALL SCORE		
366 points out of 500		

Amadeus Diamond
★★★★

This first-class rivership combines style with good food and hospitality.

Manager/operator............... Various tour operators
Entered service..2009
Registry ....Germany
Identification number ....ENI 04807380
Length (m/yds)..110.0

Number of decks (excluding sun deck) 3
Cabins (total) 62
Balcony cabins .... Yes (French)
Lift (elevator) ....No
Rivers sailed .... Danube, Rhein

The modern, smart-looking *Amadeus Diamond* is a very comfortable vessel, with decor that is really classy yet unpretentious. The cabins and bathrooms are both spacious and practical, with amenities including mini-fridges. The cuisine is varied and very creative – a notch above many others – and service is very good. A real first-class experience.

Berlitz's Ratings		
	Possible	Achieved
Hardware	100	78
Accommodation	100	77
Cuisine	100	81
Service	100	78
Miscellaneous	100	81
OVERALL SCORE		
395 points out of 500		

Amadeus Elegant
★★★★

A fine-looking rivership with excellent itineraries, food and wine.

Manager/operator............... Various tour operators
Entered service...2010
Registry ....Germany
Identification number ....ENI 04808350
Length (m/yds)..110.0

Number of decks (excluding sun deck).................3
Cabins (total) 67
Balcony cabins .... Yes (French)
Lift (elevator) ....No
Rivers sailed ....Danube, Rhein

Amadeus Elegant has an interior decor that is understated and rather classic in style. The well-designed cabins (most have French balconies) have bathrooms with large shower enclosures; nine junior suites have bathtub/showers. The cuisine and variety of food offered is excellent, with service from a well-trained crew. Overall, a good choice for anyone seeking a first-class experience.

Berlitz's Ratings		
	Possible	Achieved
Hardware	100	79
Accommodation	100	77
Cuisine	100	81
Service	100	79
Miscellaneous	100	81
OVERALL SCORE		
397 points out of 500		

Amadeus Princess
★★★★

This rivership has elegant decor and provides a decent standard.

Manager/operator............... Various tour operators
Entered service...2006
Registry ....Germany
Identification number ....ENI 04804710
Length (m/yds)..110.0

Number of decks (excluding sun deck).................3
Cabins (total) 78
Balcony cabins .... Yes (French)
Lift (elevator) ....No
Rivers sailed ....Danube, Rhein

Amadeus Princess is a good-looking, very comfortable rivership, with understated, elegant decor. The well-designed cabins (most have French balconies) include mini-fridges. The bathrooms are elegant and have large, practical shower enclosures (nine junior suites have a bathtub/shower). The cuisine is pleasantly varied, and dinners are served, with a full tablecloth setting.

Berlitz's Ratings		
	Possible	Achieved
Hardware	100	74
Accommodation	100	73
Cuisine	100	74
Service	100	75
Miscellaneous	100	76
OVERALL SCORE		
372 points out of 500		

Amadeus Rhapsody
★★★★

A first-class rivership offering plenty of style and decent hospitality.

Manager/operator............... Various tour operators
Entered service...1998
Registry ....Germany
Identification number ....ENI 08848002
Length (m/yds)...110.0

Number of decks (excluding sun deck) 3
Cabins (total) 69
Balcony cabins .... Yes (French)
Lift (elevator) ....No
Rivers sailed ....Danube, Rhein

The contemporary, smart-looking *Amadeus Rhapsody* is a very comfortable vessel, with decor that is elegant and unpretentious. The cabins are really quite spacious (mini-fridges are provided), and the bathrooms are practical. The cuisine is quite good and relatively varied. Service, too, is good. Everything you need for a good cruise experience.

Berlitz's Ratings	Possible	Achieved
Hardware	100	73
Accommodation	100	73
Cuisine	100	72
Service	100	73
Miscellaneous	100	73
OVERALL SCORE		
364 points out of 500		

Amadeus Royal
★★★★

Choose this rivership for a very comfortable, well-rounded cruise.

Manager/operator............................Grimm Touristik
Entered service...2005
Registry ....Germany
Identification number ....ENI 04803670
Length (m/yds)...110.0

Number of decks (excluding sun deck) 3
Cabins (total) 68
Balcony cabins .... Yes (French)
Lift (elevator) ....No
Rivers sailed ....Danube, Rhein

The contemporary, smart-looking *Amadeus Royal* is a very comfortable vessel, with decor that is elegant but unfussy. Most of the well-designed cabins have French balconies and nicely equipped bathrooms with large shower enclosures (four suites have bathtub/showers). The food is nicely varied, of a good standard and well presented.

Berlitz's Ratings	Possible	Achieved
Hardware	100	77
Accommodation	100	75
Cuisine	100	73
Service	100	73
Miscellaneous	100	80
OVERALL SCORE		
378 points out of 500		

Amadeus Silver
★★★★

This extremely comfortable rivership will deliver a first-class river cruise.

Manager/operator.......................... Evergreen Tours
Entered service...2013
Registry ....Netherlands
Identification number ....ENI 02335475
Length (m/yds)...135.0

Number of decks (excluding sun deck) 3
Cabins (total) 89
Balcony cabins .... Yes (French)
Lift (elevator) ....No
Rivers sailed ....Various European rivers

The interior decor of *Amadeus Silver* has some very elegant touches, and the public lounges are especially cosy. The generously sized cabins are attractively outfitted, and most have French balconies. Twelve suites also have full balconies, mini-bars, and bathrooms with bathtub/showers. Extremely good food, with plenty of variety, and fairly decent wines.

Berlitz's Ratings		
	Possible	Achieved
Hardware	100	81
Accommodation	100	81
Cuisine	100	75
Service	100	75
Miscellaneous	100	82

OVERALL SCORE
394 points out of 500

Amadeus Symphony
★★★★

A first-class rivership combining style, great food and good hospitality.

Manager/operator............... Various tour operators
Entered service...2003
Registry ....Germany
Identification number ....ENI 04802330
Length (m/yds)...110.0

Number of decks (excluding sun deck) 3
Cabins (total) 69
Balcony cabins .... Yes (French)
Lift (elevator) ....No
Rivers sailed ....Danube, Rhein

This very comfortable vessel has decor that is quite classy but unpretentious. The cabins are spacious and practical, have good soft furnishings, twin beds that convert to queen-sized beds, writing desks and mini-fridges. The bathrooms have decent-sized shower enclosures. The cuisine is varied and very creative, and the service is attentive. A real first-class experience.

Berlitz's Ratings		
	Possible	Achieved
Hardware	100	74
Accommodation	100	73
Cuisine	100	74
Service	100	76
Miscellaneous	100	74

OVERALL SCORE
371 points out of 500

Amelia
★★★★

This rivership provides good food and service in a contemporary setting.

Manager/operator.......................... Phoenix Cruises
Entered service................................. 2012
Registry .... Malta
Identification number .... ENI 07001948
Length (m/yds)................................. 135.0

Number of decks (excluding sun deck) 3
Cabins (total) 108
Balcony cabins .... Yes (French)
Lift (elevator) .... Yes
Rivers sailed .... Danube, Rhein

Amelia is an extremely comfortable and well-proportioned rivership. Cabins on the lower deck cabins have windows; all others feature French balconies. All cabins are reasonably spacious and well furnished, and bathrooms are practical with good-size shower enclosures. The restaurant spans two decks, and an aft bistro provides an alternative. Good, creative cuisine, and a decent variety of food.

Berlitz's Ratings		
	Possible	Achieved
Hardware	100	79
Accommodation	100	78
Cuisine	100	80
Service	100	76
Miscellaneous	100	76
OVERALL SCORE		
389 points out of 500		

Amsterdam
★★

A vintage rivership offering a basic, no-frills, budget cruise.

Manager/operator............... Various tour operators
Entered service................................. 1948
Registry .... Netherlands
Identification number .... ENI 02325952
Length (m/yds)................................... 78.0

Number of decks (excluding sun deck) 2
Cabins (total) 49
Balcony cabins .... No
Lift (elevator) .... No
Rivers sailed .... Rhein

Amsterdam has pleasant interior decor, but the cabins and bathrooms are tiny (having a shower means dancing with the shower curtain), storage space is limited and the air conditioning is poor. The food choice is likewise extremely limited. Overall, it's a basic, no-frills river cruise at a low price, but fine if you are travelling for the itinerary – or on a budget.

Berlitz's Ratings		
	Possible	Achieved
Hardware	100	38
Accommodation	100	35
Cuisine	100	40
Service	100	44
Miscellaneous	100	42
OVERALL SCORE		
199 points out of 500		

Andante
★★+

This rivership will provide you with a basic no-frills river cruise.

Manager/operator .... Kras Reizen
Entered service 1959
Registry .... Netherlands
Identification number .... ENI 02325292
Length (m/yds) 74.4

Number of decks (excluding sun deck) 2
Cabins (total) 48
Balcony cabins .... No
Lift (elevator) .... No
Rivers sailed .... Various European rivers

If you don't mind small cabins with little windows and slim beds, and you don't expect the food to be any more than basic, then this rivership may be acceptable. It's cheap and cheerful but rather uninspiring. It's one to choose if you're on a budget or if the destinations are your key focus.

Berlitz's Ratings		
	Possible	Achieved
Hardware	100	37
Accommodation	100	38
Cuisine	100	45
Service	100	46
Miscellaneous	100	46
OVERALL SCORE		
212 points out of 500		

Angela Esmee
★★

A vintage rivership suited to tour participants on a tight budget.

Manager/operator .... Fietsvaarvakantie
Entered service 1955
Registry .... Netherlands
Identification number .... ENI 03310386
Length (m/yds) 79.0

Number of decks (excluding sun deck) 2
Cabins (total) 41
Balcony cabins .... No
Lift (elevator) .... No
Rivers sailed .... Dutch waterways

Designed for bicycle tours, this vintage rivership will provide an inexpensive way of getting you and your bike around the region. The cabins, windows, and bathrooms are all dimensionally challenged. The food is really basic, too, because the galley is tiny and outdated. Go because the itinerary and tour are what you are looking for.

Berlitz's Ratings		
	Possible	Achieved
Hardware	100	36
Accommodation	100	35
Cuisine	100	39
Service	100	44
Miscellaneous	100	42
OVERALL SCORE		
196 points out of 500		

Anna Maria Agnes
★★

This vintage rivership is adequate for no-frills, low-budget bicycle tours.

Manager/operator........................Fietsvaarvakantie
Entered service...1910
Registry ....Netherlands
Identification number ....ENI 02211655
Length (m/yds)...72.0

Number of decks (excluding sun deck) 2
Cabins (total) 34
Balcony cabins ....No
Lift (elevator) ....No
Rivers sailed .... Dutch waterways

This vintage rivership is basically for anyone seeking transport on a cycling holiday. The cabins are really tiny, as are the windows and bathrooms. The galley is also extremely small and can only deliver the most basic food. For a river cruise, it's cheap, but it may present a convenient option of travel for you.

Berlitz's Ratings

	Possible	Achieved
Hardware	100	34
Accommodation	100	34
Cuisine	100	38
Service	100	45
Miscellaneous	100	40

OVERALL SCORE
191 points out of 500

Antonio Bellucci
★★★+

A smart, contemporary vessel that delivers a good all-round cruise experience.

Manager/operator............... Various tour operators
Entered service...2012
Registry ....Switzerland
Identification number ....ENI 02334599
Length (m/yds)..110.0

Number of decks (excluding sun deck) 3
Cabins (total) 70
Balcony cabins .... Yes (French)
Lift (elevator) .... Yes
Rivers sailed ....Various European rivers

This small, modern rivership has attractive features including a hot tub on the Sun Deck. The interiors incorporate warm woods and marble. Cabins have twins that can convert to queen-sized beds, and there are many cabins with French balconies. The bathrooms are small but functional. The cuisine is good, although not exceptional. A good all-rounder.

Berlitz's Ratings

	Possible	Achieved
Hardware	100	77
Accommodation	100	71
Cuisine	100	63
Service	100	64
Miscellaneous	100	73

OVERALL SCORE
348 points out of 500

Ariana
★★★+

This modern rivership provides a modest but good-value cruise experience.

Manager/operator.......................... Phoenix Cruises
Entered service................................2012
Registry ....Bulgaria
Identification number ....ENI 02334084
Length (m/yds)................................110.0

Number of decks (excluding sun deck) 3
Cabins (total) 81
Balcony cabins .... Yes (French)
Lift (elevator) .... Yes
Rivers sailed ....Danube

Built for Dunav Tours of Bulgaria, this small, modern vessel has a comfortable lounge. The cabins are small, with plain decor, and there's little storage space. Although many have French balconies, the bathrooms are small and basic. The food is underwhelming, and there's limited choice. It's best to choose it for the itinerary.

Berlitz's Ratings	Possible	Achieved
Hardware	100	77
Accommodation	100	72
Cuisine	100	63
Service	100	64
Miscellaneous	100	72

OVERALL SCORE
348 points out of 500

Arlene
★★★

Choose this small, dated vessel for a low-budget, no-frills cruise.

Manager/operator.................... Feenstra Rhein Line
Entered service................................1986
Registry ....Netherlands
Identification number ....ENI 02326752
Length (m/yds)................................91.2

Number of decks (excluding sun deck) 2
Cabins (total) 53
Balcony cabins ....No
Lift (elevator) ....No
Rivers sailed .... Various European rivers

Arlene is a small, older-style rivership with a lounge with uncomfortable tub chairs. The cabins are really plain, with two slim beds that fold down from wooden wall units. The bathrooms are compact. There's very limited meal choice, variety and quality. Go for the itinerary and price, not the food.

Berlitz's Ratings	Possible	Achieved
Hardware	100	57
Accommodation	100	58
Cuisine	100	58
Service	100	61
Miscellaneous	100	63

OVERALL SCORE
297 points out of 500

A-Rosa Aqua
★★★+

Modern hotel-style rivership with excellent features for a good cruise.

Manager/operator................. A-Rosa River Cruises
Entered service...2009
Registry ....Germany
Identification number ....ENI 04807500
Length (m/yds)..135.0

Number of decks (excluding sun deck) 3
Cabins (total) 99
Balcony cabins .... Yes (French)
Lift (elevator) ....No
Rivers sailed ....French rivers

This trendy rivership has very colourful interior decor in orange and yellow. Many cabins have French balconies, while others have small windows. Two slim beds can be converted into a double bed. Facilities include a fitness area with a large sauna for both men and women. The self-service buffets have plenty of fresh, healthy ingredients.

Berlitz's Ratings	Possible	Achieved
Hardware	100	72
Accommodation	100	65
Cuisine	100	65
Service	100	68
Miscellaneous	100	72
OVERALL SCORE		
342 points out of 500		

A-Rosa Bella
★★★+

A popular modern rivership ideal for youthful active types.

Manager/operator................. A-Rosa River Cruises
Entered service...2002
Registry ....Germany
Identification number ....ENI 40801170
Length (m/yds)..124.0

Number of decks (excluding sun deck) 3
Cabins (total) 100
Balcony cabins .... Yes (French)
Lift (elevator) ....No
Rivers sailed ....Danube

The interior decor is quite bright (oranges and yellows) with minimalist-style furnishings. Cabins (some have French balconies) are unfussy and plainly furnished but practical, with two slim beds that can be converted into a double bed. A wellness area includes a large (co-ed) sauna and exercise equipment. Self-service buffets are what the cuisine is all about.

Berlitz's Ratings	Possible	Achieved
Hardware	100	70
Accommodation	100	65
Cuisine	100	65
Service	100	67
Miscellaneous	100	71
OVERALL SCORE		
338 points out of 500		

A-Rosa Brava
★★★+

A very well-run, contemporary-style rivership for youthful, active types.

Manager/operator.................. A-Rosa River Cruises
Entered service...2011
Registry ....Germany
Identification number ....ENI 04809910
Length (m/yds)...135.0

Number of decks (excluding sun deck) 3
Cabins (total) 99
Balcony cabins .... Yes (French)
Lift (elevator) ....No
Rivers sailed ....French rivers

This rivership has bright, upbeat decor and soft furnishings in oranges and yellows, with cabins (some with French balconies) and bathrooms that are practical but unfussy and plain. The self-service buffets are attractively presented, but tables are without tablecloths for breakfast and lunch. A-Rosa Cruises runs well-orchestrated cruises, with excursions for active types.

Berlitz's Ratings		
	Possible	Achieved
Hardware	100	72
Accommodation	100	68
Cuisine	100	65
Service	100	68
Miscellaneous	100	72
OVERALL SCORE		
345 points out of 500		

A-Rosa Donna
★★★+

Upbeat decor and minimalist style are the features of this well-run rivership.

Manager/operator.................. A-Rosa River Cruises
Entered service...2002
Registry ....Germany
Identification number ENI04801180
Length (m/yds)...124.0

Number of decks (excluding sun deck) 3
Cabins (total) 100
Balcony cabins .... Yes (French)
Lift (elevator) ....No
Rivers sailed ....Danube

One of the first A-Rosa vessels, *A-Rosa Donna* offers excursions (including bicycle tours). The brightly coloured cabins are practical (some have French balconies) and unfussy, with two slim beds that convert to a double. Bathrooms are small and functional but plain. Go for the itinerary and destinations, not for the food, which has little flair.

Berlitz's Ratings		
	Possible	Achieved
Hardware	100	70
Accommodation	100	65
Cuisine	100	65
Service	100	67
Miscellaneous	100	72
OVERALL SCORE		
339 points out of 500		

A-Rosa Flora
Not Yet Rated

This latest-generation rivership should deliver a consistently good experience.

Manager/operator................. A-Rosa River Cruises
Entered service...2014
Registry ....Germany
Identification number ....n/a
Length (m/yds)..135.0

Number of decks (excluding sun deck) 3
Cabins (total) 99
Balcony cabins .... Yes (French)
Lift (elevator) ....No
Rivers sailed ....Danube, Rhein

A-Rosa Flora is a funky, new-generation vessel aimed at a younger market. It has bright, minimalist decor, and the cabins are bright and quite spacious (many have French balconies). The bathrooms are practical, although not luxurious. Amenities include a good spa/fitness area. Foodwise, there's a self-service buffet and grill food by day and tablecloth-service for dinner.

Berlitz's Ratings		
	Possible	Achieved
Hardware	100	NYR
Accommodation	100	NYR
Cuisine	100	NYR
Service	100	NYR
Miscellaneous	100	NYR

OVERALL SCORE
NYR points out of 500

A-Rosa Luna
★★★+

A smart, contemporary rivership well suited to active types.

Manager/operator................. A-Rosa River Cruises
Entered service...2004
Registry ....Germany
Identification number ....ENI 04803520
Length (m/yds)..125.0

Number of decks (excluding sun deck) 3
Cabins (total) 86
Balcony cabins .... Yes (French)
Lift (elevator) ....No
Rivers sailed ....French rivers

This rivership has bright, upbeat decor and soft furnishings in oranges and yellows, with cabins and bathrooms that are practical but unfussy and plain. The self-service buffets are attractively presented, but tables are without tablecloths for breakfast and lunch. A-Rosa Cruises runs well-orchestrated cruises, with excursions for active types.

Berlitz's Ratings		
	Possible	Achieved
Hardware	100	70
Accommodation	100	65
Cuisine	100	65
Service	100	67
Miscellaneous	100	72

OVERALL SCORE
339 points out of 500

A-Rosa Mia
★★★+

Upbeat decor and minimalist style for river cruising for active types.

Manager/operator.................. A-Rosa River Cruises
Entered service..2003
Registry ....Germany
Identification number ....ENI 04801870
Length (m/yds)..124.0

Number of decks (excluding sun deck) 3
Cabins (total) 100
Balcony cabins .... Yes (French)
Lift (elevator) ....No
Rivers sailed ....Danube

The decor is bright and trendy in oranges and yellows, with minimalist-style furnishings. Cabins are plainly furnished but practical, with two slim beds that can be converted into doubles; some cabins have French balconies. A fitness area includes a large (mixed) sauna. Self-service buffets are what the cuisine is all about. The wine glasses are small.

Berlitz's Ratings		
	Possible	Achieved
Hardware	100	70
Accommodation	100	65
Cuisine	100	65
Service	100	67
Miscellaneous	100	72
OVERALL SCORE		
339 points out of 500		

A-Rosa Riva
★★★+

Provides an upbeat, youthful setting for an agreeable river cruise.

Manager/operator.................. A-Rosa River Cruises
Entered service..2004
Registry ....Germany
Identification number ....ENI 04802780
Length (m/yds)..124.0

Number of decks (excluding sun deck) 3
Cabins (total) 100
Balcony cabins .... Yes (French)
Lift (elevator) ....No
Rivers sailed ....Danube

A-Rosa Riva's interior decor is bright and cheerful, in oranges and yellows. The cabins are bright, quite spacious (many have French balconies), with minimal facilities and modern bathrooms. A fitness area includes a large (co-ed) sauna. The cuisine is mostly self-service buffet-style, but with a decent variety. Organises good bicycle tours.

Berlitz's Ratings		
	Possible	Achieved
Hardware	100	70
Accommodation	100	65
Cuisine	100	65
Service	100	67
Miscellaneous	100	72
OVERALL SCORE		
339 points out of 500		

A-Rosa Silva
★★★+

A well-run trendy rivership aimed at the younger end of the market.

Manager/operator	A-Rosa River Cruises
Entered service	2012
Registry	Germany
Identification number	ENI 04810230
Length (m/yds)	135.0

Number of decks (excluding sun deck)	3
Cabins (total)	89
Balcony cabins	Yes (French)
Lift (elevator)	No
Rivers sailed	Danube, Rhein

The decor is bright and contemporary, in shades of orange and yellow. The cabins are quite spacious, bright, trendy and practical (many have French balconies), but unfussy, with two slim beds that can convert to a double. Bathrooms are small, plain and functional. Excursions include bicycle tours. Decent buffet food selection.

Berlitz's Ratings

	Possible	Achieved
Hardware	100	74
Accommodation	100	68
Cuisine	100	66
Service	100	68
Miscellaneous	100	72

OVERALL SCORE
348 points out of 500

A-Rosa Stella
★★★+

This contemporary rivership is a good option for active types.

Manager/operator	A-Rosa River Cruises
Entered service	2005
Registry	Germany
Identification number	ENI 04803530
Length (m/yds)	125.0

Number of decks (excluding sun deck)	3
Cabins (total)	86
Balcony cabins	Yes (French)
Lift (elevator)	No
Rivers sailed	Rhône

This smart rivership has bright, upbeat decor and soft furnishings in orange and yellow, with cabins and bathrooms that are practical but quite plain. The self-service buffets are nicely presented, but tables are without tablecloths for breakfast and lunch. Runs excursions (including bicycle tours) aimed at active types.

Berlitz's Ratings

	Possible	Achieved
Hardware	100	73
Accommodation	100	67
Cuisine	100	66
Service	100	66
Miscellaneous	100	72

OVERALL SCORE
344 points out of 500

A-Rosa Viva
★★★+

A well-run rivership aimed at a youthful, active clientele.

Manager/operator................. A-Rosa River Cruises
Entered service..2010
Registry ....Germany
Identification number ....ENI 04808030
Length (m/yds)..135.0

Number of decks (excluding sun deck) 3
Cabins (total) 99
Balcony cabins .... Yes (French)
Lift (elevator) ....No
Rivers sailed ....French rivers

A-Rosa Viva's brightly coloured cabins are trendy, practical and unpretentious, with two slim beds that can be converted to a double; some have French balconies. Bathrooms are small and plain but functional. Excursions, including bicycle tours, are aimed at active types. The food has little flair, so go for the destinations or excursions instead.

Berlitz's Ratings

	Possible	Achieved
Hardware	100	73
Accommodation	100	69
Cuisine	100	67
Service	100	67
Miscellaneous	100	72

OVERALL SCORE
348 points out of 500

Aurelia
★★★★

Aurelia provides good food and service in a contemporary setting.

Manager/operator.......................... Phoenix Cruises
Entered service..2006
Registry ....Switzerland
Identification number ....ENI 07001841
Length (m/yds)..110.0

Number of decks (excluding sun deck) 3
Cabins (total) 79
Balcony cabins .... Yes (French)
Lift (elevator) ....No
Rivers sailed ....Danube, Rhein

Aurelia is a really comfortable and well-proportioned rivership. The lower deck cabins have windows, while all others feature French balconies. All the cabins are reasonably spacious and nicely furnished, with practical bathrooms, including good-size shower enclosures. The restaurant spans two decks; an aft Bistro is an alternative. The cuisine is good, varied and creative.

Berlitz's Ratings

	Possible	Achieved
Hardware	100	77
Accommodation	100	68
Cuisine	100	78
Service	100	68
Miscellaneous	100	74

OVERALL SCORE
365 points out of 500

Avalon Affinity
★★★+

A pleasant, spacious rivership with decent facilities and food.

Manager/operator.......................Avalon Waterways
Entered service...2009
Registry ....Germany
Identification number ....ENI 02330846
Length (m/yds)..110.0

Number of decks (excluding sun deck) 3
Cabins (total) 69
Balcony cabins ....Yes (French)
Lift (elevator) ....Yes
Rivers sailed ....Rhein

A comfortable rivership, with many spacious cabins with French balconies. There's good underbed storage, but soundproofing is poor. The bathrooms are very nice. Some shore excursions are included, but *Avalon Affinity* disappoints in terms of only average-quality wines – drinks and wine are included with dinner, but the wine glasses are small. Food is decent enough.

Berlitz's Ratings		
	Possible	Achieved
Hardware	100	73
Accommodation	100	72
Cuisine	100	63
Service	100	63
Miscellaneous	100	72
OVERALL SCORE		
343 points out of 500		

Avalon Artistry II
★★★★

This rivership has very good facilities, smart decor and reasonable cuisine.

Manager/operator.......................Avalon Waterways
Entered service...2013
Registry ....Germany
Identification number ....ENI 02334737
Length (m/yds)..110.0

Number of decks (excluding sun deck) 3
Cabins (total) 69
Balcony cabins ....Yes (French)
Lift (elevator) ....Yes
Rivers sailed ....Various European rivers

Avalon Artistry II is a really comfortable contemporary rivership. The cabins are spacious and well designed, but they do have plain ceilings. Most have floor-to-ceiling panoramic windows, French-style balconies, river-facing beds and good bathrooms. Two delightful Royal Suites have extra-large bathrooms. The cuisine is decent, but overstated, and there's a push for extra onboard revenue.

Berlitz's Ratings		
	Possible	Achieved
Hardware	100	77
Accommodation	100	75
Cuisine	100	64
Service	100	65
Miscellaneous	100	73
OVERALL SCORE		
354 points out of 500		

Avalon Creativity
★★★+

This comfortable, contemporary rivership delivers a moderately good cruise.

Manager/operator......................Avalon Waterways
Entered service..2009
Registry ....Germany
Identification number ....ENI 02331194
Length (m/yds)..110.0

Number of decks (excluding sun deck) 3
Cabins (total) 70
Balcony cabins .... Yes (French)
Lift (elevator) ....Yes
Rivers sailed ....French rivers

Avalon Creativity's interior decor is pleasant, but quite plain and uninspiring. The cabins are well designed, with ample storage space and a mini-bar (items are at extra cost), but they are bland. The bathrooms are practical. There's a pleasant restaurant, with reasonably decent cuisine but overstated menus. There's a push for extra onboard revenue.

Berlitz's Ratings		
	Possible	Achieved
Hardware	100	72
Accommodation	100	72
Cuisine	100	63
Service	100	64
Miscellaneous	100	71
OVERALL SCORE		
342 points out of 500		

Avalon Expression
★★★★

A contemporary rivership delivering a very good cruise experience.

Manager/operator......................Avalon Waterways
Entered service..2013
Registry ....Germany
Identification number ....ENI 02334920
Length (m/yds)..135.0

Number of decks (excluding sun deck) 3
Cabins (total) 83
Balcony cabins .... Yes (French)
Lift (elevator) ....Yes
Rivers sailed .... Danube, Rhein

Avalon Expression has smart, clubby interior decor. The accommodation with French balconies is light and spacious, with queen-sized beds, and good storage space; cabins on the lowest deck have standard windows. The bathrooms are large, with decent-sized glass-door shower enclosures. The only negatives are the overstated menus, rather bland food, low-quality wines and push for extra-cost items.

Berlitz's Ratings		
	Possible	Achieved
Hardware	100	77
Accommodation	100	75
Cuisine	100	64
Service	100	66
Miscellaneous	100	73
OVERALL SCORE		
355 points out of 500		

Avalon Felicity
★★★+

This comfortable, contemporary rivership delivers a moderately good cruise.

Manager/operator.......................Avalon Waterways
Entered service...2010
Registry...Germany
Identification number.......................ENI 02332007
Length (m/yds)...110.0

Number of decks (excluding sun deck)................3
Cabins (total)...69
Balcony cabins...................................Yes (French)
Lift (elevator)... Yes
Rivers sailed...Rhein

Avalon Felicity's interior decor is rather plain and uninspiring. The well-designed cabins have ample storage space and include a mini-bar (items at extra cost), but they are quite plain. The bathrooms are practical. The restaurant is pleasant, and the cuisine is reasonably good, but the menus are overstated. There's a push for extra onboard revenue.

Berlitz's Ratings	Possible	Achieved
Hardware	100	75
Accommodation	100	76
Cuisine	100	63
Service	100	63
Miscellaneous	100	72

OVERALL SCORE
349 points out of 500

Avalon Illumination
Not Yet Rated

This rivership should deliver a reliable middle-of-the road cruise experience.

Manager/operator.......................Avalon Waterways
Entered service...2014
Registry..Switzerland
Identification number...n/a
Length (m/yds)...135.0

Number of decks (excluding sun deck)................3
Cabins (total)...83
Balcony cabins...................................Yes (French)
Lift (elevator)... Yes
Rivers sailed....................................Danube, Rhein

The accommodation with French balconies should be light and spacious, with queen-sized beds and good storage space; cabins on the lowest deck will have standard windows. The bathrooms should be large, with decent-sized glass-door shower enclosures. Foodwise, the menus are likely to be overstated, with rather bland cuisine and average-quality wines. Watch out for a push for onboard revenue.

Berlitz's Ratings	Possible	Achieved
Hardware	100	NYR
Accommodation	100	NYR
Cuisine	100	NYR
Service	100	NYR
Miscellaneous	100	NYR

OVERALL SCORE
NYR points out of 500

Avalon Impression
Not Yet Rated

This spacious rivership is likely to have state-of-the-art features but average food.

Manager/operator......................Avalon Waterways
Entered service...2014
Registry ....Switzerland
Identification number ....n/a
Length (m/yds)...135.0

Number of decks (excluding sun deck) 3
Cabins (total) 83
Balcony cabins ....Yes (French)
Lift (elevator) .... Yes
Rivers sailed ....Various European rivers

Contemporary, spacious *Avalon Impression* should have some very good features, including an aft lounge, and comfortable interior decor. The cabins with French balconies will feature queen-sized beds, good storage space and delightfully large bathrooms with glass-door shower enclosures. What will disappoint most is likely to be the food, which might lack flair and appear overstated on the menus.

Berlitz's Ratings		
	Possible	Achieved
Hardware	100	NYR
Accommodation	100	NYR
Cuisine	100	NYR
Service	100	NYR
Miscellaneous	100	NYR
OVERALL SCORE		
NYR points out of 500		

Avalon Luminary
★★★+

This spacious rivership has some notable features but disappointing cuisine.

Manager/operator......................Avalon Waterways
Entered service...2010
Registry ....Germany
Identification number ....ENI 02332637
Length (m/yds)...110.0

Number of decks (excluding sun deck) 3
Cabins (total) 69
Balcony cabins ....Yes (French)
Lift (elevator) .... Yes
Rivers sailed ....Danube, Rhein

Avalon Luminary is a nicely fitted out, very comfortable rivership, with interior decor featuring warm woods. Generously sized, well-appointed cabins (many with French balconies) have ample storage space. The attractive bathrooms have good-sized shower enclosures and L'Occitane toiletries. The cuisine is unfortunately a let-down (overstated menus, underwhelming food and low-budget wines).

Berlitz's Ratings		
	Possible	Achieved
Hardware	100	75
Accommodation	100	73
Cuisine	100	63
Service	100	63
Miscellaneous	100	72
OVERALL SCORE		
346 points out of 500		

Avalon Panorama
★★★+

This stylish contemporary rivership delivers a good all-round cruise.

Manager/operator......................Avalon Waterways
Entered service..................................2011
Registry .... Switzerland
Identification number ....ENI 02333460
Length (m/yds)...................................135.0

Number of decks (excluding sun deck) 3
Cabins (total) 83
Balcony cabins .... Yes (French)
Lift (elevator) .... Yes
Rivers sailed ....Danube

Avalon Panorama has dark-wood decor. Spacious but plain cabins with French balconies have river-facing queen-sized beds and good storage space; cabins on the lowest accommodation deck have windows only. Bathrooms are large, with generous shower enclosures. The menus are over the top and the food unfortunately bland and unvaried. Beware of the push for extra-cost items.

Berlitz's Ratings		
	Possible	Achieved
Hardware	100	75
Accommodation	100	73
Cuisine	100	63
Service	100	64
Miscellaneous	100	72
OVERALL SCORE		
347 points out of 500		

Avalon Poetry II
Not Yet Rated

This super-contemporary rivership should provide a fine cruise experience.

Manager/operator......................Avalon Waterways
Entered service..................................2014
Registry ....Germany
Identification number ....n/a
Length (m/yds)...................................110.0

Number of decks (excluding sun deck) 3
Cabins (total) 64
Balcony cabins .... Yes (French)
Lift (elevator) .... Yes
Rivers sailed .... Various European rivers

New in 2014, *Avalon Poetry II* will feature the latest in contemporary design and decor. The generously sized, well-designed cabins (most with French balconies) will have ample storage space. Well-appointed bathrooms should have good-sized shower enclosures and L'Occitane products. The restaurant is likely to be comfortable, but menus overstated and dinners underwhelming. The breakfast and lunch buffets should be good, however.

Berlitz's Ratings		
	Possible	Achieved
Hardware	100	NYR
Accommodation	100	NYR
Cuisine	100	NYR
Service	100	NYR
Miscellaneous	100	NYR
OVERALL SCORE		
NYR points out of 500		

Avalon Scenery
★★★+

This modern rivership delivers a very good all-round river cruise in France.

Manager/operator......................Avalon Waterways
Entered service..................................2008
Registry ....Germany
Identification number ....ENI 02329477
Length (m/yds)..................................110.0

Number of decks (excluding sun deck) 3
Cabins (total) 69
Balcony cabins ....Yes (French)
Lift (elevator) .... Yes
Rivers sailed ....French rivers

Avalon Scenery is a nicely outfitted, very comfortable rivership, with warm woods characteristic of the design scheme. Generously sized, well-appointed cabins (many with French balconies) have ample storage space. The attractive bathrooms have good-sized shower enclosures and L'Occitane toiletries. The food is disappointing, unfortunately, and the menus are overstated. There's a push for extra-cost items.

Berlitz's Ratings		
	Possible	Achieved
Hardware	100	71
Accommodation	100	71
Cuisine	100	63
Service	100	63
Miscellaneous	100	71
OVERALL SCORE		
339 points out of 500		

Avalon Visionary
★★★★

This rivership delivers a solid cruise experience, but disappointing food.

Manager/operator......................Avalon Waterways
Entered service..................................2012
Registry ....Germany
Identification number ....ENI 02334430
Length (m/yds)..................................135.0

Number of decks (excluding sun deck) 3
Cabins (total) 69
Balcony cabins ....Yes (French)
Lift (elevator) .... Yes
Rivers sailed ....Danube, Rhein

Avalon Visionary is in the bold club style. The accommodation with French balconies (cabins on the lowest deck have windows) is light and spacious, with queen-sized beds and good storage. The large bathrooms have decent-sized shower enclosures with glass doors. The menus are overstated and unvaried, while the food is bland and the wines young.

Berlitz's Ratings		
	Possible	Achieved
Hardware	100	76
Accommodation	100	73
Cuisine	100	64
Service	100	66
Miscellaneous	100	74
OVERALL SCORE		
353 points out of 500		

Avalon Vista
★★★★

Choose this contemporary rivership for the itinerary but not for the food.

Manager/operator......................Avalon Waterways
Entered service................................2012
Registry ....Germany
Identification number ....ENI 02333954
Length (m/yds)................................135.0

Number of decks (excluding sun deck) 3
Cabins (total) 83
Balcony cabins ....Yes (French)
Lift (elevator) .... Yes
Rivers sailed ....Various European rivers

This well-proportioned rivership has very cheerful interior decor. Most of the spacious cabins (including two extra-spacious Royal Suites) have French balconies, and abundant creature comforts. Foodwise, the menus are nicely descriptive, but overstated. Dinners are generally disappointing, but the breakfast and lunch buffets are good.

Berlitz's Ratings		
	Possible	Achieved
Hardware	100	76
Accommodation	100	75
Cuisine	100	64
Service	100	66
Miscellaneous	100	74
OVERALL SCORE		
355 points out of 500		

Azolla
★★+

A vintage rivership appealing for its no-frills, old-world ambience and style.

Manager/operator............... Various tour operators
Entered service................................1965
Registry ....Netherlands
Identification number ....ENI 02311625
Length (m/yds)................................76.5

Number of decks (excluding sun deck) 2
Cabins (total) 45
Balcony cabins ....No
Lift (elevator) ....No
Rivers sailed ....Rhein

Many people go river cruising for the itinerary and destinations. If this suits you, then this nicely refurbished rivership, with its small cabins, tiny bathrooms and very limited storage space may be suitable. Just don't expect fine food, because the galley is tiny and can only turn out fairly basic meals, albeit to a tablecloth setting.

Berlitz's Ratings		
	Possible	Achieved
Hardware	100	41
Accommodation	100	41
Cuisine	100	46
Service	100	46
Miscellaneous	100	50
OVERALL SCORE		
224 points out of 500		

Beethoven
★★★

This fuss-free French rivership is comfortable but dated.

Manager/operator .... CroisiEurope
Entered service 2004
Registry .... France
Identification number .... ENI 01823122
Length (m/yds) 110.0

Number of decks (excluding sun deck) 3
Cabins (total) 88
Balcony cabins .... No
Lift (elevator) .... No
Rivers sailed .... Danube, Rhein

Beethoven has rather dated decor, small cabins with no balconies, thin beds (most of which cannot be moved together) and tiny bathrooms with little space for toiletries. If you like a casual French-style ambience and are happy with decent food and wine, it may be suitable. Go mainly for the itinerary and destinations. Note: shore excursions cost extra.

Berlitz's Ratings

	Possible	Achieved
Hardware	100	60
Accommodation	100	57
Cuisine	100	60
Service	100	60
Miscellaneous	100	62

OVERALL SCORE
299 points out of 500

Bellefleur
★★★+

This older rivership offers a low-cost cruise with French ambience.

Manager/operator .... Various tour operators
Entered service 2001
Registry .... Germany
Identification number .... n/a
Length (m/yds) 114.3

Number of decks (excluding sun deck) 3
Cabins (total) 75
Balcony cabins .... No
Lift (elevator) .... No
Rivers sailed .... French rivers

Bellefleur's cabins are nicely appointed – all have windows (no balconies), and some have double beds (others have twins). The lounge is warmly decorated but has many pillars and uncomfortable tub chairs; it does have an outside viewing deck. The restaurant is pleasant but cramped and serves acceptable although unmemorable food (but decent cheese).

Berlitz's Ratings

	Possible	Achieved
Hardware	100	70
Accommodation	100	62
Cuisine	100	61
Service	100	60
Miscellaneous	100	64

OVERALL SCORE
317 points out of 500

Bellevue
★★★+

A stylish glass-fronted contemporary rivership delivering a good cruise experience.

Manager/operator.............. Transocean Flussreisen	Number of decks (excluding sun deck) 3
Entered service..2006	Cabins (total) 97
Registry ....Malta	Balcony cabins ....Yes (French)
Identification number ....ENI 09948013	Lift (elevator) ....No
Length (m/yds)..135.0	Rivers sailed ....Danube, Rhein

With the propulsion machinery separated from the passenger accommodation, *Bellevue's* cabins (many with French balconies) are quiet and stylish, although rather small with little storage space and compact bathrooms. Beds are fixed – one converts to a sofa by day. Large glass windows allow great views in the lounge and restaurant. The food is so-so, however.

Berlitz's Ratings		
	Possible	Achieved
Hardware	100	73
Accommodation	100	73
Cuisine	100	64
Service	100	65
Miscellaneous	100	68
OVERALL SCORE		
343 points out of 500		

Bellissima
★★★+

Good for sailing around the Venetian lagoon on a low budget.

Manager/operator................................ Nicko Tours	Number of decks (excluding sun deck) 2
Entered service..2004	Cabins (total) 67
Registry ....Germany	Balcony cabins ....Yes (French)
Identification number ....ENI 07001859	Lift (elevator) ....No
Length (m/yds)..110.0	Rivers sailed ....Po, Venetian Lagoon

Almost half of the cabins on the *Bellissima* have French balconies. Except for one double-size cabin, all the others are quite small, with little storage space and compact bathrooms. The lounge is comfortable but has low-backed chairs. The restaurant is plain with uncomfortable chairs. The food is uninspiring and of limited variety.

Berlitz's Ratings		
	Possible	Achieved
Hardware	100	72
Accommodation	100	70
Cuisine	100	66
Service	100	66
Miscellaneous	100	66
OVERALL SCORE		
340 points out of 500		

Bellriva
★★★

An adequate but very high-density and dated rivership for a low-cost cruise.

Manager/operator............................ 1A Vista Reisen
Entered service..1971
Registry ....Germany
Identification number ....ENI 07001702
Length (m/yds)..104.6

Number of decks (excluding sun deck) 2
Cabins (total) 90
Balcony cabins ....No
Lift (elevator) ....No
Rivers sailed ....Rhein

This older rivership feels rather cramped but has pleasant decor. The cabins (all of which have windows) are really quite small, with little storage space, poor reading lights and compact bathrooms. The restaurant has tight seating, with four people per table. The galley is small, as is the range and choice of meals. Go for the itinerary offered.

Berlitz's Ratings		
	Possible	Achieved
Hardware	100	56
Accommodation	100	56
Cuisine	100	58
Service	100	60
Miscellaneous	100	62
OVERALL SCORE		
292 points out of 500		

Belvedere
★★★+

Choose this fairly stylish rivership for a good-quality river cruise experience.

Manager/operator.............. Transocean Flussreisen
Entered service..2006
Registry ....Malta
Identification number ....ENI 09948010
Length (m/yds)..126.0

Number of decks (excluding sun deck) 3
Cabins (total) 88
Balcony cabins .... Yes (French)
Lift (elevator) ....No
Rivers sailed ....Danube

Belvedere is a modern-looking vessel, with attractive, unfussy interior decor. Many of the generously sized cabins have French balconies, while others have windows. All except the four suites are the same size and well-appointed, with river-facing beds and good bathroom facilities. Wellness area includes a sauna. There's a nice restaurant, but the food lacks variety.

Berlitz's Ratings		
	Possible	Achieved
Hardware	100	73
Accommodation	100	71
Cuisine	100	66
Service	100	67
Miscellaneous	100	68
OVERALL SCORE		
345 points out of 500		

Bizet
★★★+

Choose this rivership for the itinerary and destinations, not the food.

Manager/operator..............Grand Circle Cruise Line
Entered service...2002
Registry ....Malta
Identification number ....ENI 07001815
Length (m/yds)..110.0

Number of decks (excluding sun deck) 2
Cabins (total) 60
Balcony cabins .... Yes (French)
Lift (elevator) .... Yes
Rivers sailed ....French rivers

This modern yet dated rivership lacks flair. Some cabins have French balconies and are hence lighter than others, which are small and plain, with slim beds that fold down from the wall. Bathrooms are compact and basic, with curtained-off showers and little space for toiletries. The French cuisine is disappointing, and the wine glasses are small.

Berlitz's Ratings		
	Possible	Achieved
Hardware	100	60
Accommodation	100	68
Cuisine	100	65
Service	100	64
Miscellaneous	100	73
OVERALL SCORE 330 points out of 500		

Bolero
★★★+

A consistent middle-of-the-road rivership that lacks panache.

Manager/operator........................ Lippstadter Tours
Entered service...2003
Registry ....Germany
Identification number ....ENI 09948004
Length (m/yds)..126.7

Number of decks (excluding sun deck) 3
Cabins (total) 90
Balcony cabins .... Yes (French)
Lift (elevator) ....No
Rivers sailed ....Various European rivers

This is a pleasant rivership, but the lounge, while comfortable, is small. Two full decks feature reasonably spacious cabins with French balconies (the cabins on the lowest deck have windows) and good storage space, but the beds are short. Bathrooms are practical but have poor amenities. The cuisine is so-so, and service is rushed.

Berlitz's Ratings		
	Possible	Achieved
Hardware	100	61
Accommodation	100	74
Cuisine	100	66
Service	100	67
Miscellaneous	100	68
OVERALL SCORE 336 points out of 500		

Botticelli
★★★

A consistent, standard-quality river cruise for Francophiles on a budget.

Manager/operator .... CroisiEurope
Entered service 2004
Registry .... France
Identification number .... ENI 01823123
Length (m/yds) 110.0

Number of decks (excluding sun deck) 2
Cabins (total) 77
Balcony cabins .... No
Lift (elevator) .... No
Rivers sailed .... French rivers

Botticelli's interior decor is quite plain. The cabins are rather dull, with short beds and tiny bathrooms with very little space for toiletries. On the plus side, it offers decent French food and wine, a chic French ambience and a good itinerary – and the price is modest. Note shore excursions cost extra.

Berlitz's Ratings		
	Possible	Achieved
Hardware	100	61
Accommodation	100	59
Cuisine	100	59
Service	100	56
Miscellaneous	100	61
OVERALL SCORE		
296 points out of 500		

Brillant
★★+

This rivership delivers a very basic cruise for tight budgets.

Manager/operator .. BTR International River Cruises
Entered service 1948
Registry .... Netherlands
Identification number .... ENI 02312870
Length (m/yds) 63.4

Number of decks (excluding sun deck) 2
Cabins (total) 40
Balcony cabins .... No
Lift (elevator) .... No
Rivers sailed .... Rhein

If you don't mind dated, tiny cabins with slim, short beds, small windows and poor soundproofing, and you don't expect the food to be any more than basic, then this rivership may be acceptable. It's 'cheap and cheerful' and no frills but uninspiring. Go for the destinations and the price.

Berlitz's Ratings		
	Possible	Achieved
Hardware	100	41
Accommodation	100	44
Cuisine	100	52
Service	100	50
Miscellaneous	100	50
OVERALL SCORE		
237 points out of 500		

Britannia
★★+

A passable vintage rivership for travellers on very tight budgets.

Manager/operator .... Nicko Tours
Entered service 1969
Registry .... Switzerland
Identification number .... ENI 07001701
Length (m/yds) 110.0

Number of decks (excluding sun deck) 2
Cabins (total) 92
Balcony cabins .... No
Lift (elevator) .... No
Rivers sailed .... Rhein

The cabins on *Britannia* are really tiny, as are the windows and bathrooms. Most cabins have fold-down beds, although the larger cabins do have twins. There's a cosy ambience, however, and amenities include a little heated open-deck pool. The galley is small and can only deliver basic meals. Good if you're on a tight budget.

Berlitz's Ratings		
	Possible	Achieved
Hardware	100	45
Accommodation	100	44
Cuisine	100	51
Service	100	48
Miscellaneous	100	52
OVERALL SCORE		
240 points out of 500		

Calypso
★★★

This rivership is best chosen for the itinerary and destinations, not the food.

Manager/operator .... Phoenix Cruises
Entered service 1978
Registry .... Netherlands
Identification number .... ENI 2321970
Length (m/yds) 75.6

Number of decks (excluding sun deck) 2
Cabins (total) 49
Balcony cabins .... No
Lift (elevator) .... No
Rivers sailed .... Rhein

This rivership can take you on a river cruise, but because it's an older vessel, the galley is small and so the food choice is basic and limited. The cabins are very small, as are the bathrooms and storage space. Overall, it's a basic, no-frills river cruise at a low price, so it's best to go because of the itinerary.

Berlitz's Ratings		
	Possible	Achieved
Hardware	100	52
Accommodation	100	52
Cuisine	100	56
Service	100	58
Miscellaneous	100	60
OVERALL SCORE		
278 points out of 500		

Camargue
★★★

This standard-quality, unfussy and casual rivership is comfortable, but dated.

Manager/operator.................................CroisiEurope
Entered service...1995
Registry ....France
Identification number ....ENI 01822739
Length (m/yds)...110.0

Number of decks (excluding sun deck) 2
Cabins (total) 73
Balcony cabins ....No
Lift (elevator) ....No
Rivers sailed ....French rivers

Camargue will provide you with a decent middle-of-the road cruise experience. However, the cabins are disappointingly small, as are the bathrooms (think: dancing with shower curtain!), and storage space is poor. Unstuffy French food lacks creativity (the galley is small, as are the wine glasses). Shore excursions cost extra.

Berlitz's Ratings		
	Possible	Achieved
Hardware	100	57
Accommodation	100	56
Cuisine	100	58
Service	100	56
Miscellaneous	100	60
OVERALL SCORE		
287 points out of 500		

Casanova
★★★

This rivership has elegant decor and provides a decent overall experience.

Manager/operator................................. Nicko Tours
Entered service...2001
Registry ....Switzerland
Identification number ....ENI 04800110
Length (m/yds)...103.0

Number of decks (excluding sun deck) 2
Cabins (total) 48
Balcony cabins .... Yes (French)
Lift (elevator) ....No
Rivers sailed ....Various European rivers

Casanova features some fine artwork. The cabins (particularly the bathrooms) have either a short double bed or two slim beds (one converts to a sofa by day), but are bright and cheerful. The restaurant (you must reserve your table for the whole cruise) is cramped. The galley is small, so the variety of meals is disappointing. Breakfasts are repetitious.

Berlitz's Ratings		
	Possible	Achieved
Hardware	100	62
Accommodation	100	58
Cuisine	100	58
Service	100	57
Miscellaneous	100	61
OVERALL SCORE		
296 points out of 500		

Cezanne
★★★

This older rivership will provide a fairly decent river cruise experience.

Manager/operator................................ Nicko Tours
Entered service..1993
Registry .... Switzerland
Identification number ....ENI 05117120
Length (m/yds)..118.0

Number of decks (excluding sun deck) 2
Cabins (total) 51
Balcony cabins ....No
Lift (elevator) ....No
Rivers sailed ....French rivers

Cezanne is a popular ship on the River Seine. Facilities are limited, but the ambience is chic. Although there are no balcony cabins, the cabins themselves are actually quite spacious; some have a double bed, but others have two (couple-unfriendly) slim beds that fold down from the wall. The cuisine is unadventurous.

Berlitz's Ratings

	Possible	Achieved
Hardware	100	58
Accommodation	100	58
Cuisine	100	58
Service	100	56
Miscellaneous	100	60

OVERALL SCORE
290 points out of 500

Clara Schumann
★★★+

This older Elbe rivership delivers a well-rehearsed pleasing cruise experience.

Manager/operator................... Viking River Cruises
Entered service..1991
Registry .... Switzerland
Identification number ....ENI 05113920
Length (m/yds)..94.8

Number of decks (excluding sun deck) 2
Cabins (total) 60
Balcony cabins ....No
Lift (elevator) ....No
Rivers sailed ....Elbe

There are limited facilities in this older rivership, but the cabins are actually quite spacious (there are no balcony cabins), although the bathroom and shower enclosure are dimensionally challenged. Some cabins have a double bed; others have two fold-down beds. The food is decent enough and unfussy, but lacks spirit.

Berlitz's Ratings

	Possible	Achieved
Hardware	100	57
Accommodation	100	64
Cuisine	100	66
Service	100	67
Miscellaneous	100	71

OVERALL SCORE
325 points out of 500

Classica
★★★+

Smart-looking rivership should deliver a good all-round cruise experience.

Manager/operator .... Nicko Tours
Entered service 2000
Registry .... Malta
Identification number .... ENI 09948009
Length (m/yds) 111.2

Number of decks (excluding sun deck) 2
Cabins (total) 74
Balcony cabins .... No
Lift (elevator) .... Yes
Rivers sailed .... Various European rivers

While the decently-sized cabins are comfortable, they are bland; many have large, but non-opening windows (no balconies). Small, but practical bathroom and shower. They have either a sofa bed and fold-away bed, or two sofa beds (none can be pushed together). Comfortable restaurant, with a reasonable variety of tasty food.

Berlitz's Ratings		
	Possible	Achieved
Hardware	100	65
Accommodation	100	60
Cuisine	100	61
Service	100	60
Miscellaneous	100	66

OVERALL SCORE
312 points out of 500

Cyrano de Bergerac
★★★+

This smart-looking rivership has good features, and a French ambience.

Manager/operator .... CroisiEurope
Entered service 2013
Registry .... France
Identification number .... MMSI 22600810
Length (m/yds) 110.0

Number of decks (excluding sun deck) 3
Cabins (total) 88
Balcony cabins .... Yes (French)
Lift (elevator) .... No
Rivers sailed .... French rivers

This modern vessel has chic, quirky interior decor and some delightful artwork. The cabins (many feature French balconies) are bland, but very functional; twin beds can convert to doubles (but bedside reading lights are poor). Bathrooms have a good-sized circular glazed shower enclosure. Fairly decent, not outstanding French cuisine (but good cheeses), and young wines.

Berlitz's Ratings		
	Possible	Achieved
Hardware	100	74
Accommodation	100	72
Cuisine	100	63
Service	100	64
Miscellaneous	100	68

OVERALL SCORE
341 points out of 500

DCS Amethyst
★★★+

A fairly attractive rivership offering a good-quality river cruise experience.

Manager/operator .... DCS
Entered service 2004
Registry .... Malta
Identification number .... ENI 09948007
Length (m/yds) 126.7

Number of decks (excluding sun deck) 3
Cabins (total) 89
Balcony cabins .... Yes (French)
Lift (elevator) .... No
Rivers sailed .... Various European rivers

DCS Amethyst is a fairly modern-looking vessel with attractive, unfussy interior decor. Many of the spacious cabins have French balconies. All except the four suites are the same size and well-appointed, with river-facing beds and good bathrooms. A wellness area includes a hot tub and sauna. Pleasant restaurant, but the food lacks variety and flair.

Berlitz's Ratings		
	Possible	Achieved
Hardware	100	72
Accommodation	100	76
Cuisine	100	65
Service	100	63
Miscellaneous	100	67
OVERALL SCORE		
343 points out of 500		

Da Vinci
★★★

This pleasant, slightly tired, rivership is decent for a low-cost cruise.

Manager/operator .... Various tour operators
Entered service 1995
Registry .... Switzerland
Identification number .... ENI 07001839
Length (m/yds) 105.0

Number of decks (excluding sun deck) 2
Cabins (total) 57
Balcony cabins .... Yes (full)
Lift (elevator) .... No
Rivers sailed .... Various European rivers

Da Vinci is a pleasant rivership, but some interior furnishings are tired. The cabins have windows and two slim beds that fold up for use as sofas by day. Facilities include a small sauna and fitness area. The restaurant is pleasant, but the food, although adequate, is underwhelming and unvaried.

Berlitz's Ratings		
	Possible	Achieved
Hardware	100	58
Accommodation	100	60
Cuisine	100	58
Service	100	61
Miscellaneous	100	61
OVERALL SCORE		
298 points out of 500		

Danubia
★★★

An older-style rivership offering a modestly priced, basic cruise.

Manager/operator............................ Polster & Pohl	Number of decks (excluding sun deck) 2
Entered service... 1980	Cabins (total) 71
Registry .... Romania	Balcony cabins .... No
Identification number .... ENI 46000113	Lift (elevator) .... No
Length (m/yds).. 102.0	Rivers sailed .... Danube, Rhein

With its nostalgic, rich wood interiors, *Danubia* has a calming ambience, although it is quite cramped when full. The small cabins have windows (no balconies) and two fixed, unromantic, short beds. The bathrooms are compact with tiny shower enclosures. The restaurant is comfortable, with food that is actually quite good, and there's a decent variety.

Berlitz's Ratings

	Possible	Achieved
Hardware	100	54
Accommodation	100	57
Cuisine	100	58
Service	100	62
Miscellaneous	100	60

OVERALL SCORE
291 points out of 500

Delta Star
★★★

This rivership delivers a basic no-frills river cruise for restricted budgets.

Manager/operator................................ Nicko Tours	Number of decks (excluding sun deck) 2
Entered service... 1991	Cabins (total) 83
Registry .... Romania	Balcony cabins .... No
Identification number .... ENI 46000141	Lift (elevator) .... No
Length (m/yds).. 107.3	Rivers sailed .... Danube

Delta Star is a very high-density vessel with rather tired decor. The cabins are reasonably spacious, but bland, with two single beds; upper-deck cabins have windows that open. The bathrooms are decidedly small. The restaurant is very comfortable, but the food is hearty rather than high quality, and the variety is limited.

Berlitz's Ratings

	Possible	Achieved
Hardware	100	51
Accommodation	100	51
Cuisine	100	52
Service	100	54
Miscellaneous	100	57

OVERALL SCORE
265 points out of 500

Der Kleine Prinz
★★+

An older, intimate, budget rivership with sombre decor but good artworks.

Manager/operator.......................Value World Tours
Entered service...............................1992
Registry ....Germany
Identification number ....ENI 04803150
Length (m/yds)....................................93.3

Number of decks (excluding sun deck) 2
Cabins (total) 45
Balcony cabins ....No
Lift (elevator) .... Yes
Rivers sailed ....Danube

For anyone looking for a cruise at a low price, then *Der Kleine Prinz* may be suitable. It's an older vessel, lacking the bells and whistles of newer riverships, but it will give you all the basics. Cabins are very small and dated (with couple-unfriendly fixed beds that cannot be moved together) and dimensionally challenged bathrooms.

Berlitz's Ratings	Possible	Achieved
Hardware	100	48
Accommodation	100	44
Cuisine	100	51
Service	100	52
Miscellaneous	100	53
OVERALL SCORE		
248 points out of 500		

Dertour Amadeus
★★★+

A good choice for a well-rounded medium-budget river cruise.

Manager/operator...........................Dertour Cruises
Entered service...............................1997
Registry ....Germany
Identification number ....ENI 08848003
Length (m/yds)....................................110.0

Number of decks (excluding sun deck) 3
Cabins (total) 73
Balcony cabins ....No
Lift (elevator) ....No
Rivers sailed ....Various European rivers

The smart, modern-looking *Dertour Amadeus* is a very comfortable vessel, with decor that is elegant but unstuffy. The cabins are really quite spacious and have mini-fridges and practical bathrooms. The cuisine is quite good and includes a decent amount of variety. Service, too, is good. You should have a very pleasant experience aboard this rivership.

Berlitz's Ratings	Possible	Achieved
Hardware	100	73
Accommodation	100	68
Cuisine	100	67
Service	100	68
Miscellaneous	100	71
OVERALL SCORE		
347 points out of 500		

Dertour Mozart
★★★+

This double-width rivership provides ample space but average cuisine.

Manager/operator...........................Dertour Cruises
Entered service.................................1987
Registry ....Malta
Identification number ....ENI 04805980
Length (m/yds)................................120.6

Number of decks (excluding sun deck) 3
Cabins (total) 103
Balcony cabins .... Yes (French)
Lift (elevator) ....No
Rivers sailed ....Danube

Built for the Danube, this is a comfortable vessel, with pleasant ocean-liner-style decor. Two (one-bedroom) suites are lovely. 'Tamino Deck' cabins are spacious and have French balconies; all others have windows only and small bathrooms. An indoor pool and spa occupies the front of one deck. The mid-ship restaurant has dark decor and unstartling cuisine.

Berlitz's Ratings		
	Possible	Achieved
Hardware	100	74
Accommodation	100	74
Cuisine	100	60
Service	100	63
Miscellaneous	100	72
OVERALL SCORE		
343 points out of 500		

Diana
★★+

A vintage rivership offering no-frills cruises to budget travellers.

Manager/operator............... Various tour operators
Entered service.................................1964
Registry ....Netherlands
Identification number ....ENI 02325126
Length (m/yds)................................78.0

Number of decks (excluding sun deck) 2
Cabins (total) 39
Balcony cabins ....No
Lift (elevator) ....No
Rivers sailed .... Various European rivers

Small, with limited facilities, this vessel is intimate, with comfortable decor. The cabins, though, are really tiny, with slim, short beds. The restaurant is pleasant enough, but with a tiny galley, so don't expect much in terms of cuisine – it's quite basic. *Diana* is best chosen for its itinerary and low cost.

Berlitz's Ratings		
	Possible	Achieved
Hardware	100	42
Accommodation	100	41
Cuisine	100	50
Service	100	51
Miscellaneous	100	55
OVERALL SCORE		
239 points out of 500		

Dnepr
★★+

This older-style rivership is suited to travellers on tight budgets.

Manager/operator................................. Nicko Tours
Entered service..................................1971
Registry ....Ukraine
Identification number ....ENI 42000004
Length (m/yds)................................105.9

Number of decks (excluding sun deck) 2
Cabins (total) 80
Balcony cabins ....No
Lift (elevator) ....No
Rivers sailed ....Danube

If you can cope with extremely small cabins with slim beds, and you don't expect the food to be any more than basic, then this rivership may be acceptable. It's cheap and cheerful, but uninspiring, with decor that is quite dark. Best to prioritise the destinations rather than the amenities on this no-frills rivership.

Berlitz's Ratings		
	Possible	Achieved
Hardware	100	46
Accommodation	100	50
Cuisine	100	50
Service	100	50
Miscellaneous	100	52
OVERALL SCORE		
248 points out of 500		

Donau Star
★★★

This rivership delivers a no-frills river cruise for restricted budgets.

Manager/operator............... Various tour operators
Entered service..................................1987
Registry ....Romania
Identification number ....ENI 46000140
Length (m/yds)................................107.0

Number of decks (excluding sun deck) 2
Cabins (total) 82
Balcony cabins ....No
Lift (elevator) ....No
Rivers sailed ....Danube

Donau Star is a high-density vessel, with dated interior decor. The cabins are, however, reasonably spacious (but bland), have windows that open (upper deck cabins only) and two single beds. Bathrooms are decidedly small. The restaurant is very comfortable, but the food is hearty rather than high quality, and the variety is limited.

Berlitz's Ratings		
	Possible	Achieved
Hardware	100	62
Accommodation	100	58
Cuisine	100	58
Service	100	58
Miscellaneous	100	61
OVERALL SCORE		
297 points out of 500		

Douce France
★★★

This middle-of-the-road rivership is dated but comfortable.

Manager/operator..................................CroisiEurope
Entered service...1997
Registry ....France
Identification number ....ENI 01822845
Length (m/yds)...105.0

Number of decks (excluding sun deck) 2
Cabins (total) 71
Balcony cabins ....No
Lift (elevator) ....No
Rivers sailed ....Rhein

Despite its small plain cabins with short beds and small bathrooms with poor storage space, this rivership may still be suitable for you. Its interior decor is uninspiring, so choose it mainly for its comfortable ambience, the reasonably decent French food and wine and the itinerary. Shore excursions cost extra, but drinks and wine are included.

Berlitz's Ratings

	Possible	Achieved
Hardware	100	58
Accommodation	100	56
Cuisine	100	60
Service	100	57
Miscellaneous	100	61

OVERALL SCORE
292 points out of 500

Douro Queen
★★★+

A smart rivership with good features for stylish Douro cruises.

Manager/operator............... Various tour operators
Entered service...2005
Registry ....Portugal
Identification number ....IMO 9329356
Length (m/yds)...77.4

Number of decks (excluding sun deck) 2
Cabins (total) 65
Balcony cabins .... Yes (French)
Lift (elevator) ....No
Rivers sailed .... Douro

Douro Queen is a small, comfortable vessel with rich interior decor. Cabins on the upper accommodation deck have French balconies, are quite spacious and have decent soundproofing. Bathrooms are small but practical. The restaurant is on the lowest deck and is quite cramped. The cuisine includes many Portuguese and international dishes, which are attractively presented.

Berlitz's Ratings

	Possible	Achieved
Hardware	100	72
Accommodation	100	72
Cuisine	100	66
Service	100	68
Miscellaneous	100	68

OVERALL SCORE
346 points out of 500

Douro Spirit
★★★★

This stylish rivership is recommended for a decent Douro cruise.

Manager/operator .... Vantage River Cruises
Entered service 2011
Registry .... Portugal
Identification number .... n/a
Length (m/yds) 79.5

Number of decks (excluding sun deck) 3
Cabins (total) 65
Balcony cabins .... Yes (French)
Lift (elevator) .... Yes
Rivers sailed .... Douro

Douro Spirit is an attractive rivership. Even the smallest cabin is quite spacious and comfortable, with good soundproofing – the top grades are especially stylish. Most rooms have French balconies, and light colours abound. There's also an appealing restaurant offering attractively presented Portuguese and international dishes.

Berlitz's Ratings	Possible	Achieved
Hardware	100	75
Accommodation	100	73
Cuisine	100	67
Service	100	73
Miscellaneous	100	72
OVERALL SCORE		
360 points out of 500		

Edelweiss
★★★★

A high-quality contemporary rivership for a first-class cruise.

Manager/operator .... Thurgau Travel
Entered service 2013
Registry .... Switzerland
Identification number .... ENI 07001964
Length (m/yds) 110.0

Number of decks (excluding sun deck) 3
Cabins (total) 90
Balcony cabins .... Yes (full)
Lift (elevator) .... Yes
Rivers sailed .... Various European rivers

The interiors of the stylish *Edelweiss* are all about high-quality fittings and furnishings, including hardwood panelling and fine carpeting. The well-appointed, practical cabins have ample storage space, and the bathrooms, with fully glazed shower enclosures, are really pleasing. High-quality, great-tasting food is provided, and there's a good variety. Overall, this rivership delivers a fine-quality cruise.

Berlitz's Ratings	Possible	Achieved
Hardware	100	79
Accommodation	100	77
Cuisine	100	73
Service	100	72
Miscellaneous	100	76
OVERALL SCORE		
377 points out of 500		

Elegant Lady
★★★+

A smart-looking rivership that provides good-value cruises.

Manager/operator	Plantours Cruises	Number of decks (excluding sun deck)	2
Entered service	2002	Cabins (total)	64
Registry	Bulgaria	Balcony cabins	No
Identification number	ENI 08923003	Lift (elevator)	No
Length (m/yds)	110.0	Rivers sailed	Various European rivers

Elegant Lady has nicely appointed interiors but limited public rooms (lounge and restaurant), which makes it feel cramped. The well-designed cabins are quite spacious (each has two slim beds), although the bathrooms are small (but practical). The restaurant is pleasantly decorated. The food is hearty, but choices are limited and the quality and creativity disappointing.

Berlitz's Ratings

	Possible	Achieved
Hardware	100	68
Accommodation	100	67
Cuisine	100	62
Service	100	62
Miscellaneous	100	64

OVERALL SCORE
323 points out of 500

Emerald Sky
Not Yet Rated

This smart rivership will have state-of-the-art features and stylish cabins.

Manager/operator	Emerald Waterways	Number of decks (excluding sun deck)	3
Entered service	2014	Cabins (total)	92
Registry	Malta	Balcony cabins	Yes (French)
Identification number	n/a	Lift (elevator)	Yes
Length (m/yds)	135.0	Rivers sailed	Various European rivers

Emerald Sky will be a really stylish but high-density vessel with nicely appointed interiors; aft there will be a small pool that can be covered and turned into a cinema by night. The cabins should be delightful and spacious; all except those on the lowest deck will have French balconies. Trendy bathrooms should have large shower enclosures. The restaurant is likely to be rather cramped, but with attractive decor.

Berlitz's Ratings

	Possible	Achieved
Hardware	100	NYR
Accommodation	100	NYR
Cuisine	100	NYR
Service	100	NYR
Miscellaneous	100	NYR

OVERALL SCORE
NYR points out of 500

Emerald Star
Not Yet Rated

This smart, contemporary rivership is designed for the youthful traveller.

Manager/operator .... Emerald Waterways
Entered service 2014
Registry .... Malta
Identification number .... n/a
Length (m/yds) 135.0

Number of decks (excluding sun deck) 3
Cabins (total) 92
Balcony cabins .... Yes (French)
Lift (elevator) .... Yes
Rivers sailed .... Various European rivers

The high-density *Emerald Sky* will have well-appointed interiors. The cabins should be lovely and spacious, with bathrooms with large showers; all cabins except those on the lowest deck will have French balconies. Aft will be a small (heated) pool that can be covered and the room turned into a cinema by night. The restaurant will probably have cramped seating but appealing décor.

Berlitz's Ratings		
	Possible	Achieved
Hardware	100	NYR
Accommodation	100	NYR
Cuisine	100	NYR
Service	100	NYR
Miscellaneous	100	NYR

OVERALL SCORE
NYR points out of 500

Esmeralda
★★★

This older vessel provides the basics for no-frills cruising.

Manager/operator .... Shearings Holidays
Entered service 1995
Registry .... Netherlands
Identification number .... ENI 02315764
Length (m/yds) 90.0

Number of decks (excluding sun deck) 2
Cabins (total) 63
Balcony cabins .... No
Lift (elevator) .... Yes
Rivers sailed .... Various European rivers

This pleasant, older, small rivership has limited facilities, but the lounge/bar is comfortable enough. The basic cabins are extremely small and have two pull-down beds; soundproofing is poor. The bathrooms are tiny. The food isn't great either: it lacks both taste and variety, and the breakfast buffets are particularly poor.

Berlitz's Ratings		
	Possible	Achieved
Hardware	100	60
Accommodation	100	57
Cuisine	100	60
Service	100	57
Miscellaneous	100	58

OVERALL SCORE
292 points out of 500

Excellence Coral
★★★+

A charming, compact rivership offers a basic yet decent cruise.

Manager/operator.. Swiss Excellence River Cruises
Entered service...1998
Registry ....Switzerland
Identification number ....ENI 07001711
Length (m/yds)...82.0

Number of decks (excluding sun deck) 2
Cabins (total) 45
Balcony cabins ....No
Lift (elevator) ....No
Rivers sailed .... Elbe, Havel, Oder

Excellence Coral, while small, has pleasant interior decor with warm wood and brass accenting. A lounge and restaurant are the only two public rooms, so it feels cramped inside. Although the cabins are small (as are the bathrooms), they are attractively decorated and have windows (no balconies). Meals are adequate, but there's no flair.

Berlitz's Ratings		
	Possible	Achieved
Hardware	100	63
Accommodation	100	62
Cuisine	100	65
Service	100	72
Miscellaneous	100	71
OVERALL SCORE		
333 points out of 500		

Excellence Queen
★★★+

This contemporary, elegant rivership delivers a good-quality cruise experience.

Manager/operator.. Swiss Excellence River Cruises
Entered service...2011
Registry ....Switzerland
Identification number ....ENI 02333632
Length (m/yds)...110.0

Number of decks (excluding sun deck) 3
Cabins (total) 76
Balcony cabins .... Yes (French)
Lift (elevator) .... Yes
Rivers sailed ....Various European rivers

Excellence Queen features very elegant and stylish dark-wood interiors, with intricate wrought-iron railings. The richly-appointed cabins are comfortable and each has a double bed; bathrooms have a glazed-door shower enclosure. Nice restaurant. The cuisine is good, but doesn't really stand out (more variety and flair are needed).

Berlitz's Ratings		
	Possible	Achieved
Hardware	100	75
Accommodation	100	67
Cuisine	100	65
Service	100	68
Miscellaneous	100	70
OVERALL SCORE		
345 points out of 500		

Excellence Rhône
★★★+

A modern rivership that's reliable for a well-rounded cruise.

Manager/operator.. Swiss Excellence River Cruises
Entered service...2006
Registry ....Switzerland
Identification number ....ENI 07001833
Length (m/yds)...110.0

Number of decks (excluding sun deck) 3
Cabins (total) 76
Balcony cabins .... Yes (French)
Lift (elevator) ....No
Rivers sailed ....French rivers

This stylish vessel has a wide variety of cabin types. Two accommodation decks have cabins with French balconies; others have non-opening windows. All are pleasantly decorated and have either a double or two single beds, plus decent bathrooms. The restaurant is comfortable, with warm decor. Foodwise, there's limited choice, but it's quite good.

Berlitz's Ratings		
	Possible	Achieved
Hardware	100	73
Accommodation	100	68
Cuisine	100	65
Service	100	67
Miscellaneous	100	69
OVERALL SCORE		
342 points out of 500		

Excellence Royal
★★★+

This contemporary, elegant rivership delivers a good-quality cruise experience.

Manager/operator.. Swiss Excellence River Cruises
Entered service...2010
Registry ....Switzerland
Identification number ....ENI 02332815
Length (m/yds)...110.0

Number of decks (excluding sun deck) 3
Cabins (total) 76
Balcony cabins .... Yes (French)
Lift (elevator) ....No
Rivers sailed ....French rivers

Excellence Royal has elegant and stylish dark-wood interiors, with intricate wrought-iron railings and accents. The cabins are richly appointed and comfortable, with double beds; bathrooms have glass shower enclosures. The cuisine is good, although nothing really stands out, and more variety is needed.

Berlitz's Ratings		
	Possible	Achieved
Hardware	100	76
Accommodation	100	67
Cuisine	100	65
Service	100	68
Miscellaneous	100	70
OVERALL SCORE		
346 points out of 500		

Fernão de Magalhães (Ferdinand Magellan)
★★★+

An older Douro rivership for a middle-of-the-road river cruise.

Manager/operator............... Various tour operators
Entered service...2003
Registry ....Portugal
Identification number ....n/a
Length (m/yds)...75.0

Number of decks (excluding sun deck) 3
Cabins (total) 75
Balcony cabins ....No
Lift (elevator) ....No
Rivers sailed .... Douro

This rivership is pleasant enough but has dated interior decor and a rather cramped main lounge. The cabins are small with slim beds that generally can't be moved together and no balconies. Bathrooms are tiny too, with little storage space for toiletries. The cuisine, focussed on local Portuguese food, is adequate, nothing more.

Berlitz's Ratings		
	Possible	Achieved
Hardware	100	71
Accommodation	100	60
Cuisine	100	63
Service	100	62
Miscellaneous	100	62
OVERALL SCORE		
318 points out of 500		

Filia Rheni II
★★★★

This smart-looking rivership delivers fine food and a quality cruise.

Manager/operator....................................Saga Travel
Entered service...2000
Registry ....Germany
Identification number ....ENI 04608050
Length (m/yds)...110.0

Number of decks (excluding sun deck) 3
Cabins (total) 75
Balcony cabins ....No
Lift (elevator) ....No
Rivers sailed .... Various European rivers

Filia Rheni II is a well-appointed vessel, with a large lounge with Scandinavian decor and panoramic windows. The cabins are small but practical and very comfortable. The food is creative, with oodles of variety and taste, and is well presented, with tablecloths and crisp napkins for dinner. This is a well-organised Saga Travel product.

Berlitz's Ratings		
	Possible	Achieved
Hardware	100	73
Accommodation	100	72
Cuisine	100	76
Service	100	74
Miscellaneous	100	74
OVERALL SCORE		
369 points out of 500		

Flamenco
★★★+

Contemporary and casual, this rivership provides a good-value experience.

Manager/operator .... Nicko Tours
Entered service 2005
Registry .... Malta
Identification number .... ENI 09948011
Length (m/yds) 135.0

Number of decks (excluding sun deck) 3
Cabins (total) 96
Balcony cabins .... Yes (French)
Lift (elevator) .... No
Rivers sailed .... Danube

A 'twin cruiser', with the propulsion machinery separated from passenger accommodation, *Flamenco* offers small, stylish, quiet cabins, many with French balconies. Beds are fixed, and one converts to a sofa by day. Large glass windows allow great views from both the lounge and restaurant, but the food is nothing special.

Berlitz's Ratings

	Possible	Achieved
Hardware	100	76
Accommodation	100	75
Cuisine	100	63
Service	100	62
Miscellaneous	100	68

OVERALL SCORE
344 points out of 500

Florentina
★★★

This older-style rivership may suit if you're on a tight budget.

Manager/operator .... Nicko Tours
Entered service 1981
Registry .... Netherlands
Identification number .... ENI 32108292
Length (m/yds) 80.0

Number of decks (excluding sun deck) 2
Cabins (total) 47
Balcony cabins .... No
Lift (elevator) .... No
Rivers sailed .... Elbe, Moldau

If you don't mind really small cabins with slim beds and you don't expect the food to be any more than basic, then this rivership may be suitable for you. It's cheap and cheerful but a little uninspiring. Choose it for the destinations or if the budget is tight, not for the rivership itself.

Berlitz's Ratings

	Possible	Achieved
Hardware	100	63
Accommodation	100	58
Cuisine	100	56
Service	100	57
Miscellaneous	100	56

OVERALL SCORE
290 points out of 500

Fluvius
★★

This rivership is known for its budget-conscious bicycle tours.

Manager/operator................ Various tour operators
Entered service...1929
Registry ....Netherlands
Identification number ....ENI 23155535
Length (m/yds)...69.9

Number of decks (excluding sun deck) 2
Cabins (total) 19
Balcony cabins ....No
Lift (elevator) ....No
Rivers sailed .... Elbe, Oder, Havel

This is a vintage rivership, used mainly for transportation on low-cost bicycle tours. It has small cabins without balconies and tiny bathrooms, and, foodwise, the self-service buffets are poor, with minimal choice (the galley is tiny). This really is no-frills river cruising, so go because of your ride or to suit a minimal budget.

Berlitz's Ratings		
	Possible	Achieved
Hardware	100	36
Accommodation	100	35
Cuisine	100	41
Service	100	42
Miscellaneous	100	44
OVERALL SCORE		
198 points out of 500		

Fortuna
★★★

This rather dated rivership provides the basics only for a no-frills cruise.

Manager/operator................ Various tour operators
Entered service...1974
Registry ....Netherlands
Identification number ....ENI 02321035
Length (m/yds)...66.0

Number of decks (excluding sun deck) 2
Cabins (total) 48
Balcony cabins ....No
Lift (elevator) ....No
Rivers sailed ....Various European rivers

If you are not too fussy about food and wine and could cope with a very small, plain cabin with slim beds and a bathroom with a small amount of storage space, then this no-frills rivership may be suitable for you. Choose it mainly for the itinerary and destinations rather than the vessel itself.

Berlitz's Ratings		
	Possible	Achieved
Hardware	100	55
Accommodation	100	54
Cuisine	100	53
Service	100	55
Miscellaneous	100	61
OVERALL SCORE		
278 points out of 500		

France
★★★

This unpretentious rivership provides a standard, decent-value river cruise.

Manager/operator	CroisiEurope
Entered service	2001
Registry	France
Identification number	ENI 01823029
Length (m/yds)	110.0

Number of decks (excluding sun deck)	2
Cabins (total)	78
Balcony cabins	No
Lift (elevator)	No
Rivers sailed	French rivers

The decor of this fairly modern rivership is quite bland. The cabins are small, with inferior sound insulation and a lack of storage space, but they are practical. Bathrooms are tight. The restaurant is cramped and serves average food and wines, of limited variety, although good cheeses. Choose it for the itinerary and French ambience.

Berlitz's Ratings

	Possible	Achieved
Hardware	100	61
Accommodation	100	57
Cuisine	100	60
Service	100	57
Miscellaneous	100	58

OVERALL SCORE
293 points out of 500

Frederic Chopin
★★★+

A small but smart-looking rivership, just adequate for a basic cruise.

Manager/operator	Various tour operators
Entered service	2002
Registry	Switzerland
Identification number	ENI 04801240
Length (m/yds)	83.0

Number of decks (excluding sun deck)	2
Cabins (total)	42
Balcony cabins	No
Lift (elevator)	No
Rivers sailed	Elbe, Havel, Oder

Frederic Chopin has small, cramped interiors, and facilities are limited. The cabins are adequate (and they do have mini-fridges), although dimensionally challenged; and most have either a double bed or two lower beds. Bathrooms are tiny, too. The cuisine is reasonably decent, as are the wines.

Berlitz's Ratings

	Possible	Achieved
Hardware	100	66
Accommodation	100	63
Cuisine	100	64
Service	100	56
Miscellaneous	100	62

OVERALL SCORE
311 points out of 500

Gérard Schmitter
★★★+

This smart-looking rivership has good features and a French ambience.

Manager/operator................................CroisiEurope
Entered service.................................2012
Registry ....France
Identification number ....ENI 01831335
Length (m/yds).................................110.0

Number of decks (excluding sun deck) 3
Cabins (total) 88
Balcony cabins .... Yes (French)
Lift (elevator) ....No
Rivers sailed .... Danube, Rhein

This modern rivership has chic, rather quaint, decor with nice artworks. The cabins are fairly plain but practical, with twin beds that convert to a double and, frequently, French balconies. Downsides include the lack of storage space. Bathrooms have outdated curtained showers. There's decent, rich cuisine (especially the cheeses), but the wines are young.

Berlitz's Ratings		
	Possible	Achieved
Hardware	100	74
Accommodation	100	64
Cuisine	100	61
Service	100	66
Miscellaneous	100	68
OVERALL SCORE		
333 points out of 500		

Heidelberg
★★★+

This modern rivership would be a good choice for a well-rounded cruise.

Manager/operator................................ Nicko Tours
Entered service.................................2004
Registry ....Switzerland
Identification number ....ENI 04802890
Length (m/yds).................................110.0

Number of decks (excluding sun deck) 2
Cabins (total) 56
Balcony cabins .... Yes (French)
Lift (elevator) ....No
Rivers sailed .... Mosel, Rhein

Heidelberg has nicely designed interiors but a confined lobby. Most cabins are spacious, well-appointed and have French balconies (lowest deck cabins have non-opening portholes); some have double beds or one bed and a fold-down (sofa) bed. Amenities include a small wellness centre. The cuisine is average, but you should have a very comfortable cruise.

Berlitz's Ratings		
	Possible	Achieved
Hardware	100	73
Accommodation	100	68
Cuisine	100	67
Service	100	66
Miscellaneous	100	71
OVERALL SCORE		
345 points out of 500		

Heinrich Heine
★★★

This now-dated rivership has some good features for a comfortable cruise.

Manager/operator .... Phoenix Reisen
Entered service 1991
Registry .... Bulgaria
Identification number .... ENI 08948008
Length (m/yds) 106.6

Number of decks (excluding sun deck) 2
Cabins (total) 55
Balcony cabins .... No
Lift (elevator) .... Yes
Rivers sailed .... Danube

Heinrich Heine is compact with a small reception lobby and a wellness area. All cabins have opening windows, one fixed bed and one fold-down bed (one larger cabin has a double bed); bathrooms are very small. The attractive restaurant is cramped. The galley is small, as is the food choice, but what there is tastes good.

Berlitz's Ratings		
	Possible	Achieved
Hardware	100	57
Accommodation	100	55
Cuisine	100	55
Service	100	56
Miscellaneous	100	60
OVERALL SCORE		
283 points out of 500		

Infante Don Henrique
★★★

Expect a comfortable, standard cruise on this small Douro rivership.

Manager/operator .... CroisiEurope
Entered service 2003
Registry .... France
Identification number .... ENI 01823121
Length (m/yds) 75.0

Number of decks (excluding sun deck) 2
Cabins (total) 71
Balcony cabins .... No
Lift (elevator) .... Yes
Rivers sailed .... Douro

This rivership has a compact, nicely decorated lounge and restaurant but limited facilities. Most cabins have large windows, two beds (some are convertible to a double, while some are fixed); reading lights are poor, and bathrooms are very small. Although limited, the cuisine includes several Portuguese and some international dishes; wine glasses are small.

Berlitz's Ratings		
	Possible	Achieved
Hardware	100	61
Accommodation	100	58
Cuisine	100	60
Service	100	58
Miscellaneous	100	61
OVERALL SCORE		
298 points out of 500		

Inspire
Not Yet Rated

A fine rivership that should offer excellent features and delightful decor.

Manager/operator	Tauck Tours	Number of decks (excluding sun deck)	3
Entered service	2014	Cabins (total)	67
Registry	Malta	Balcony cabins	Yes (French)
Identification number	n/a	Lift (elevator)	Yes
Length (m/yds)	135.0	Rivers sailed	Various European rivers

Inspire will be contemporary with restrained, elegant decor. The spacious cabins and 22 double-size suites (the latter offering room service for breakfast) will have French balconies (cabins on the lowest deck have windows), excellent bed linen and Molton Brown toiletries. Beverages will be unlimited. The main restaurant is forward; an alternative venue for light food is located aft.

Berlitz's Ratings

	Possible	Achieved
Hardware	100	NYR
Accommodation	100	NYR
Cuisine	100	NYR
Service	100	NYR
Miscellaneous	100	NYR

OVERALL SCORE
NYR points out of 500

Invicta
★★★

A small, older Douro rivership for a basic, inexpensive cruise.

Manager/operator	CroisiEurope	Number of decks (excluding sun deck)	2
Entered service	1963	Cabins (total)	40
Registry	Portugal	Balcony cabins	No
Identification number	ENI 02315334	Lift (elevator)	No
Length (m/yds)	68.0	Rivers sailed	Douro

Pleasant, but dated, *Invicta* has extremely compact cabins with twin beds, some of which are not fixed and can be pushed together to form doubles. The dinky bathrooms are passable – just. The cuisine includes many regional dishes, but don't expect much because the galley is tiny. Overall, an inexpensive way to cruise the Douro.

Berlitz's Ratings

	Possible	Achieved
Hardware	100	52
Accommodation	100	53
Cuisine	100	56
Service	100	57
Miscellaneous	100	58

OVERALL SCORE
276 points out of 500

Johann Strauss
★★★+

This attractive rivership delivers a fine experience to its international clientele.

Manager/operator .... Various tour operators
Entered service 2004
Registry .... Malta
Identification number .... ENI 09948006
Length (m/yds) 126.7

Number of decks (excluding sun deck) 2
Cabins (total) 90
Balcony cabins .... Yes (French)
Lift (elevator) .... No
Rivers sailed .... Various European rivers

Johann Strauss is a well-designed vessel, with restful rather than trendy decor. The blonde wood of the large cabins, more than 60 of which have French balconies, is warm. There is ample storage space, and the bathrooms are nicely appointed. There's an attractive central dining room, but the cuisine is disappointing. Internet connectivity costs extra.

Berlitz's Ratings		
	Possible	Achieved
Hardware	100	71
Accommodation	100	68
Cuisine	100	65
Service	100	65
Miscellaneous	100	72
OVERALL SCORE		
341 points out of 500		

Johannes Brahms
★★★

A shallow draught vessel for budget cruises on the Oder.

Manager/operator .... Various tour operators
Entered service 1998
Registry .... Germany
Identification number .... ENI 04033510
Length (m/yds) 81.9

Number of decks (excluding sun deck) 2
Cabins (total) 40
Balcony cabins .... No
Lift (elevator) .... No
Rivers sailed .... Oder

Johannes Brahms is a modestly comfortable vessel, but with limited facilities due to its small size. The small, cramped cabins have windows (no balconies) and short beds, but they are still modestly comfortable; bathrooms are dimensionally challenged. There's a pleasant dining room, but uninspiring food and limited choice. One for the destinations or tight budgets.

Berlitz's Ratings		
	Possible	Achieved
Hardware	100	62
Accommodation	100	59
Cuisine	100	56
Service	100	60
Miscellaneous	100	61
OVERALL SCORE		
298 points out of 500		

Katharina von Bora
★★★+

This small, smart-looking rivership is adequate for a basic cruise.

Manager/operator............... Various tour operators
Entered service.................................2000
Registry ....Switzerland
Identification number ....ENI 05803950
Length (m/yds)....................................83.0

Number of decks (excluding sun deck) 2
Cabins (total) 42
Balcony cabins ....No
Lift (elevator) ....No
Rivers sailed ....Various European rivers

Katharina von Bora's interiors are small and cramped, and the facilities are limited. The cabins are adequate although dimensionally challenged with tiny bathrooms; most have either double beds or two lower beds, as well as a mini-fridge. The galley is tiny, so the cuisine is pretty basic, as are the wines.

Berlitz's Ratings		
	Possible	Achieved
Hardware	100	66
Accommodation	100	70
Cuisine	100	66
Service	100	65
Miscellaneous	100	66
OVERALL SCORE		
333 points out of 500		

Koenigstein
★★★

This small, standard-quality rivership is dated but characterful.

Manager/operator................................ Nicko Tours
Entered service.................................1992
Registry ....Germany
Identification number ....ENI 05502420
Length (m/yds)....................................68.0

Number of decks (excluding sun deck) 2
Cabins (total) 30
Balcony cabins ....No
Lift (elevator) ....No
Rivers sailed ....Elbe, Havel, Moldau, Vltava

Koenigstein's interior decor is rather dark, but there are some interesting artworks and the vessel is surprisingly cosy. The cabins have slim, short beds, and the bathrooms are very small; storage space is very tight. The galley is small, so food variety is quite limited. Fine for a no-frills experience and decent itineraries.

Berlitz's Ratings		
	Possible	Achieved
Hardware	100	61
Accommodation	100	54
Cuisine	100	57
Service	100	58
Miscellaneous	100	60
OVERALL SCORE		
290 points out of 500		

L'Europe
★★★

A relatively modern rivership offering a decent French-style cruise.

Manager/operator	CroisiEurope
Entered service	2006
Registry	France
Identification number	ENI 01823178
Length (m/yds)	110.0
Number of decks (excluding sun deck)	3
Cabins (total)	80
Balcony cabins	No
Lift (elevator)	No
Rivers sailed	Danube, Rhein

This rivership's decor is quite warm. The cabins are practical but small (storage space is tight), with poor reading lights. The bathrooms are quite cramped, but L'Occitane toiletries are provided. The restaurant is pleasant, but the meals are nothing special, although the cheese selection is good. Choose it for the destination over the rivership itself.

Berlitz's Ratings		
	Possible	Achieved
Hardware	100	64
Accommodation	100	58
Cuisine	100	60
Service	100	55
Miscellaneous	100	59
OVERALL SCORE		
296 points out of 500		

La Belle de Cadix
★★★

This high-density rivership provides a decent but hectic cruise experience.

Manager/operator	CroisiEurope
Entered service	2005
Registry	Belgium
Identification number	IMO 9068938
Length (m/yds)	110.0
Number of decks (excluding sun deck)	3
Cabins (total)	89
Balcony cabins	No
Lift (elevator)	No
Rivers sailed	Guadalquiver

Modern, with warm interior decor, this rivership has very small cabins, some with double beds, some with twins that convert to a double. Bathrooms are also dinky. Other negatives include too few crew members. On the plus side, there's a compact but pleasantly decorated restaurant. The French cuisine is average, but there's a good cheese selection.

Berlitz's Ratings		
	Possible	Achieved
Hardware	100	64
Accommodation	100	59
Cuisine	100	60
Service	100	55
Miscellaneous	100	60
OVERALL SCORE		
298 points out of 500		

La Boheme
★★★

This older rivership will deliver a standard-quality cruise experience.

Manager/operator .... CroisiEurope
Entered service 1995
Registry .... France
Identification number .... ENI 01822744
Length (m/yds) 110.0

Number of decks (excluding sun deck) 2
Cabins (total) 80
Balcony cabins .... No
Lift (elevator) .... No
Rivers sailed .... Danube, Rhein

La Boheme's cabins (none with French balconies) have either a double bed, a two-bed configuration or even a third bed. Bathrooms are very small and functional, with little storage space for toiletries. Go because of its relaxed French ambience, unfussy food and light wines, and for the itinerary. Note that shore excursions cost extra.

Berlitz's Ratings		
	Possible	Achieved
Hardware	100	60
Accommodation	100	57
Cuisine	100	60
Service	100	57
Miscellaneous	100	60
OVERALL SCORE		
294 points out of 500		

Lady Anne
★★+

A tired granny of a rivership for budget, no-frills cruising.

Manager/operator .... Nicko Tours
Entered service 1963
Registry .... Netherlands
Identification number .... ENI 02007059
Length (m/yds) 70.0

Number of decks (excluding sun deck) 2
Cabins (total) 53
Balcony cabins .... No
Lift (elevator) .... Yes
Rivers sailed .... Rhein

Everything about the *Lady Anne* is really basic, but the crew is amiable and the ambience intimate. The cabins have fixed beds, and the bathrooms really are tiny. It's best described as a vintage water taxi with food that passengers view as between barely and reasonably adequate. Go for the itinerary and the low price.

Berlitz's Ratings		
	Possible	Achieved
Hardware	100	43
Accommodation	100	41
Cuisine	100	47
Service	100	45
Miscellaneous	100	48
OVERALL SCORE		
224 points out of 500		

Leonardo da Vinci
★★★

This French-style rivership delivers a good-value, comfortable cruise.

Manager/operator .... CroisiEurope
Entered service 2003
Registry .... France
Identification number .... ENI 01823119
Length (m/yds) 105.0

Number of decks (excluding sun deck) 2
Cabins (total) 72
Balcony cabins .... No
Lift (elevator) .... No
Rivers sailed .... Danube, Rhein

If you like straightforward French food and wine and are happy with a comfortable but small (no balcony) cabin, slim beds and tiny bathroom with limited storage space, then *Leonardo da Vinci* may be suitable for you. Choose it for its laid-back French ambience, itinerary and destinations. Note that excursions cost extra.

Berlitz's Ratings		
	Possible	Achieved
Hardware	100	62
Accommodation	100	57
Cuisine	100	60
Service	100	56
Miscellaneous	100	60
OVERALL SCORE		
295 points out of 500		

Lord Byron
★★★★+

A high-quality contemporary rivership for a first-class cruise experience.

Manager/operator .... Riviera Travel (UK)
Entered service 2012
Registry .... UK
Identification number .... ENI 65000004
Length (m/yds) 110.0

Number of decks (excluding sun deck) 3
Cabins (total) 74
Balcony cabins .... Yes (French)
Lift (elevator) .... No
Rivers sailed .... Various European rivers

The interiors of the stylish *Lord Byron* are all about high-quality fittings and furnishings, such as hardwood panelling and plush carpeting. Well-appointed, practical cabins have ample storage space, and the bathrooms, with fully glazed shower enclosures, are a pleasure. In addition, the cuisine is high quality, creative, tasty and varied. A quality product.

Berlitz's Ratings		
	Possible	Achieved
Hardware	100	84
Accommodation	100	84
Cuisine	100	78
Service	100	77
Miscellaneous	100	82
OVERALL SCORE		
405 points out of 500		

Maribelle
★★★+

An attractive, well-appointed rivership for French river cruises.

Manager/operator .... Various tour operators
Entered service 2000
Registry .... Malta
Identification number .... ENI 04802070
Length (m/yds) 110.0

Number of decks (excluding sun deck) 2
Cabins (total) 77
Balcony cabins .... No
Lift (elevator) .... Yes
Rivers sailed .... Rhône

Nicely outfitted with the emphasis on blonde wood, *Maribelle*'s interior is minimalist and fairly comfortable. The cabins have good soundproofing; some have two beds, while others have one fixed and one fold-down bed (acting as a sofa by day), and windows that open (Upper Deck only). The restaurant is pleasant and serves French regional cuisine.

Berlitz's Ratings		
	Possible	Achieved
Hardware	100	69
Accommodation	100	68
Cuisine	100	65
Service	100	63
Miscellaneous	100	64
OVERALL SCORE		
329 points out of 500		

Michaelangelo
★★★

Choose this French rivership for a standard but consistent experience.

Manager/operator .... CroisiEurope
Entered service 2000
Registry .... France
Identification number .... n/a
Length (m/yds) 110.0

Number of decks (excluding sun deck) 2
Cabins (total) 74
Balcony cabins .... No
Lift (elevator) .... No
Rivers sailed .... Po, Venetian Lagoon

Michaelangelo's interior decor is rather plain and looks tired. The cabins are practical, although diminutive – the beds are small and short – and the bathroom has basic amenities and little space for toiletries. The food is so-so. Shore excursions cost extra. Choose it mainly for its French ambience and for the itinerary.

Berlitz's Ratings		
	Possible	Achieved
Hardware	100	61
Accommodation	100	57
Cuisine	100	60
Service	100	56
Miscellaneous	100	60
OVERALL SCORE		
294 points out of 500		

Modigliani
★★★

A consistent, standard-quality Venetian Lagoon cruise with French food.

Manager/operator .... CroisiEurope
Entered service 2001
Registry .... France
Identification number .... ENI 01823030
Length (m/yds) 110.0

Number of decks (excluding sun deck) 2
Cabins (total) 78
Balcony cabins .... No
Lift (elevator) .... No
Rivers sailed .... Danube, Rhein

This rivership offers comfortable and unpretentious (no-balcony) cabins with short beds and small bathrooms that are low on storage space. It does, however, provide decent but unfussy French (not Italian) food and wine. Choose it mainly for its friendly ambience, itinerary and destinations. Note that shore excursions cost extra.

Berlitz's Ratings		
	Possible	Achieved
Hardware	100	62
Accommodation	100	57
Cuisine	100	60
Service	100	56
Miscellaneous	100	60
OVERALL SCORE		
295 points out of 500		

Moldavia
★★+

This older-style rivership is passable for anyone on a tight budget.

Manager/operator .... Nicko Tours
Entered service 1979
Registry .... Ukraine
Identification number .... ENI 42000002
Length (m/yds) 115.7

Number of decks (excluding sun deck) 2
Cabins (total) 80
Balcony cabins .... No
Lift (elevator) .... No
Rivers sailed .... Danube

The decor is tired and sombre but characterful. The cabins are small and utilitarian (with windows or portholes) and have fixed or pull-down beds; some have lower and upper berths. The tiny bathrooms have showers with curtains, rather than glazed doors. The galley is small, and the food – served in the cramped restaurant – is uninspiring.

Berlitz's Ratings		
	Possible	Achieved
Hardware	100	48
Accommodation	100	45
Cuisine	100	48
Service	100	51
Miscellaneous	100	51
OVERALL SCORE		
243 points out of 500		

Mona Lisa
★★★

Disappointingly small, plain cabins, but good French ambience and food.

Manager/operator .... CroisiEurope
Entered service 2000
Registry .... France
Identification number .... ENI 01822875
Length (m/yds) 82.5

Number of decks (excluding sun deck) 2
Cabins (total) 50
Balcony cabins .... No
Lift (elevator) .... No
Rivers sailed .... Danube, Rhein

If you like unpretentious French food and wine and are happy with a comfortable but small (no-balcony) cabin, slim beds and tiny bathroom with limited storage space, then *Mona Lisa* may be a suitable choice. It's best to consider it mainly for its French ambience, itinerary and destinations. Shore excursions cost extra.

Berlitz's Ratings		
	Possible	Achieved
Hardware	100	61
Accommodation	100	57
Cuisine	100	60
Service	100	56
Miscellaneous	100	60
OVERALL SCORE		
294 points out of 500		

Monet
★★★

This comfortable, but now dated, rivership has French flair.

Manager/operator .... CroisiEurope
Entered service 1999
Registry .... France
Identification number .... ENI 01822874
Length (m/yds) 110.0

Number of decks (excluding sun deck) 2
Cabins (total) 83
Balcony cabins .... No
Lift (elevator) .... No
Rivers sailed .... Danube, Rhein

Monet has dated interior decor, small (no-balcony) cabins with slim beds (most can't be moved together) and tiny bathrooms with poor storage space for toiletries. But if you like an unpretentious, casual ambience, fairly decent food and wine (limited choice), it may be suitable for you. Travel for the itinerary. Note that shore excursions cost extra.

Berlitz's Ratings		
	Possible	Achieved
Hardware	100	58
Accommodation	100	57
Cuisine	100	60
Service	100	56
Miscellaneous	100	58
OVERALL SCORE		
289 points out of 500		

My Story
★★+

A rivership for the itinerary and destinations but not the food.

Manager/operator.............. Transocean Flussreisen
Entered service.................................1971
Registry ....Netherlands
Identification number ....ENI 07001704
Length (m/yds)..................................105.0

Number of decks (excluding sun deck) 2
Cabins (total) 100
Balcony cabins ....No
Lift (elevator) .... Yes
Rivers sailed .... Various European rivers

This fairly smart-looking, older rivership has had many name changes, but is comfortable. Often used for bicycle-tour participants, it has pleasant public areas, but the cabins are small (as are the bathrooms) and have no balconies, little storage space and poor soundproofing. The galley is small, and the food is just so-so.

Berlitz's Ratings		
	Possible	Achieved
Hardware	100	48
Accommodation	100	47
Cuisine	100	48
Service	100	51
Miscellaneous	100	54
OVERALL SCORE		
248 points out of 500		

Nestroy
★★★+

This stylish, modern rivership delivers a standard cruise experience.

Manager/operator............... Various tour operators
Entered service.................................2007
Registry ....Switzerland
Identification number ....ENI 08001848
Length (m/yds)..................................124.8

Number of decks (excluding sun deck) 3
Cabins (total) 113
Balcony cabins .... Yes (French)
Lift (elevator) .... Yes
Rivers sailed .... Various European rivers

Nestroy is a smart-looking vessel, with an attractive, comfortable lounge, but it can get crowded. While suites have queen-sized beds, all other cabins are extremely compact, with slim pull-down beds that can't be pushed together (these act as sofas by day). The bathrooms are functional. The restaurant is uninspiring and serves average food.

Berlitz's Ratings		
	Possible	Achieved
Hardware	100	73
Accommodation	100	68
Cuisine	100	66
Service	100	62
Miscellaneous	100	65
OVERALL SCORE		
334 points out of 500		

Normandie
★★★

Choose this French rivership for a standard but consistent experience.

Manager/operator .... Various tour operators
Entered service 1989
Registry .... Netherlands
Identification number .... ENI 02327268
Length (m/yds) 91.2

Number of decks (excluding sun deck) 2
Cabins (total) 51
Balcony cabins .... No
Lift (elevator) .... No
Rivers sailed .... Various European rivers

If you like unpretentious French food and wine and can accept a small (no-balcony) but practical cabin, with slim beds and a small bathroom with limited space for toiletries, then *Normandie* may be suitable. Go mainly for its comfortable ambience and for the itinerary and destinations. Note that shore excursions cost extra.

Berlitz's Ratings		
	Possible	Achieved
Hardware	100	60
Accommodation	100	58
Cuisine	100	58
Service	100	58
Miscellaneous	100	56
OVERALL SCORE		
290 points out of 500		

Olympia
★★★

This small, older-style, nicely furnished rivership has a warm atmosphere.

Manager/operator .... Newmarket Holidays
Entered service 1984
Registry .... Switzerland
Identification number .... ENI 07001846
Length (m/yds) 88.5

Number of decks (excluding sun deck) 2
Cabins (total) 51
Balcony cabins .... No
Lift (elevator) .... No
Rivers sailed .... Rhein

Olympia is a comfortable rivership. The cabins are compact and basic but they have large windows and reasonable storage; most have two (fixed, rather short) slim beds, while three cabins have double beds. The bathrooms are tiny but functional. Downsides include dim lighting in the accommodation hallway. The standard-quality food is tailored to British passengers.

Berlitz's Ratings		
	Possible	Achieved
Hardware	100	61
Accommodation	100	52
Cuisine	100	56
Service	100	60
Miscellaneous	100	58
OVERALL SCORE		
287 points out of 500		

Polonaise
★★+

A small, comfortable but basic rivership for cruising Poland's Vistula.

Manager/operator....................................Intercruise
Entered service...1982
Registry ....Poland
Identification number ....ENI 04031590
Length (m/yds)..82.5

Number of decks (excluding sun deck)................2
Cabins (total) 43
Balcony cabins ....No
Lift (elevator) ....No
Rivers sailed .... Vistula (Poland)

This is a small, older-style, two-deck rivership with small but comfortable cabins with windows (those on the lowest deck are smaller than the others) and basic bathrooms with curtained-off showers. Just don't expect fine food, because the galley is tiny and can only turn out fairly basic meals. Choose *Polonaise* for the itinerary and destinations.

Berlitz's Ratings

	Possible	Achieved
Hardware	100	51
Accommodation	100	50
Cuisine	100	45
Service	100	47
Miscellaneous	100	53
OVERALL SCORE		
246 points out of 500		

Poseidon
★★★

A small, older rivership with dated facilities offering no-frills cruising.

Manager/operator............................... Triton Reisen
Entered service...1980
Registry ....Netherlands
Identification number ....ENI 02204965
Length (m/yds)..78.0

Number of decks (excluding sun deck)................2
Cabins (total) 49
Balcony cabins ....No
Lift (elevator) ....No
Rivers sailed ....Various European rivers

The delightful bird's-eye-maple interior, old-world style and comfortable chairs help make this a comfortable rivership, despite its interior looking generally tired. Small cabins have one pull-down bed (creating space when pushed up in the daytime) and one sofa bed. The bathrooms are tiny. There's uninspiring food (tiny galley), so make the itinerary your priority.

Berlitz's Ratings

	Possible	Achieved
Hardware	100	57
Accommodation	100	56
Cuisine	100	51
Service	100	54
Miscellaneous	100	58
OVERALL SCORE		
276 points out of 500		

Primadonna
★★★+

This double-width rivership with ample space provides comfortable river cruises.

Manager/operator...............Euro Shipping Voyages	Number of decks (excluding sun deck) 3
Entered service..................................1998	Cabins (total) 76
Registry ....Malta	Balcony cabins .... Yes (French)
Identification number ....ENI 09240010	Lift (elevator) .... Yes
Length (m/yds)..................................113.3	Rivers sailed ....Danube

Built on two hulls and only operating on the Danube, *Primadonna* has a spacious two-deck-high interior lobby. Many cabins (and bathrooms), though, are small, and storage space is tight; 40 cabins have small wedge-shaped French balconies. The food is just so-so and needs more variety, so go for the itinerary.

Berlitz's Ratings		
	Possible	Achieved
Hardware	100	71
Accommodation	100	58
Cuisine	100	60
Service	100	58
Miscellaneous	100	61
OVERALL SCORE		
308 points out of 500		

Princess
★★★

A small, dumpy-looking rivership for basic, no-frills river cruising.

Manager/operator........ Swiss International Cruises	Number of decks (excluding sun deck) 2
Entered service..................................1984	Cabins (total) 50
Registry ....Netherlands	Balcony cabins ....No
Identification number ....ENI 02323525	Lift (elevator) ....No
Length (m/yds)..................................80.0	Rivers sailed ....Various European Rivers

The exterior won't win any Prince Charming contest, but the interior decor is nicely restrained and comfortable. The cabins are compact and simple, with fold-away beds, as are the bathrooms – you can dance with the shower curtain. Choose it for the itinerary and for its cheap-and-cheerful price, but not for the food, which is basic.

Berlitz's Ratings		
	Possible	Achieved
Hardware	100	61
Accommodation	100	55
Cuisine	100	56
Service	100	58
Miscellaneous	100	58
OVERALL SCORE		
288 points out of 500		

Princess Sophie
★★★

This dated rivership delivers an average, but good-value, cruise experience.

Manager/operator............... Various tour operators
Entered service..1994
Registry ....Switzerland
Identification number ....ENI 07001903
Length (m/yds)..105.0

Number of decks (excluding sun deck) 2
Cabins (total) 74
Balcony cabins ....No
Lift (elevator) ....No
Rivers sailed ....Various European rivers

A high-density vessel with bland, non-descript interior decor. The cabins are very, very small, with short (double or twin) beds, and partially opening windows; the bathrooms are tiny with curtained-off showers only. The banquet-style restaurant is plain. The cuisine is unmemorable, and there's little choice. Decent value, though.

Berlitz's Ratings		
	Possible	Achieved
Hardware	100	61
Accommodation	100	57
Cuisine	100	58
Service	100	58
Miscellaneous	100	61
OVERALL SCORE		
295 points out of 500		

Princesse d'Aquitaine
★★★

This smart French rivership delivers a standard, but good-value cruise.

Manager/operator................................CroisiEurope
Entered service..2001
Registry ....France
Identification number ....IMO 8919805
Length (m/yds)..110.0

Number of decks (excluding sun deck) 2
Cabins (total) 69
Balcony cabins ....No
Lift (elevator) ....No
Rivers sailed ....French rivers

This attractive rivership has fairly bland interior decor, but if you are happy with rustic French-style cuisine and wine and a comfortable but small (no-balcony) cabin, thin beds and a small bathroom with little storage space, then this rivership may be suitable. Go for its pleasant ambience, good itinerary and destinations. Shore excursions cost extra.

Berlitz's Ratings		
	Possible	Achieved
Hardware	100	60
Accommodation	100	57
Cuisine	100	60
Service	100	57
Miscellaneous	100	60
OVERALL SCORE		
294 points out of 500		

Princesse de Provence
★★★

An elegantly decorated rivership offering decent hospitality.

Manager/operator.................................. Nicko Tours
Entered service...................................1992
Registry ....Switzerland
Identification number ....IMO 8643353
Length (m/yds)...............................110.0

Number of decks (excluding sun deck) 2
Cabins (total) 72
Balcony cabins ....No
Lift (elevator) ....No
Rivers sailed ....French rivers

This vessel's lovely, old-world interior decor includes an abundance of rich woods and brass fittings, especially in the Panorama Salon. The cabins are very small and include two fixed beds (one folds into the wall by day) and tiny but functional bathrooms. The food is adequate, but the variety is limited by the tiny galley.

Berlitz's Ratings		
	Possible	Achieved
Hardware	100	61
Accommodation	100	61
Cuisine	100	57
Service	100	58
Miscellaneous	100	60
OVERALL SCORE		
297 points out of 500		

Prinses Christina
★★+

This older rivership provides a no-frills cruise for tight budgets.

Manager/operator............... Various tour operators
Entered service...................................1969
Registry ....Netherlands
Identification number ....ENI 02326420
Length (m/yds).....................................72.0

Number of decks (excluding sun deck) 2
Cabins (total) 54
Balcony cabins ....No
Lift (elevator) ....No
Rivers sailed ....French rivers

If you can accept very small cabins with slim beds, and you don't expect the food to be any more than basic, *Prinses Christina* may be adequate. The interior decor includes nicely polished wood. Go for the destinations, and not for this no-frills cheap-and-cheerful vessel, with its noisy engines.

Berlitz's Ratings		
	Possible	Achieved
Hardware	100	42
Accommodation	100	41
Cuisine	100	44
Service	100	46
Miscellaneous	100	48
OVERALL SCORE		
221 points out of 500		

Prinzessin Isabella
★★★+

A very good choice for a well-rounded river cruise.

Manager/operator.......................... Phoenix Cruises
Entered service...2002
Registry ....Malta
Identification number ....ENI 04804660
Length (m/yds)...125.5

Number of decks (excluding sun deck) 3
Cabins (total) 84
Balcony cabins .... Yes (French)
Lift (elevator) .... Yes
Rivers sailed ....Danube

The cabins are quite spacious and comfortable, with the more costly grades featuring French balconies and twin beds that can be converted to doubles. Other cabins have large windows, with fold-down beds that act as sofas by day. The small bathrooms are practical, with glazed showers. The food is reasonably good but of inadequate variety.

Berlitz's Ratings

	Possible	Achieved
Hardware	100	65
Accommodation	100	64
Cuisine	100	66
Service	100	59
Miscellaneous	100	63

OVERALL SCORE
317 points out of 500

Prinzessin Katharina
★★★+

This delightful, grand hotel-style rivership delivers charm and good cuisine.

Manager/operator...............................SE Tours/KVS
Entered service...1991
Registry ....Malta
Identification number ....ENI 09948003
Length (m/yds)...110.0

Number of decks (excluding sun deck) 2
Cabins (total) 76
Balcony cabins .... Yes (French)
Lift (elevator) ....No
Rivers sailed .... Douro

Named after a late Greek princess, this small, older rivership has a beautiful lounge/bar and glamorous traditional interior decor. 'Upper Deck' cabins have French balconies, with one fixed bed and one pull-down 'Pullman' bed. 'Main Deck' cabins have non-opening windows and fixed beds in an 'L'-shape. The grand, hotel-style dining room does good food.

Berlitz's Ratings

	Possible	Achieved
Hardware	100	60
Accommodation	100	58
Cuisine	100	64
Service	100	60
Miscellaneous	100	62

OVERALL SCORE
304 points out of 500

Queen Isabel
★★★★

This smart-looking rivership provides a fine Douro cruise.

Manager/operator..... Uniworld Grand River Cruises
Entered service.................................2013
Registry ....Portugal
Identification number ....n/a
Length (m/yds).................................79.0

Number of decks (excluding sun deck) 3
Cabins (total) 58
Balcony cabins .... Yes (French and full)
Lift (elevator) .... Yes
Rivers sailed .... Douro

Queen Isabel features some beautiful Portuguese furniture and fittings and has a small pool and mini-spa. The cabins, most of which have full or French balconies, are nicely appointed and have decent-sized bathrooms with L'Occitane toiletries. The cuisine is good and features many Portuguese specialities. A delightful way to travel on the River Douro.

Berlitz's Ratings		
	Possible	Achieved
Hardware	100	80
Accommodation	100	80
Cuisine	100	75
Service	100	70
Miscellaneous	100	75
OVERALL SCORE		
380 points out of 500		

Regina Rheni
★★★★

Choose this smart-looking vessel for a high-quality cruise with good food.

Manager/operator............... Various tour operators
Entered service.................................2000
Registry ....Netherlands
Identification number ....ENI 02324591
Length (m/yds).................................110.0

Number of decks (excluding sun deck) 3
Cabins (total) 77
Balcony cabins ....No
Lift (elevator) ....No
Rivers sailed ....Rhein, Danube

A nicely appointed rivership, *Regina Rheni* has a large lounge with panoramic windows. The interior decor is Scandinavian minimalist and very comfortable. The galley turns out a wide variety of food that is really good, with plenty of taste and attractive presentation. Overall, this is a well-run product.

Berlitz's Ratings		
	Possible	Achieved
Hardware	100	75
Accommodation	100	68
Cuisine	100	73
Service	100	74
Miscellaneous	100	77
OVERALL SCORE		
367 points out of 500		

Rembrandt
★★★+

A small rivership known for its high-quality cuisine and service.

Manager/operator............... Various tour operators
Entered service..2003
Registry .... Switzerland
Identification number ....ENI 07001819
Length (m/yds)..82.0

Number of decks (excluding sun deck) 2
Cabins (total) 39
Balcony cabins ....Yes (French in 4 suites)
Lift (elevator) ....No
Rivers sailed ....French rivers

Rembrandt is smart-looking, small and cosy with delightfully warm interior decor and fine soft furnishings. Four suites have double beds and French balconies, while all other cabins have twin beds that convert to sofas by day. The intimate dining room has tablecloths for dinner. The food comes in minimalist portions but it's creative and tasty.

Berlitz's Ratings		
	Possible	Achieved
Hardware	100	72
Accommodation	100	63
Cuisine	100	70
Service	100	65
Miscellaneous	100	70
OVERALL SCORE		
340 points out of 500		

Rembrandt von Rijn
★★★

This older-style rivership offers a basic, no-frills river cruise.

Manager/operator...................................Travelmaxx
Entered service..1985
Registry ....Netherlands
Identification number ....ENI 07001819
Length (m/yds)..110.0

Number of decks (excluding sun deck) 2
Cabins (total) 63
Balcony cabins ....No
Lift (elevator) .... Yes
Rivers sailed ....Various European rivers

This older, but nicely refurbished, rivership has warm interiors, including a lovely lounge, accented by lots of polished wood. The cabins are small, with short twin beds, and the bathrooms are diminutive, too, with limited storage space. Go for the itinerary but not for the food, which is limited due to the small galley.

Berlitz's Ratings		
	Possible	Achieved
Hardware	100	61
Accommodation	100	56
Cuisine	100	60
Service	100	57
Miscellaneous	100	58
OVERALL SCORE		
292 points out of 500		

Renoir
★★★

This little French vessel offers standard cruising but lacks panache.

Manager/operator...............................CroisiEurope
Entered service...1999
Registry ....France
Identification number ....ENI 01822865
Length (m/yds)..110.0

Number of decks (excluding sun deck) 2
Cabins (total) 78
Balcony cabins ....No
Lift (elevator) ....No
Rivers sailed ....French rivers

The *Renoir* will provide you with a well-organised middle-of-the road cruise experience, although the cabins are quite small (with a wide choice of bed configurations), as are the bathrooms, plus storage space is limited and there are no balconies. The cuisine lacks creativity and variety (the galley is tiny), and the wine glasses are small.

Berlitz's Ratings

	Possible	Achieved
Hardware	100	60
Accommodation	100	58
Cuisine	100	60
Service	100	56
Miscellaneous	100	62
OVERALL SCORE		
296 points out of 500		

Rex Rheni
★★★+

This small, high-density rivership delivers an average basic cruise experience.

Manager/operator....................................Saga Travel
Entered service...1979
Registry ....Netherlands
Identification number ....ENI 02007993
Length (m/yds)..90.5

Number of decks (excluding sun deck) 3
Cabins (total) 78
Balcony cabins ....No
Lift (elevator) ....No
Rivers sailed .... Mosel, Rhein

Rex Rheni is an older type of rivership with just a lounge/bar and restaurant, plus an open sundeck, so it feels cramped. The stairways between decks have steep steps. The cabins are really small and utilitarian, with bathrooms that have curtained-off showers only. The food is uninspiring, and the variety is minimal.

Berlitz's Ratings

	Possible	Achieved
Hardware	100	57
Accommodation	100	56
Cuisine	100	60
Service	100	72
Miscellaneous	100	61
OVERALL SCORE		
306 points out of 500		

Rhein Prinzessin
★★★

This smartish rivership delivers a standard river cruise product.

Manager/operator........................... Phoenix Cruises
Entered service...1999
Registry ....Switzerland
Identification number ....ENI 07001717
Length (m/yds)..110.0

Number of decks (excluding sun deck) 2
Cabins (total) 70
Balcony cabins ....Yes (French)
Lift (elevator) .... Yes
Rivers sailed ....Various European rivers

This rivership has dated interior decor but is pleasingly comfortable. Except for a few cabins with French balconies, the accommodation is disappointingly small, and the soundproofing and lighting are poor. The beds are very slim (many fold down from the walls), and the bathrooms are tiny. It's not for food lovers, either. A proper no-frills experience.

Berlitz's Ratings

	Possible	Achieved
Hardware	100	57
Accommodation	100	53
Cuisine	100	54
Service	100	55
Miscellaneous	100	56

OVERALL SCORE
275 points out of 500

Rhine Princess
★★

An older rivership suitable only if you are on a really tight budget.

Manager/operator............... Various tour operators
Entered service...1960
Registry ....Malta
Identification number ....ENI 07000661
Length (m/yds)..83.2

Number of decks (excluding sun deck) 2
Cabins (total) 60
Balcony cabins ....No
Lift (elevator) ....No
Rivers sailed .... Mosel, Rhein

This is an old, much-rebuilt and not very handsome vessel. The cabins are very small and really basic, with slim, short beds and poor soundproofing. Bathrooms are minimal. The galley is tiny and can only turn out the most basic meals. Best advice: look for something better, unless the budget really can't stretch any further.

Berlitz's Ratings

	Possible	Achieved
Hardware	100	40
Accommodation	100	37
Cuisine	100	38
Service	100	42
Miscellaneous	100	40

OVERALL SCORE
197 points out of 500

Rigoletto
★★★

This dated rivership offers a standard, no-frills cruise.

Manager/operator .... Various tour operators
Entered service 1987
Registry .... Netherlands
Identification number .... ENI 02325887
Length (m/yds) 105.0

Number of decks (excluding sun deck) 2
Cabins (total) 60
Balcony cabins .... No
Lift (elevator) .... No
Rivers sailed .... Various European rivers

Extended by 10m (33ft) in 2003, *Rigoletto* is reasonably comfortable and typical of 1980s-built vessels without French-balcony cabins. The cabins are really small, however; most have couple-unfriendly beds that fold down from opposite walls. Bathrooms are tight. The restaurant is pleasant enough, but the galley is small and cannot deliver much variety.

Berlitz's Ratings		
	Possible	Achieved
Hardware	100	60
Accommodation	100	56
Cuisine	100	55
Service	100	56
Miscellaneous	100	60
OVERALL SCORE		
287 points out of 500		

River Adagio
★★★+

A comfortable rivership offering a decent but dated cruise experience.

Manager/operator .... Grand Circle Cruise Line
Entered service 2003
Registry .... Malta
Identification number .... ENI 07001803
Length (m/yds) 125.0

Number of decks (excluding sun deck) 2
Cabins (total) 82
Balcony cabins .... Yes (French)
Lift (elevator) .... Yes
Rivers sailed .... Various European rivers

River Adagio is comfortable, with brass fittings featuring heavily in its design scheme, but it's now dated. All the cabins are the same size; some have French balconies. The twin beds are fixed, with one converting to a sofa by day. The bathrooms are pleasant enough, but the toilets are noisy. The cuisine is unmemorable.

Berlitz's Ratings		
	Possible	Achieved
Hardware	100	71
Accommodation	100	67
Cuisine	100	61
Service	100	62
Miscellaneous	100	63
OVERALL SCORE		
324 points out of 500		

River Allegro
★★★+

A rivership for the itinerary and destinations, not the food.

Manager/operator..............Grand Circle Cruise Line
Entered service...1991
Registry ....Malta
Identification number ....ENI 02315025
Length (m/yds)..110.0

Number of decks (excluding sun deck) 2
Cabins (total) 48
Balcony cabins .... Yes
Lift (elevator) ....No
Rivers sailed ....Elbe, Havel, Moldau, Vltava

This small rivership navigates Europe's smaller waterways. The interior decor includes lots of brass and dark wood. The cabins and bathrooms are really very small, but they do have character and balconies. The food is so-so, because the galley is small. Go for the itineraries and the old-world comfort.

Berlitz's Ratings		
	Possible	Achieved
Hardware	100	61
Accommodation	100	65
Cuisine	100	60
Service	100	60
Miscellaneous	100	60

OVERALL SCORE
306 points out of 500

River Ambassador
★★★+

This rivership has oodles of panache and delivers an 'inclusive' cruise.

Manager/operator............... Various tour operators
Entered service...1993
Registry ....Netherlands
Identification number ....ENI 02320666
Length (m/yds)..110.0

Number of decks (excluding sun deck) 2
Cabins (total) 64
Balcony cabins .... Yes (French)
Lift (elevator) ....No
Rivers sailed ....Various European rivers

River Ambassador is a small, older vessel, but it's comfortable, with elegant interiors. The cabins are dimensionally challenged, but functional and nicely decorated, with windows (some open, some don't) and fixed queen-sized beds. The bathrooms and showers are compact, however, with little space for toiletries. The lovely, open-seating restaurant provides reasonable food, but young wines.

Berlitz's Ratings		
	Possible	Achieved
Hardware	100	62
Accommodation	100	65
Cuisine	100	61
Service	100	60
Miscellaneous	100	61

OVERALL SCORE
309 points out of 500

River Aria
★★★+

This rivership should provide you with a decent cruise experience.

Manager/operator..............Grand Circle Cruise Line
Entered service..................................2001
Registry ....Malta
Identification number ....ENI 07001740
Length (m/yds)..................................125.0

Number of decks (excluding sun deck) 3
Cabins (total) 82
Balcony cabins .... Yes (French)
Lift (elevator) .... Yes
Rivers sailed ....Various European rivers

River Adagio is comfortable, with brass fittings featuring heavily in its design scheme, but it's now dated. All the cabins are the same size; some have French balconies. The twin beds are fixed, with one converting to a sofa by day. The bathrooms are pleasant enough, but the toilets are noisy. The cuisine is unmemorable.

Berlitz's Ratings		
	Possible	Achieved
Hardware	100	70
Accommodation	100	64
Cuisine	100	63
Service	100	63
Miscellaneous	100	66
OVERALL SCORE		
326 points out of 500		

River Art
★★★+

This modern vessel is a good choice for a well-rounded cruise.

Manager/operator............... Various tour operators
Entered service..................................2005
Registry ....Switzerland
Identification number ....ENI 07001812
Length (m/yds)..................................110.0

Number of decks (excluding sun deck) 2
Cabins (total) 67
Balcony cabins .... Yes (French)
Lift (elevator) ....No
Rivers sailed ....Various European rivers

River Art has very pleasant, comfortable interior decor. The cabins are all nicely appointed (the upper deck cabins have French balconies) and are spacious enough, as are the bathrooms. Two slim, short beds fold away during the day; just one cabin has a double bed. The cuisine is standard, with no flair and little variety.

Berlitz's Ratings		
	Possible	Achieved
Hardware	100	74
Accommodation	100	66
Cuisine	100	65
Service	100	66
Miscellaneous	100	69
OVERALL SCORE		
340 points out of 500		

River Baroness
★★★+

This rivership has oodles of panache and provides an 'inclusive' cruise.

Manager/operator..... Uniworld Grand River Cruises
Entered service..1995
Registry ....Netherlands
Identification number ....ENI 02320666
Length (m/yds)..110.0

Number of decks (excluding sun deck) 2
Cabins (total) 64
Balcony cabins .... Yes (French)
Lift (elevator) ....No
Rivers sailed ....French rivers

River Baroness is a small, older vessel, but it's comfortable, with elegant interiors. The cabins are dimensionally challenged, but functional and nicely decorated, with windows (some open, some don't) and fixed queen-sized beds. The bathrooms and showers are compact, however, with little space for toiletries. The lovely, open-seating restaurant provides good food, but young wines.

Berlitz's Ratings		
	Possible	Achieved
Hardware	100	61
Accommodation	100	62
Cuisine	100	62
Service	100	60
Miscellaneous	100	62
OVERALL SCORE		
307 points out of 500		

River Beatrice
★★★★

This boutique rivership offers elegant decor and chic, quality cruising.

Manager/operator..... Uniworld Grand River Cruises
Entered service..2007
Registry ....Netherlands
Identification number ....ENI 02329007
Length (m/yds)..125.0

Number of decks (excluding sun deck) 3
Cabins (total) 80
Balcony cabins .... Yes (French)
Lift (elevator) .... Yes
Rivers sailed ....Danube

River Beatrice has elegant interior decor in its cabins and restaurant, with white featuring heavily. The cabins are fairly spacious (most have twin beds convertible to queen-sized beds). Many cabins feature French balconies, good storage space and welcoming bathrooms. The open-seating restaurant provides good food, but young wines. Facilities include a complimentary passenger laundry.

Berlitz's Ratings		
	Possible	Achieved
Hardware	100	73
Accommodation	100	76
Cuisine	100	68
Service	100	67
Miscellaneous	100	73
OVERALL SCORE		
357 points out of 500		

River Cloud II
★★★★

This handsome retro-look rivership has tasteful features and lovely decor.

Manager/operator......................Sea Cloud Cruises
Entered service..2001
Registry ....Malta
Identification number ....ENI 04800450
Length (m/yds)..103.0

Number of decks (excluding sun deck) 2
Cabins (total) 44
Balcony cabins ....No
Lift (elevator) ....No
Rivers sailed ....Various European rivers

River Cloud II's attractive wood-and-brass interiors are in the 1930s grand-hotel style. The cabins are quite spacious and nicely furnished and appointed. All have windows (no balconies), some of which can be opened. The bathrooms are quite small, however. The restaurant is comfortable and the cuisine good-quality, but it lacks panache. Amenities include a hair salon and sauna.

Berlitz's Ratings		
	Possible	Achieved
Hardware	100	71
Accommodation	100	76
Cuisine	100	75
Service	100	73
Miscellaneous	100	73
OVERALL SCORE		
368 points out of 500		

River Concerto
★★★+

This older, well-proportioned rivership will deliver a decent cruise experience.

Manager/operator..............Grand Circle Cruise Line
Entered service..2000
Registry ....Malta
Identification number ....ENI 07001728
Length (m/yds)..110.0

Number of decks (excluding sun deck) 3
Cabins (total) 70
Balcony cabins ....Yes (French)
Lift (elevator) ....Yes
Rivers sailed ....Various European rivers

River Concerto is a comfortable vessel, but the interior decor is rather dated. Most cabins have windows, but a few have French balconies. Best described as 'small but sufficient', the cabins have immovable (couple-unfriendly) fixed, thin beds. The restaurant is pleasant enough, but the food is limited in variety and lacks flair.

Berlitz's Ratings		
	Possible	Achieved
Hardware	100	73
Accommodation	100	67
Cuisine	100	63
Service	100	61
Miscellaneous	100	63
OVERALL SCORE		
327 points out of 500		

River Countess
★★★+

Choose this comfortable rivership for its good-quality furnishings and itinerary.

Manager/operator..... Uniworld Grand River Cruises
Entered service...2003
Registry .... Switzerland
Identification number ....ENI 07001802
Length (m/yds)..110.0

Number of decks (excluding sun deck) 3
Cabins (total) 67
Balcony cabins .... Yes (French)
Lift (elevator) .... Yes
Rivers sailed ....Po, Venetian Lagoon

The *River Countess* is a nicely appointed vessel. Cabins are small, with limited storage– the 'Rhein Deck' suites and cabins have French balconies, while all others have windows only. The bathrooms are also small. The open-seating aft restaurant is comfortable. The cuisine is decent and includes a healthy choice menu. Amenities include a fitness area.

Berlitz's Ratings		
	Possible	Achieved
Hardware	100	73
Accommodation	100	68
Cuisine	100	63
Service	100	66
Miscellaneous	100	69
OVERALL SCORE		
339 points out of 500		

River Discovery II
★★★+

Good facilities and decent food make this rivership a sound choice.

Manager/operator................. Vantage River Cruises
Entered service...2013
Registry ....Germany
Identification number ....ENI 02334834
Length (m/yds)..135.0

Number of decks (excluding sun deck) 3
Cabins (total) 85
Balcony cabins .... Yes (French)
Lift (elevator) .... Yes
Rivers sailed ....French rivers

Designed for American tastes, with classy interior decor, this contemporary vessel has a good range of cabins, most of which have French balconies and twin beds that convert to doubles. The open-seating restaurant is comfortable. The cuisine is reasonably good – it includes a healthy choice menu – but lacks flair. Complimentary bicycles are carried on board.

Berlitz's Ratings		
	Possible	Achieved
Hardware	100	78
Accommodation	100	72
Cuisine	100	61
Service	100	65
Miscellaneous	100	70
OVERALL SCORE		
346 points out of 500		

River Duchess
★★★+

An elegant rivership with attractive features for a decent cruise.

Manager/operator................ Various tour operators
Entered service...2003
Registry ....Switzerland
Identification number ....ENI 08001805
Length (m/yds)..110.0

Number of decks (excluding sun deck) 3
Cabins (total) 67
Balcony cabins .... Yes (French)
Lift (elevator) .... Yes
Rivers sailed ....Various European rivers

The *River Duchess* is a nicely appointed vessel. Cabins are small, with limited storage– the 'Rhein Deck' suites and cabins have French balconies, while all others have windows only. The bathrooms are also small. The open-seating aft restaurant is comfortable. The cuisine is reasonably good and includes a healthy choice menu, although lacking in finesse and unmemorable. Amenities include a fitness area.

Berlitz's Ratings

	Possible	Achieved
Hardware	100	68
Accommodation	100	67
Cuisine	100	58
Service	100	62
Miscellaneous	100	66

OVERALL SCORE
321 points out of 500

River Empress
★★★+

This modern rivership might be a good choice for a well-rounded cruise.

Manager/operator..... Uniworld Grand River Cruises
Entered service...2002
Registry ....Switzerland
Identification number ....ENI 08001740
Length (m/yds)..110.0

Number of decks (excluding sun deck) 3
Cabins (total) 65
Balcony cabins .... Yes (French)
Lift (elevator) .... Yes
Rivers sailed ....Various European rivers

River Empress is a nicely appointed vessel. Cabins are small, with limited storage– the 'Rhein Deck' suites and cabins have French balconies, while all others have windows only. The bathrooms are also small. The open-seating aft restaurant is comfortable. The cuisine is reasonably good and includes a healthy choice menu, although lacking in finesse and unmemorable. Amenities include a fitness area.

Berlitz's Ratings

	Possible	Achieved
Hardware	100	68
Accommodation	100	76
Cuisine	100	65
Service	100	68
Miscellaneous	100	69

OVERALL SCORE
346 points out of 500

River Harmony
★★★+

This small rivership is dated but has decent practical features.

Manager/operator..............Grand Circle Cruise Line
Entered service...1999
Registry ....Malta
Identification number ....ENI 07001721
Length (m/yds)...110.0

Number of decks (excluding sun deck).................3
Cabins (total) 70
Balcony cabins ....Yes (French)
Lift (elevator) .... Yes
Rivers sailed ....Various European rivers

River Harmony is now rather dated, with plain interior decor. Some cabins have French balconies, with twin beds that convert to doubles and ample storage space. Other cabins have two pull-down (couple-unfriendly) beds. Other downsides include the lack of bathroom space, poor reading lights and inferior sound insulation. The restaurant is cramped and serves average food, but offers good service.

Berlitz's Ratings

	Possible	Achieved
Hardware	100	66
Accommodation	100	68
Cuisine	100	61
Service	100	67
Miscellaneous	100	65

OVERALL SCORE
327 points out of 500

River Melody
★★★+

This dated rivership still provides a decent backdrop for a river cruise.

Manager/operator..............Grand Circle Cruise Line
Entered service...1999
Registry ....Malta
Identification number ....ENI 07001718
Length (m/yds)...110.0

Number of decks (excluding sun deck).................3
Cabins (total) 70
Balcony cabins ....Yes (15 with French)
Lift (elevator) .... Yes
Rivers sailed ....Various European rivers

This small rivership with plain decor is comfortable, if dated. Some cabins have French balconies; others have windows that don't open. Some have twin beds that can be converted to doubles, while others have fixed beds. Downsides include the space, reading lights, sound insulation and cramped restaurant. The food is average, with slim choice.

Berlitz's Ratings

	Possible	Achieved
Hardware	100	67
Accommodation	100	68
Cuisine	100	61
Service	100	66
Miscellaneous	100	66

OVERALL SCORE
328 points out of 500

River Navigator
★★★+

This rivership provides good facilities for a comfortable cruise experience.

Manager/operator .... Vantage River Cruises
Entered service 2002
Registry .... Malta
Identification number .... ENI 04804650
Length (m/yds) 110.0

Number of decks (excluding sun deck) 3
Cabins (total) 72
Balcony cabins .... Yes (French)
Lift (elevator) .... Yes
Rivers sailed .... Danube

River Navigator's decor is comfortable rather than stylish. There's a 'Rat Pack'-themed lounge/bar within the main lounge. The good range of cabins includes some singles and some with French balconies; most are small, but all have twin beds that convert to doubles. Bathrooms are small but have glazed shower enclosures. The food is just so-so.

Berlitz's Ratings		
	Possible	Achieved
Hardware	100	66
Accommodation	100	72
Cuisine	100	61
Service	100	65
Miscellaneous	100	65
OVERALL SCORE		
329 points out of 500		

River Odyssey
★★★+

This comfortable rivership provides a good range of features.

Manager/operator .... Vantage River Cruises
Entered service 2002
Registry .... Germany
Identification number .... ENI 04804660
Length (m/yds) 125.0

Number of decks (excluding sun deck) 2
Cabins (total) 85
Balcony cabins .... Yes (French)
Lift (elevator) .... Yes
Rivers sailed .... Various European rivers

This vessel is comfortable rather than stylish. There's a neat 'Rat Pack'-themed lounge/bar within the main lounge. About half the cabins have French balconies and twin beds that convert to doubles; the others are small, with two pull-down beds. The bathrooms are small but adequate. The food is so-so, and the wines are young.

Berlitz's Ratings		
	Possible	Achieved
Hardware	100	67
Accommodation	100	72
Cuisine	100	61
Service	100	65
Miscellaneous	100	66
OVERALL SCORE		
331 points out of 500		

River Princess
★★★+

This modern rivership might be a good choice for a well-rounded cruise.

Manager/operator..... Uniworld Grand River Cruises
Entered service..2001
Registry ....Netherlands
Identification number ....ENI 02325078
Length (m/yds)..110.0

Number of decks (excluding sun deck) 3
Cabins (total) 65
Balcony cabins .... Yes (French)
Lift (elevator) .... Yes
Rivers sailed ....Various European rivers

River Princess is a nicely appointed vessel. Cabins are small, with limited storage – the 'Rhein Deck' suites and cabins have French balconies, while all others have windows only. The bathrooms are also small. The open-seating aft restaurant is comfortable. The cuisine is reasonably good and includes a healthy choice menu, although lacking in finesse. Amenities include a fitness area.

Berlitz's Ratings

	Possible	Achieved
Hardware	100	68
Accommodation	100	72
Cuisine	100	62
Service	100	69
Miscellaneous	100	70

OVERALL SCORE
341 points out of 500

River Queen
★★★+

A retro-look boutique rivership with tasteful features and bags of style.

Manager/operator..... Uniworld Grand River Cruises
Entered service..1999
Registry ....Netherlands
Identification number ....ENI 02323692
Length (m/yds)..110.0

Number of decks (excluding sun deck) 3
Cabins (total) 70
Balcony cabins ....No
Lift (elevator) .... Yes
Rivers sailed ....Various European rivers

The interior of the *River Queen* is in the elegant Art Deco style. The spacious cabins are well equipped and comfortable, but their windows don't open. The open-seating restaurant is delightful, although cramped. The disappointing food, however, lacks variety (breakfast buffets are repetitive). Amenities include a wellness area with sauna, a launderette and complimentary bicycles.

Berlitz's Ratings

	Possible	Achieved
Hardware	100	67
Accommodation	100	72
Cuisine	100	62
Service	100	71
Miscellaneous	100	70

OVERALL SCORE
342 points out of 500

River Rhapsody
★★★+

This small, dated rivership has decent basic features, and is good value.

Manager/operator..............Grand Circle Cruise Line
Entered service...1999
Registry .... Malta
Identification number ....ENI 07001722
Length (m/yds)..110.0

Number of decks (excluding sun deck) 3
Cabins (total) 70
Balcony cabins .... Yes (French)
Lift (elevator) .... Yes
Rivers sailed .... Various European rivers

This small rivership with plain decor is comfortable, if dated. Some cabins have French balconies; others have windows that don't open. Some have twin beds that can be converted to doubles, while others have fixed beds. Downsides include the space, reading lights, sound insulation and cramped restaurant. The food is average and lacks flair.

Berlitz's Ratings		
	Possible	Achieved
Hardware	100	67
Accommodation	100	68
Cuisine	100	62
Service	100	66
Miscellaneous	100	68
OVERALL SCORE		
331 points out of 500		

River Royale
★★★★

This modern rivership could be a good choice for a well-rounded cruise.

Manager/operator..... Uniworld Grand River Cruises
Entered service...2006
Registry ....Netherlands
Identification number ....ENI 02327301
Length (m/yds)..110.0

Number of decks (excluding sun deck) 3
Cabins (total) 70
Balcony cabins .... Yes (French)
Lift (elevator) .... Yes
Rivers sailed ....French rivers

River Royale is a nicely appointed vessel, with light, modernist interior decor. Cabins are small, with limited storage– the 'Rhein Deck' suites and cabins have French balconies, while all others have windows only. The bathrooms are also small. The open-seating aft restaurant is comfortable. The cuisine is reasonably good and includes a healthy choice list, but the menus are overstated.

Berlitz's Ratings		
	Possible	Achieved
Hardware	100	74
Accommodation	100	75
Cuisine	100	67
Service	100	71
Miscellaneous	100	71
OVERALL SCORE		
358 points out of 500		

River Splendor
★★★★

With fine facilities and features, this contemporary rivership is a good choice.

Manager/operator .... Vantage River Cruises	Number of decks (excluding sun deck) 3
Entered service 2013	Cabins (total) 85
Registry .... Germany	Balcony cabins .... Yes (French)
Identification number .... ENI 02334836	Lift (elevator) .... Yes
Length (m/yds) 135.0	Rivers sailed .... Various European rivers

Designed for American tastes, with tasteful interior decor, this contemporary vessel has a good range of cabins, most of which have French balconies and twin beds that convert to doubles. The open-seating restaurant is comfortable. The cuisine is reasonably good – it includes a healthy choice menu – but lacks flair. Complimentary bicycles are carried on board.

Berlitz's Ratings

	Possible	Achieved
Hardware	100	78
Accommodation	100	78
Cuisine	100	63
Service	100	68
Miscellaneous	100	72

OVERALL SCORE
359 points out of 500

River Venture
★★★★

This contemporary rivership, with its excellent facilities, makes a good choice.

Manager/operator .... Vantage River Cruises	Number of decks (excluding sun deck) 3
Entered service 2013	Cabins (total) 78
Registry .... Germany	Balcony cabins .... Yes (French)
Identification number .... ENI 02334835	Lift (elevator) .... No
Length (m/yds) 110.0	Rivers sailed .... Various European rivers

Designed for American tastes, with classy interior decor, this contemporary vessel has a good range of cabins, most of which have French balconies and twin beds that convert to doubles. The open-seating restaurant is comfortable. The cuisine is reasonably good – it includes a healthy choice menu – but lacks flair. Complimentary bicycles are carried on board.

Berlitz's Ratings

	Possible	Achieved
Hardware	100	78
Accommodation	100	78
Cuisine	100	63
Service	100	68
Miscellaneous	100	71

OVERALL SCORE
358 points out of 500

Rossini
★★★

A rivership for the itinerary, not the food or space.

Manager/operator..............Grand Circle Cruise Line
Entered service..1983
Registry ....Germany
Identification number ....ENI 05116760
Length (m/yds)..111.0

Number of decks (excluding sun deck) 2
Cabins (total) 95
Balcony cabins ....No
Lift (elevator) ....No
Rivers sailed ....Danube

Rossini is an older rivership with rich wood interiors (nice bar counter) and Old Master-style paintings. The very small, functional cabins have windows (except for 11 interior ones) and, usually, two L-shaped beds (some have single beds). The restaurant is cramped and dark. The cuisine is cheap and cheerful, with limited choice.

Berlitz's Ratings		
	Possible	Achieved
Hardware	100	58
Accommodation	100	57
Cuisine	100	57
Service	100	58
Miscellaneous	100	63
OVERALL SCORE		
293 points out of 500		

Rotterdam
★★★

This small, older rivership is passable for a no-frills cruise experience.

Manager/operator.................... Shearings Holidays
Entered service..1969
Registry ....Switzerland
Identification number ....ENI 07001417
Length (m/yds)..75.5

Number of decks (excluding sun deck) 2
Cabins (total) 60
Balcony cabins ....No
Lift (elevator) ....No
Rivers sailed ....Various European rivers

Rotterdam is a much-rebuilt vessel, with very limited facilities – basically just a lounge/bar. The cabins are quite plain but cosy and adequate. They have windows (some can be opened), not balconies. There are three single-occupancy cabins. Unusually, there are cabins between the kitchen and the restaurant, which gets in the way of getting hot meals.

Berlitz's Ratings		
	Possible	Achieved
Hardware	100	46
Accommodation	100	50
Cuisine	100	53
Service	100	57
Miscellaneous	100	59
OVERALL SCORE		
265 points out of 500		

Rousse
★★★

This high-density rivership is adequate for a basic no-frills experience.

Manager/operator	Various tour operators
Entered service	1984
Registry	Bulgaria
Identification number	ENI 47000014
Length (m/yds)	113.5
Number of decks (excluding sun deck)	2
Cabins (total)	98
Balcony cabins	No
Lift (elevator)	Yes
Rivers sailed	Danube

This older vessel is rather cramped when full, but it does have a sauna and massage room. The cabins are extremely compact; most have two slim beds (one of which folds away for daytime); some have a third berth. The bathroom is basic, but does include a shower. The food is passable, not gourmet.

Berlitz's Ratings

	Possible	Achieved
Hardware	100	58
Accommodation	100	58
Cuisine	100	58
Service	100	59
Miscellaneous	100	60

OVERALL SCORE
293 points out of 500

Rousse Prestige
★★★+

A consistent, good-value river cruise aboard a modern rivership.

Manager/operator	Phoenix Cruises
Entered service	2004
Registry	Bulgaria
Identification number	ENI 08923002
Length (m/yds)	110.0
Number of decks (excluding sun deck)	3
Cabins (total)	79
Balcony cabins	No
Lift (elevator)	No
Rivers sailed	Danube

Rousse Prestige has rather bland interior decor. The compact cabins (except those on the lowest deck) have opening windows, but little in the way of storage space. The bathrooms are small, but manageable. The restaurant has comfortable seating, but no armrests on the chairs. The food is so-so, and there's little variety. Amenities include a small wellness area and laundry service.

Berlitz's Ratings

	Possible	Achieved
Hardware	100	73
Accommodation	100	69
Cuisine	100	60
Service	100	68
Miscellaneous	100	68

OVERALL SCORE
338 points out of 500

Royal Crown
★★★★

This grand hotel-style rivership evokes the past with flair.

Manager/operator............... Various tour operators
Entered service...1994
Registry ....Switzerland
Identification number ....ENI 07001647
Length (m/yds)..110.0

Number of decks (excluding sun deck) 2
Cabins (total) 47
Balcony cabins ....No
Lift (elevator) ....No
Rivers sailed ....Various European rivers

This vessel's lovely grand-hotel-style interior decor recreates the 1930s, with teak decks, wood-rich, elegant public rooms, chic marble finishes and luxurious soft furnishings. The cabins are a decent size and ornately decorated (six royal suites have king-size beds; others have either queen-sized beds or twin beds). There's also an appealing restaurant, despite the small galley, and pleasant meals.

Berlitz's Ratings		
	Possible	Achieved
Hardware	100	75
Accommodation	100	71
Cuisine	100	70
Service	100	74
Miscellaneous	100	73
OVERALL SCORE		
363 points out of 500		

Rugen
★★★

This small, older rivership provides just the basics for no-frills cruising.

Manager/operator................Vantage River Cruises
Entered service...1979
Registry ....Germany
Identification number ....ENI 04031590
Length (m/yds)..82.5

Number of decks (excluding sun deck) 2
Cabins (total) 44
Balcony cabins ....No
Lift (elevator) ....No
Rivers sailed ....Elbe

If you are not too fussy about food and wine and would be happy with a comfortable but unpretentious cabin and bathroom with a small amount of storage space, then this rivership may be right for you. Choose it mainly for the itinerary and destinations.

Berlitz's Ratings		
	Possible	Achieved
Hardware	100	48
Accommodation	100	48
Cuisine	100	60
Service	100	57
Miscellaneous	100	51
OVERALL SCORE		
264 points out of 500		

Sainte Odile
★★★

This comfortable rivership has French flair but is really dated.

Manager/operator.................................CroisiEurope
Entered service...1992
Registry ....France
Identification number .... ENI 0182262N
Length (m/yds)..90.0

Number of decks (excluding sun deck) 2
Cabins (total) 63
Balcony cabins ....No
Lift (elevator) ....No
Rivers sailed .... Rhein, Mosel

Sainte Odile has dated interior decor, small (no-balcony) cabins with slim beds (most can't be moved together) and tiny bathrooms with poor storage space for toiletries. But if you like an unpretentious, casual ambience, fairly decent food and wine (limited choice), it may be suitable for you. Travel for the itinerary. Note that shore excursions cost extra.

Berlitz's Ratings

	Possible	Achieved
Hardware	100	58
Accommodation	100	56
Cuisine	100	58
Service	100	56
Miscellaneous	100	60

OVERALL SCORE
288 points out of 500

Salvinia
★★

This vintage, high-density rivership is for a basic, no-frills cruise.

Manager/operator............................. Favorit Reisen
Entered service...1939
Registry ....Netherlands
Identification number ....ENI 02315334
Length (m/yds)..91.5

Number of decks (excluding sun deck) 2
Cabins (total) 65
Balcony cabins ....No
Lift (elevator) .... Yes
Rivers sailed ....Rhein

Salvinia is an old lady but she still has plenty of character and decor to match. The cabins have poor soundproofing and are very small (almost all have one fixed and one fold-down bed), as are the bathrooms, which have curtained-off showers and limited storage. The cuisine in the cramped restaurant is limited but passable.

Berlitz's Ratings

	Possible	Achieved
Hardware	100	35
Accommodation	100	36
Cuisine	100	40
Service	100	40
Miscellaneous	100	41

OVERALL SCORE
192 points out of 500

Sans Souci
★★★

Specially designed for Elbe cruises, this rivership is a good choice.

Manager/operator............... Various tour operators
Entered service...................................2000
Registry ....Germany
Identification number ....ENI 02324117
Length (m/yds)....................................82.0

Number of decks (excluding sun deck) 2
Cabins (total) 41
Balcony cabins .... Yes (French)
Lift (elevator) .... Yes
Rivers sailed ....Elbe-Saal, Havel, Oder

Sans Souci is a smart, compact vessel, with well-designed cabins. Ruby Deck cabins have French balconies; others have windows. The fold-away beds are short, and the bathrooms are really small. There's a charming restaurant serving food of limited variety, although generally good (the buffet breakfasts are repetitious). Dinners come with (young) regional wines.

Berlitz's Ratings

	Possible	Achieved
Hardware	100	60
Accommodation	100	60
Cuisine	100	60
Service	100	57
Miscellaneous	100	61

OVERALL SCORE
298 points out of 500

Savor
Not Yet Rated

This new rivership will have state-of-the-art features, plus spacious cabins.

Manager/operator.................................. Nicko Tours
Entered service...................................2014
Registry ....Switzerland
Identification number ....n/a
Length (m/yds)....................................135.0

Number of decks (excluding sun deck) 3
Cabins (total) 67
Balcony cabins .... Yes (French)
Lift (elevator) .... Yes
Rivers sailed ....Danube

Savor will be contemporary with restrained, elegant decor. The spacious cabins and 22 double-size suites (the latter offering room service for breakfast) will have French balconies (cabins on the lowest deck have windows), excellent bed linen and Molton Brown toiletries. Beverages will be unlimited. The main restaurant is forward; an alternative venue for light food is located aft.

Berlitz's Ratings

	Possible	Achieved
Hardware	100	NYR
Accommodation	100	NYR
Cuisine	100	NYR
Service	100	NYR
Miscellaneous	100	NYR

OVERALL SCORE
NYR points out of 500

Saxonia
★★★+

This small rivership has elegant decor and provides a decent cruise.

Manager/operator .... Phoenix Cruises
Entered service 2001
Registry .... Switzerland
Identification number .... ENI 07001736
Length (m/yds) 82.0

Number of decks (excluding sun deck) 2
Cabins (total) 45
Balcony cabins .... No
Lift (elevator) .... No
Rivers sailed .... Various European rivers

This pleasant rivership will provide you with a good middle-of-the road cruise experience. Although the cabins are quite small, as are the bathrooms, they are comfortable. The food variety and choice are both rather limited, and wines are of the basic variety, but it's fine if the destinations are your priority.

Berlitz's Ratings		
	Possible	Achieved
Hardware	100	66
Accommodation	100	61
Cuisine	100	63
Service	100	64
Miscellaneous	100	63
OVERALL SCORE		
317 points out of 500		

Scenic Crystal
★★★★

This rivership is just the ticket for a really fine cruise experience.

Manager/operator .... Saga Travel
Entered service 2012
Registry .... Malta
Identification number .... ENI 02334159
Length (m/yds) 135.0

Number of decks (excluding sun deck) 3
Cabins (total) 85
Balcony cabins .... Yes (French)
Lift (elevator) .... Yes
Rivers sailed .... Danube, Rhein

Scenic Crystal is a lovely vessel with delightful decor. Most cabins have French balconies and are spacious, with high-quality linens. The well-designed bathrooms feature L'Occitane toiletries. The restaurant is quite cramped, but offers multiple table configurations. The cuisine is very good. Amenities include good, although small, wellness facilities. An 'all-inclusive' product, but 'premium' drinks cost extra.

Berlitz's Ratings		
	Possible	Achieved
Hardware	100	80
Accommodation	100	78
Cuisine	100	70
Service	100	70
Miscellaneous	100	77
OVERALL SCORE		
375 points out of 500		

Scenic Diamond
★★★★

This rivership is a good choice for a well-programmed cruise experience.

Manager/operator............................ 1AVista Reisen
Entered service...2009
Registry ....Malta
Identification number ....ENI 07001905
Length (m/yds)..135.0

Number of decks (excluding sun deck) 3
Cabins (total) 85
Balcony cabins ....Yes (French)
Lift (elevator) .... Yes
Rivers sailed ....Various European rivers

Scenic Diamond is a good vessel with elegant decor and a small but decent wellness area. Most cabins have French balconies, are spacious and feature high-quality linens. The well-designed bathrooms feature L'Occitane products. The restaurant is quite cramped, but offers multiple table configurations. The cuisine is good. An 'all-inclusive' product, but 'premium' drinks cost extra.

Berlitz's Ratings		
	Possible	Achieved
Hardware	100	77
Accommodation	100	75
Cuisine	100	69
Service	100	67
Miscellaneous	100	73
OVERALL SCORE		
361 points out of 500		

Scenic Emerald
★★★★

This rivership is a fine choice for a well-organised cruise experience.

Manager/operator............... Various tour operators
Entered service...2008
Registry ....Malta
Identification number ....ENI 07001869
Length (m/yds)..135.0

Number of decks (excluding sun deck) 3
Cabins (total) 85
Balcony cabins ....Yes (French)
Lift (elevator) .... Yes
Rivers sailed ....French rivers

Scenic Emerald is a good vessel with elegant decor and a small but decent wellness area. Most cabins have French balconies, are spacious and feature high-quality linens. The well-designed bathrooms feature L'Occitane products. The restaurant is cramped, but offers multiple table configurations. The cuisine is good but lacks finesse. 'All inclusive', but 'premium' drinks cost extra.

Berlitz's Ratings		
	Possible	Achieved
Hardware	100	76
Accommodation	100	75
Cuisine	100	69
Service	100	67
Miscellaneous	100	73
OVERALL SCORE		
360 points out of 500		

Scenic Gem
Not Yet Rated

This will be a good choice for an efficiently run cruise.

Manager/operator................ Various tour operators
Entered service.................................2014
Registry ....Malta
Identification number ....n/a
Length (m/yds)..................................110.0

Number of decks (excluding sun deck) 3
Cabins (total) 63
Balcony cabins .... Yes (French)
Lift (elevator) .... Yes
Rivers sailed ....French rivers

This new rivership has all the latest rivership features imaginable, including a tiled, heated indoor pool and movie screen. The spacious cabins with French balconies have convertible beds, large bathrooms and a decent amount of storage space. The food is likely to be good, but nothing special. It's an 'all-inclusive' product, but 'premium' drinks will cost extra.

Berlitz's Ratings		
	Possible	Achieved
Hardware	100	NYR
Accommodation	100	NYR
Cuisine	100	NYR
Service	100	NYR
Miscellaneous	100	NYR
OVERALL SCORE		
NYR points out of 500		

Scenic Jade
Not Yet Rated

This rivership would be a good choice for a tasteful cruise experience.

Manager/operator.............. Transocean Flussreisen
Entered service.................................2014
Registry ....Malta
Identification number ....n/a
Length (m/yds)..................................135.0

Number of decks (excluding sun deck) 3
Cabins (total) 63
Balcony cabins .... Yes (French)
Lift (elevator) .... Yes
Rivers sailed ....Various European rivers

Scenic Jade will be a fine vessel with tasteful decor and limited but good wellness facilities. Most cabins will have French balconies, be spacious and feature high-quality linens. The well-designed bathrooms are due to feature L'Occitane products. The restaurant is likely to be cramped, but offer multiple table configurations and cuisine that is good but lacks flair. 'All inclusive', but 'premium' drinks will cost extra.

Berlitz's Ratings		
	Possible	Achieved
Hardware	100	NYR
Accommodation	100	NYR
Cuisine	100	NYR
Service	100	NYR
Miscellaneous	100	NYR
OVERALL SCORE		
NYR points out of 500		

Scenic Jewel
★★★★

This rivership is just the ticket for a really fine cruise experience.

Manager/operator .... Tauck Tours
Entered service 2013
Registry .... Malta
Identification number .... ENI 07001906
Length (m/yds) 135.0

Number of decks (excluding sun deck) 3
Cabins (total) 63
Balcony cabins .... Yes (French)
Lift (elevator) .... Yes
Rivers sailed .... Various European rivers

Scenic Jewel is a fine vessel with delightful decor and limited but good wellness facilities. Most cabins have French balconies, are spacious and feature high-quality linens. The well-designed bathrooms feature L'Occitane products. The restaurant is cramped, but offers multiple table configurations. The cuisine is good but not outstanding. 'All inclusive', but 'premium' drinks cost extra.

Berlitz's Ratings		
	Possible	Achieved
Hardware	100	80
Accommodation	100	78
Cuisine	100	70
Service	100	73
Miscellaneous	100	78
OVERALL SCORE		
379 points out of 500		

Scenic Pearl
★★★★

A stylish rivership offering a well-programmed cruise.

Manager/operator .... Phoenix Cruises
Entered service 2011
Registry .... Malta
Identification number .... ENI 65000002
Length (m/yds) 135.0

Number of decks (excluding sun deck) 2
Cabins (total) 85
Balcony cabins .... Yes (French)
Lift (elevator) .... Yes
Rivers sailed .... Various European rivers

Scenic Pearl is an elegantly decorated vessel. Most cabins have 'Sun Lounge' French balconies, are spacious and feature high-quality linens. The well-designed bathrooms feature L'Occitane products. The restaurant is cramped, but offers multiple table configurations. The cuisine is very good. Facilities include a small, decent wellness area. It's 'all inclusive', but 'premium' drinks cost extra.

Berlitz's Ratings		
	Possible	Achieved
Hardware	100	78
Accommodation	100	75
Cuisine	100	70
Service	100	68
Miscellaneous	100	73
OVERALL SCORE		
364 points out of 500		

Scenic Ruby
★★★★

Choose this stylish rivership for a good-quality river cruise experience.

Manager/operator ....Scenic Tours
Entered service 2009
Registry ....Malta
Identification number ....ENI 07001907
Length (m/yds)...135.0

Number of decks (excluding sun deck) 2
Cabins (total) 84
Balcony cabins ....Yes (French)
Lift (elevator) ....Yes
Rivers sailed ....Various European rivers

Scenic Ruby is a tastefully decorated, contemporary vessel. Most cabins have 'Sun Lounge' French balconies and are very spacious with ample storage space. The well-designed bathrooms feature L'Occitane products. The restaurant is quite cramped, but offers multiple table configurations. The cuisine is very good but not outstanding. It's 'all inclusive', but 'premium' drinks cost extra.

Berlitz's Ratings		
	Possible	Achieved
Hardware	100	77
Accommodation	100	75
Cuisine	100	70
Service	100	67
Miscellaneous	100	68
OVERALL SCORE		
357 points out of 500		

Scenic Sapphire
★★★★

This sound rivership offers a well-programmed cruise experience.

Manager/operator ....Scenic Tours
Entered service 2008
Registry ....Malta
Identification number ....ENI 07001865
Length (m/yds)...135.0

Number of decks (excluding sun deck) 3
Cabins (total) 84
Balcony cabins ....Yes (French)
Lift (elevator) ....Yes
Rivers sailed ....Various European rivers

Scenic Sapphire is an elegantly decorated vessel. Most cabins have 'Sun Lounge' French balconies, are spacious and feature high-quality linens. The well-designed bathrooms feature L'Occitane products. The restaurant is cramped, but offers multiple table configurations. The cuisine is very good. Facilities include a small, decent wellness area. It's 'all inclusive', but 'premium' drinks cost extra.

Berlitz's Ratings		
	Possible	Achieved
Hardware	100	77
Accommodation	100	75
Cuisine	100	69
Service	100	72
Miscellaneous	100	68
OVERALL SCORE		
361 points out of 500		

Seine Princess
★★★

This French rivership delivers a standard, good-value cruise experience.

Manager/operator ....CroisiEurope
Entered service 2002
Registry ....France
Identification number ....ENI 01823132
Length (m/yds)...110.0

Number of decks (excluding sun deck) 2
Cabins (total) 78
Balcony cabins ....No
Lift (elevator) ....No
Rivers sailed ....French rivers

This small rivership offers a good middle-of-the road cruise experience and pleasant itineraries, although the cabins and bathrooms (curtained-off showers only) are quite small, and storage space is tight. The unpretentious food lacks creativity (most likely due to a small galley), and the wine glasses are not large.

Berlitz's Ratings		
	Possible	Achieved
Hardware	100	60
Accommodation	100	57
Cuisine	100	60
Service	100	57
Miscellaneous	100	58
OVERALL SCORE		
292 points out of 500		

Serena
★★

A vintage rivership suited to bicycle tourists and tight budgets.

Manager/operator .... Various tour operators
Entered service 1935
Registry ....Netherlands
Identification number ....ENI 02322470
Length (m/yds)...89.6

Number of decks (excluding sun deck) 2
Cabins (total) 53
Balcony cabins ....No
Lift (elevator) ....No
Rivers sailed ....Various European rivers

Serena will provide you and your bicycle with cheap transportation, but it's cramped on board. The cabins (with two fixed, slim, short beds), bathrooms and windows are all tiny. The food is really basic, too, because the galley is tiny and outdated. Go for the itinerary or the price point rather than the facilities.

Berlitz's Ratings		
	Possible	Achieved
Hardware	100	36
Accommodation	100	37
Cuisine	100	40
Service	100	44
Miscellaneous	100	41
OVERALL SCORE		
198 points out of 500		

Serenade 1
★★★+

Although not extraordinary, this offers a consistent, comfortable river cruise.

Manager/operator................................Travelsphere
Entered service..2005
Registry ....Netherlands
Identification number ....ENI 02326953
Length (m/yds)..110.0

Number of decks (excluding sun deck) 2
Cabins (total) 68
Balcony cabins .... Yes (French)
Lift (elevator) .... Yes
Rivers sailed .... Various European rivers

Serenade I is a very comfortable rivership, and, while not luxurious, its decor is quite contemporary. The cabins are quite large and include twin beds, ample storage space, mini-fridges and tea- and coffee-making facilities; the bathrooms feature small bathtubs and separate glazed shower enclosures. The cuisine is just so-so.

Berlitz's Ratings		
	Possible	Achieved
Hardware	100	72
Accommodation	100	68
Cuisine	100	63
Service	100	67
Miscellaneous	100	68
OVERALL SCORE		
338 points out of 500		

Serenade 2
★★★★

This rivership is a decent choice for a good-value cruise.

Manager/operator............... Various tour operators
Entered service..2007
Registry ....Netherlands
Identification number ....ENI 02328761
Length (m/yds)..110.0

Number of decks (excluding sun deck) 2
Cabins (total) 70
Balcony cabins .... Yes (French)
Lift (elevator) .... Yes
Rivers sailed .... Danube, Rhein

This vessel's interior decor includes lots of wood and glass. While the cabins (many with French balconies) are a little plain, they feature Tempur memory-foam mattresses and generous bathrooms. The restaurant seating is rather cramped, but the cuisine is reasonably good, although the variety is limited.

Berlitz's Ratings		
	Possible	Achieved
Hardware	100	74
Accommodation	100	71
Cuisine	100	66
Service	100	70
Miscellaneous	100	72
OVERALL SCORE		
353 points out of 500		

Serenity
★★★+

A high-density modern rivership notable for its distinctive bold exterior.

Manager/operator............... Various tour operators
Entered service..................................2006
Registry ....Netherlands
Identification number ....ENI 07001831
Length (m/yds)..................................110.0

Number of decks (excluding sun deck) 2
Cabins (total) 95
Balcony cabins .... Yes (French)
Lift (elevator) .... Yes
Rivers sailed ....Danube, Rhein

Serenity has a wine-coloured exterior and restful interior decoration. 'Panorama Deck' cabins have French balconies; all others have windows (some open, some don't). The cabins are small, with twin beds (these cannot be pushed together) that fold down to become daytime seats. The bathrooms are cramped. The cuisine is generally good, but needs more variety.

Berlitz's Ratings		
	Possible	Achieved
Hardware	100	73
Accommodation	100	70
Cuisine	100	66
Service	100	67
Miscellaneous	100	70
OVERALL SCORE		
346 points out of 500		

Sir Winston
★★+

A very small, vintage, no-frills rivership specialising in bicycle tours.

Manager/operator.... Various bicycle tour operators
Entered service..................................1946
Registry ....Netherlands
Identification number ....ENI 02311506
Length (m/yds)..................................67.2

Number of decks (excluding sun deck) 2
Cabins (total) 35
Balcony cabins ....No
Lift (elevator) ....No
Rivers sailed ....Various European rivers

This vintage rivership is for anyone seeking basic water-bound transportation with their bicycles. The cabins are tiny (beds are in an 'L'-shape), as are the bathrooms and windows (which do open). The galley is very small and can only deliver the most basic food. One for the convenience, the bike-friendly approach and the budget price.

Berlitz's Ratings		
	Possible	Achieved
Hardware	100	41
Accommodation	100	40
Cuisine	100	42
Service	100	46
Miscellaneous	100	47
OVERALL SCORE		
216 points out of 500		

Sofia
★★★

This high-density older vessel will provide a decent-value cruise.

Manager/operator................ Various tour operators
Entered service..1983
Registry ....Bulgaria
Identification number ....ENI 47000013
Length (m/yds)..113.5

Number of decks (excluding sun deck) 3
Cabins (total) 101
Balcony cabins ....No
Lift (elevator) ....No
Rivers sailed ....Danube

Sofia packs its travellers into especially small cabins with only the most basic facilities. In the bathrooms, you'll dance with the shower curtain! It does, however, have a small wellness area with a sauna. The mid-ship restaurant is attractive, but the seating is very cramped. The food is reasonably good, but lacks creativity and variety.

Berlitz's Ratings		
	Possible	Achieved
Hardware	100	57
Accommodation	100	53
Cuisine	100	54
Service	100	56
Miscellaneous	100	57
OVERALL SCORE		
277 points out of 500		

Sound of Music
★★★+

One for the itinerary and price rather than the food.

Manager/operator................ Various tour operators
Entered service..2006
Registry ....Netherlands
Identification number ....ENI 07001861
Length (m/yds)..110.0

Number of decks (excluding sun deck) 3
Cabins (total) 64
Balcony cabins .... Yes (French)
Lift (elevator) ....No
Rivers sailed .... Various European rivers

The *Sound of Music* is a fairly stylish modern rivership, which includes a small wellness area. Cabins range from very tight to moderately large; some have double beds (some, although not all, of these can also be split into two). The restaurant is attractive but cramped and serves decent cuisine, though lacking creativity, quality and variety.

Berlitz's Ratings		
	Possible	Achieved
Hardware	100	72
Accommodation	100	67
Cuisine	100	66
Service	100	67
Miscellaneous	100	71
OVERALL SCORE		
343 points out of 500		

Spirit of Chartwell
★★★★

Choose this regal rivership for a fine Douro cruise experience.

Manager/operator............... Various tour operators
Entered service................................1997
Registry ....Portugal
Identification number ....ENI 07001842
Length (m/yds)......................................53.8

Number of decks (excluding sun deck) 2
Cabins (total) 15
Balcony cabins ....No
Lift (elevator) ....No
Rivers sailed .... Douro

Famed for being chartered in 2012 as the royal barge for Queen Elizabeth II's Diamond Jubilee celebrations, *Spirit of Chartwell* is all about British country-house style. The wood-rich cabins have two fixed beds and bedside reading lamps from the *SS France* and *Olympia*. The restaurant has mostly banquette-style seating. The food is unfussy Portuguese fare.

Berlitz's Ratings		
	Possible	Achieved
Hardware	100	81
Accommodation	100	72
Cuisine	100	66
Service	100	68
Miscellaneous	100	71
OVERALL SCORE		
358 points out of 500		

S.S. Antoinette
★★★★

This top-range rivership has some state-of-the-art features and good food.

Manager/operator..... Uniworld Grand River Cruises
Entered service...2011
Registry ....Netherlands
Identification number ....ENI 07001935
Length (m/yds)......................................135.0

Number of decks (excluding sun deck) 3
Cabins (total) 82
Balcony cabins .... Yes (French and full)
Lift (elevator) .... Yes
Rivers sailed ....Rhein

This rivership's ornate decor pays homage to its elegant namesake (Marie Antoinette). Each finely decorated, very spacious cabin has a Nespresso machine, ample storage, full or French balcony, a bathroom with large shower enclosure, heated towel rails and L'Occitane products. There's also a heated indoor pool-cum-cinema, good food and service, and a neat Leopard Bar.

Berlitz's Ratings		
	Possible	Achieved
Hardware	100	80
Accommodation	100	81
Cuisine	100	68
Service	100	71
Miscellaneous	100	76
OVERALL SCORE		
376 points out of 500		

S.S. Catherine
Not Yet Rated

Choose this stylish rivership for a high-quality river cruise experience.

Manager/operator..... Uniworld Grand River Cruises
Entered service..2014
Registry ....Switzerland
Identification number ....n/a
Length (m/yds)..135.0

Number of decks (excluding sun deck) 3
Cabins (total) 82
Balcony cabins .... Yes (French and full)
Lift (elevator) .... Yes
Rivers sailed ....French rivers

Uniworld's riverships are hallmarked by classic, elegant style. The very spacious, finely decorated cabins have full balconies (sometimes also French balconies) and large bathrooms with L'Occitane toiletries. Soundproofing is good. This vessel will feature a tiled, heated indoor pool, whimsical artworks and antiques, an abundance of mirrors, and an ample choice of well-crafted meals.

Berlitz's Ratings		
	Possible	Achieved
Hardware	100	NYR
Accommodation	100	NYR
Cuisine	100	NYR
Service	100	NYR
Miscellaneous	100	NYR
OVERALL SCORE		
NYR points out of 500		

Swiss Corona
★★★+

This very comfortable vessel offers a good-quality cruise experience.

Manager/operator.......................Hansa + SE Tours
Entered service..2004
Registry ....Switzerland
Identification number ....ENI 07001807
Length (m/yds)..110.0

Number of decks (excluding sun deck) 3
Cabins (total) 75
Balcony cabins .... Yes (French)
Lift (elevator) .... Yes
Rivers sailed ....French rivers

Swiss Corona is a very attractive vessel, with a mix of classic and modern decor. There are six suites with beds that face the river (nice views when you wake up). Some cabins have French balconies, but many only have windows. All are nicely appointed. The cuisine is good and quite varied, but not outstanding.

Berlitz's Ratings		
	Possible	Achieved
Hardware	100	72
Accommodation	100	67
Cuisine	100	63
Service	100	66
Miscellaneous	100	71
OVERALL SCORE		
339 points out of 500		

Swiss Crown
★★★+

This modern rivership will provide you with a well-rounded cruise.

Manager/operator............... Various tour operators
Entered service...................................2000
Registry .... Switzerland
Identification number ....ENI 07001725
Length (m/yds)..................................110.0

Number of decks (excluding sun deck) 3
Cabins (total) 75
Balcony cabins .... Yes (French)
Lift (elevator) .... Yes
Rivers sailed ....Danube, Rhein

Nicely appointed, *Swiss Crown* is a very comfortable rivership with unfussy interior decor. Cabins are quite plain but comfortable; some have twin beds that can be converted to doubles, while others have one or two slim beds that convert to sofas by day. The restaurant is attractive, while the cuisine is adequate but underwhelming.

Berlitz's Ratings

	Possible	Achieved
Hardware	100	68
Accommodation	100	67
Cuisine	100	66
Service	100	68
Miscellaneous	100	70

OVERALL SCORE
339 points out of 500

Swiss Crystal
★★★+

This rivership is a good choice for a well-rounded cruise.

Manager/operator.....................Nicko Tours (Japan)
Entered service...................................1995
Registry .... Switzerland
Identification number ....ENI 07001643
Length (m/yds)..................................101.3

Number of decks (excluding sun deck) 2
Cabins (total) 63
Balcony cabins ....No
Lift (elevator) ....No
Rivers sailed ....Main, Mosel, Rhein

This smaller-than-average rivership has fuss-free yet elegant decoration. The cabins are on the bland side, and some have televisions in an awkward viewing position. All have windows, mini-fridges and twin beds, one of which converts to a sofa. Bathrooms are compact. The food is decent but nothing special. An open-deck hot tub is a bonus.

Berlitz's Ratings

	Possible	Achieved
Hardware	100	63
Accommodation	100	60
Cuisine	100	66
Service	100	66
Miscellaneous	100	66

OVERALL SCORE
321 points out of 500

Swiss Diamond
★★★+

A simply designed rivership offering a well-rounded river cruise.

Manager/operator............... Various tour operators
Entered service.. 1996
Registry .... Switzerland
Identification number .... ENI 07001646
Length (m/yds).. 101.3

Number of decks (excluding sun deck) 2
Cabins (total) 61
Balcony cabins ....No
Lift (elevator) ....No
Rivers sailed .... Main, Mosel, Rhein

This smaller-than-average rivership has fuss-free yet elegant decoration. The cabins are plain but comfortable, and some have televisions in an awkward viewing position. All have windows, mini-fridges and twin beds, one of which converts to a sofa. Bathrooms are compact. The food is decent but nothing special. An open-deck hot tub is a bonus.

Berlitz's Ratings		
	Possible	Achieved
Hardware	100	64
Accommodation	100	61
Cuisine	100	66
Service	100	68
Miscellaneous	100	67
OVERALL SCORE		
326 points out of 500		

Swiss Emerald
★★★★

A well-run rivership offering very comfortable cruising and great cuisine.

Manager/operator................................. Tauck Tours
Entered service.. 2006
Registry .... Switzerland
Identification number .... ENI 07001825
Length (m/yds).. 110.0

Number of decks (excluding sun deck) 3
Cabins (total) 62
Balcony cabins .... Yes (French)
Lift (elevator) .... Yes
Rivers sailed .... French rivers

This well-designed contemporary rivership has a very pleasant lounge and extremely elegant interior decor. It has very comfortable, extra-large cabins, some with French balconies, good beds (some with direct river views) and mini-fridges. The bathrooms have large shower enclosures. The unpretentious, varied cuisine is well above rivership average, packing in plenty of taste.

Berlitz's Ratings		
	Possible	Achieved
Hardware	100	72
Accommodation	100	67
Cuisine	100	68
Service	100	71
Miscellaneous	100	76
OVERALL SCORE		
354 points out of 500		

Swiss Gloria
★★★+

A very comfortable vessel offering a well-rounded cruise.

Manager/operator.......................... Phoenix Cruises
Entered service................................2005
Registry ....Switzerland
Identification number ....ENI 07001814
Length (m/yds)................................110.0

Number of decks (excluding sun deck) 3
Cabins (total) 76
Balcony cabins .... Yes (French)
Lift (elevator) .... Yes
Rivers sailed .... Danube, Main, Rhein

Swiss Gloria is a very nicely appointed vessel featuring a wellness area with a sauna and hot tub. The cabins are quite spacious and practical, and many have French balconies. The restaurant is very comfortable, with rich wood decoration. The cuisine is pretty good, and there's a decent choice, particularly for the buffet breakfasts.

Berlitz's Ratings

	Possible	Achieved
Hardware	100	71
Accommodation	100	67
Cuisine	100	68
Service	100	66
Miscellaneous	100	72

OVERALL SCORE
344 points out of 500

Swiss Jewel
★★★★

Choose this stylish rivership for an excellent, well-organised river cruise.

Manager/operator................................ Tauck Tours
Entered service................................2009
Registry ....Switzerland
Identification number ....ENI 07001906
Length (m/yds)................................110.0

Number of decks (excluding sun deck) 3
Cabins (total) 76
Balcony cabins .... Yes (French)
Lift (elevator) .... Yes
Rivers sailed .... Danube, Main, Rhein

This vessel features lovely decoration reminiscent of Victorian-era grand hotels. The cabins feel spacious – some have French balconies, some have floor-to-ceiling windows – and all have good soundproofing and decent bathrooms, the largest with mini-bathtubs. The cuisine is good, offering ample choice and quality ingredients. Facilities include a hot tub on the sun deck and bicycles.

Berlitz's Ratings

	Possible	Achieved
Hardware	100	74
Accommodation	100	68
Cuisine	100	67
Service	100	71
Miscellaneous	100	76

OVERALL SCORE
356 points out of 500

Swiss Pearl
★★★+

An older rivership that still delivers a good-value cruise experience.

Manager/operator............... Various tour operators
Entered service..................................1993
Registry ....Switzerland
Identification number ....ENI 08001632
Length (m/yds)...................................110.0

Number of decks (excluding sun deck) 2
Cabins (total) 62
Balcony cabins ....No
Lift (elevator) ....No
Rivers sailed ....French rivers

Despite being rather dated, *Swiss Pearl* has comfortable interiors and features a fitness room with hot tub. The cabins are a reasonable size – all have mini-fridges, safes, good wardrobe space and windows. The largest cabins have generous-sized bathrooms with bathtubs. The galley is small, so meal choice and variety is limited.

Berlitz's Ratings		
	Possible	Achieved
Hardware	100	60
Accommodation	100	58
Cuisine	100	64
Service	100	65
Miscellaneous	100	64
OVERALL SCORE		
311 points out of 500		

Swiss Ruby
★★★+

Choose this small rivership for a decent-quality river cruise experience.

Manager/operator............... Various tour operators
Entered service..................................2002
Registry ....Switzerland
Identification number ....ENI 07001742
Length (m/yds)...................................85.0

Number of decks (excluding sun deck) 2
Cabins (total) 44
Balcony cabins ....Yes (French)
Lift (elevator) ....No
Rivers sailed ....French rivers

Specially designed for shallow river cruising, *Swiss Ruby* has decent facilities, with pleasant, restful decoration. The cabins are very small and cramped with twin or double beds (those on the lower deck have couple-unfriendly fixed twins). The restaurant is pleasant, but meal choice is limited due to the small galley. Go mainly for the itinerary.

Berlitz's Ratings		
	Possible	Achieved
Hardware	100	71
Accommodation	100	68
Cuisine	100	65
Service	100	66
Miscellaneous	100	70
OVERALL SCORE		
340 points out of 500		

Swiss Sapphire
★★★★

Another winner from Tauck, offering an upmarket, excellent all-round cruise.

Manager/operator.................................. Tauck Tours
Entered service...2008
Registry .... Switzerland
Identification number ....ENI 07001858
Length (m/yds)..110.0

Number of decks (excluding sun deck) 3
Cabins (total) 59
Balcony cabins .... Yes (French)
Lift (elevator) .... Yes
Rivers sailed .... Seine

This well-designed contemporary rivership has a pleasant lounge and elegant interior. It has very spacious cabins, with mini-fridges; most have French balconies and floor-to-ceiling windows. Fourteen of the cabins can sleep three people. The bathrooms are well outfitted, with large shower enclosures and L'Occitane toiletries. The unpretentious cuisine is tasty, and there's ample choice.

Berlitz's Ratings		
	Possible	Achieved
Hardware	100	74
Accommodation	100	68
Cuisine	100	67
Service	100	71
Miscellaneous	100	76
OVERALL SCORE		
356 points out of 500		

Swiss Tiara
★★★+

This modern vessel is a good choice for a decent-quality cruise.

Manager/operator........................ Plantours Cruises
Entered service...2006
Registry .... Switzerland
Identification number ....ENI 07001832
Length (m/yds)..110.0

Number of decks (excluding sun deck) 3
Cabins (total) 76
Balcony cabins .... Yes (French)
Lift (elevator) .... Yes
Rivers sailed .... Danube, Rhein

This well-built, very comfortable rivership has unfussy interior decoration. The cabins (many with French balconies) are, however, quite small, although they do include mini-fridges, extremely comfortable beds and fine linens. The bathrooms have glazed shower enclosures and are very practical. The food is so-so with little variety, and the wine glasses are small.

Berlitz's Ratings		
	Possible	Achieved
Hardware	100	71
Accommodation	100	68
Cuisine	100	66
Service	100	68
Miscellaneous	100	70
OVERALL SCORE		
343 points out of 500		

Switzerland II
★★★+

An older vessel with restful decor offering a decent cruise.

Manager/operator .... Various tour operators
Entered service 1991
Registry .... Netherlands
Identification number .... ENI 02329015
Length (m/yds) 100.0

Number of decks (excluding sun deck) 2
Cabins (total) 53
Balcony cabins .... No
Lift (elevator) .... No
Rivers sailed .... Danube, Rhein

Switzerland II has tasteful interior decor, accented with rich woods and brass. The cabins are small but adequate, with windows rather than balconies; many have beds in an 'L'-shape. The dimly lit restaurant has reasonable cuisine that lacks flair and creativity. Facilities include a small fitness area with sauna. Overall, it's a comfortable, older vessel.

Berlitz's Ratings

	Possible	Achieved
Hardware	100	61
Accommodation	100	60
Cuisine	100	65
Service	100	67
Miscellaneous	100	68

OVERALL SCORE
321 points out of 500

Symphonie
★★★

A French rivership for a straightforward but reliable cruise.

Manager/operator .... CroisiEurope
Entered service 1997
Registry .... France
Identification number .... ENI 01822862
Length (m/yds) 110.0

Number of decks (excluding sun deck) 2
Cabins (total) 77
Balcony cabins .... No
Lift (elevator) .... No
Rivers sailed .... Danube, Rhein

If you like unpretentious French food and wine and are happy with a comfortable but small cabin with no balcony, limited soundproofing, slim beds and a bathroom with very small shower enclosure and minimal storage space, then *Symphonie* may be suitable. Go mainly for its chic ambience and for the itinerary. Shore excursions cost extra.

Berlitz's Ratings

	Possible	Achieved
Hardware	100	58
Accommodation	100	56
Cuisine	100	58
Service	100	56
Miscellaneous	100	58

OVERALL SCORE
286 points out of 500

Theodor Fontane
★★★

This rivership offers a fairly basic, no-frills cruise.

Manager/operator............... Various tour operators
Entered service...1991
Registry ....Germany
Identification number ....ENI 05113670
Length (m/yds)...94.8

Number of decks (excluding sun deck) 2
Cabins (total) 55
Balcony cabins .... Yes (French)
Lift (elevator) ....No
Rivers sailed ....Elbe

Most people take a river cruise because of the itinerary and destinations. If this suits you, then this rivership, with its tiny cabins and bathrooms and virtually zero storage space may be acceptable. Just don't expect fine food, because the galley is tiny and unable to turn out gourmet dishes.

Berlitz's Ratings		
	Possible	Achieved
Hardware	100	58
Accommodation	100	48
Cuisine	100	46
Service	100	48
Miscellaneous	100	53
OVERALL SCORE		
253 points out of 500		

Theodor Körner
★★+

This vintage rivership is good for bicycle tour participants on a tight budget.

Manager/operator.... Various bicycle tour operators
Entered service...1965
Registry ....Germany
Identification number ....MMSI 203999376
Length (m/yds)...87.0

Number of decks (excluding sun deck) 2
Cabins (total) 65
Balcony cabins ....No
Lift (elevator) ....No
Rivers sailed ....Danube

Theodor Körner is a real vintage rivership, with Art Deco interiors. It has limited facilities and very noisy engines (take earplugs) at night. The cabins are utterly basic, and include twin beds, a shower, washbasin and toilet. The food includes some good, hearty fare for breakfast, but the other meals are pretty elementary.

Berlitz's Ratings		
	Possible	Achieved
Hardware	100	41
Accommodation	100	40
Cuisine	100	47
Service	100	48
Miscellaneous	100	50
OVERALL SCORE		
226 points out of 500		

Travelmarvel Diamond
★★★★

A stylish rivership with good facilities for a decent-standard cruise.

Manager/operator	Travel Marvel (APT)	
Entered service	2007	
Registry	Malta	
Identification number	ENI 09948014	
Length (m/yds)	135.0	

Number of decks (excluding sun deck) 3
Cabins (total) 81
Balcony cabins .... Yes (French)
Lift (elevator) .... No
Rivers sailed .... Danube, Rhein

This 'twin cruiser' offers quiet cabins, because the propulsion unit is separate from the accommodation. Many cabins have French balconies and are stylish but small, although storage space is good. Large glass windows afford great views in the lounge and restaurant. Cheaper than the riverships of the parent company APT, but with inferior food.

Berlitz's Ratings	Possible	Achieved
Hardware	100	75
Accommodation	100	75
Cuisine	100	66
Service	100	67
Miscellaneous	100	73

OVERALL SCORE
356 points out of 500

Travelmarvel Jewel
★★★★

This stylish, glass-fronted, contemporary vessel delivers a quality cruise.

Manager/operator	Travel Marvel (APT)	
Entered service	2007	
Registry	Malta	
Identification number	ENI 09948015	
Length (m/yds)	135.0	

Number of decks (excluding sun deck) 3
Cabins (total) 81
Balcony cabins .... Yes (French)
Lift (elevator) .... No
Rivers sailed .... Danube, Rhein

With the propulsion machinery separated from the passenger accommodation, all cabins (many with French balconies) are quiet, in addition to being stylish and small. Beds are fixed (one converts to a sofa), and bathrooms are compact. Large glass windows afford great views in the lounge and restaurant. The food is nothing special, but it serves the purpose.

Berlitz's Ratings	Possible	Achieved
Hardware	100	75
Accommodation	100	75
Cuisine	100	66
Service	100	66
Miscellaneous	100	73

OVERALL SCORE
355 points out of 500

Treasures
★★★★

This comfortable modern rivership offers a well-rounded river cruise.

Manager/operator .... Tauck Tours
Entered service 2011
Registry .... Switzerland
Identification number .... ENI 07001943
Length (m/yds) 110.0

Number of decks (excluding sun deck) 3
Cabins (total) 62
Balcony cabins .... Yes (French)
Lift (elevator) .... Yes
Rivers sailed .... Various European rivers

Nicely appointed, *Treasures* is a very comfortable rivership, with unfussy interior decor. The seven suites are delightful spaces. The cabins are well designed and practically laid out, as are the bathrooms, which have L'Occitane toiletries. The cuisine is pretty good, with good ingredients used and ample choice. Amenities include a hot tub on the sun deck and bicycles.

Berlitz's Ratings		
	Possible	Achieved
Hardware	100	77
Accommodation	100	78
Cuisine	100	72
Service	100	72
Miscellaneous	100	74
OVERALL SCORE		
373 points out of 500		

TUI Allegra
★★★+

A chic, stylish, glass-fronted rivership affording a good cruise.

Manager/operator .... TUI Travel
Entered service 2011
Registry .... Malta
Identification number .... ENI 04809190
Length (m/yds) 135.0

Number of decks (excluding sun deck) 3
Cabins (total) 89
Balcony cabins .... Yes (French)
Lift (elevator) .... No
Rivers sailed .... Various European rivers

This 'twin cruiser' means quiet cabins for everyone, because the propulsion unit is separate from the accommodation. Many cabins have French balconies and are quite stylish, but small, although storage space is good. Large glass windows offer great views in both the lounge and restaurant. The food is nothing special and could be more creative. TUI will operate this rivership until the end of summer 2014 only.

Berlitz's Ratings		
	Possible	Achieved
Hardware	100	76
Accommodation	100	68
Cuisine	100	63
Service	100	64
Miscellaneous	100	71
OVERALL SCORE		
342 points out of 500		

TUI Maxima
★★★+

This modern rivership provides a decent cruise experience.

Manager/operator......................................TUI Travel
Entered service...2003
Registry ....Malta
Identification number ....ENI 09948005
Length (m/yds)...126.0

Number of decks (excluding sun deck) 3
Cabins (total) 76
Balcony cabins .... Yes (French and full)
Lift (elevator) ....No
Rivers sailed ....Danube, Rhein

The nicely outfitted *TUI Maxima* has decent facilities, although the interior decor lacks character somewhat. The cabins (many featuring French balconies) have double beds or twin singles, mini-fridges and personal safes. The bathrooms are small, but practical. The restaurant is reasonably comfortable, but seating is cramped. The cuisine is quite underwhelming. TUI will operate this rivership until the end of summer 2014 only.

Berlitz's Ratings

	Possible	Achieved
Hardware	100	69
Accommodation	100	68
Cuisine	100	63
Service	100	64
Miscellaneous	100	70

OVERALL SCORE
334 points out of 500

TUI Melodia
★★★+

This trendy, contemporary, glass-fronted rivership delivers a good cruise.

Manager/operator......................................TUI Travel
Entered service...2011
Registry ....Germany
Identification number ....ENI 04809200
Length (m/yds)...135.0

Number of decks (excluding sun deck) 3
Cabins (total) 89
Balcony cabins .... Yes (French)
Lift (elevator) ....No
Rivers sailed ....Various European rivers

With the propulsion machinery separated from the passenger accommodation, all this twin cruiser's stylish cabins (many with French balconies) are quiet, although small. Beds are fixed (one converts to a sofa). Large glass windows allow great views from the lounge and restaurant. The food is so-so, with plenty of variety but no 'wow' factor. TUI will operate this rivership until the end of summer 2014 only.

Berlitz's Ratings

	Possible	Achieved
Hardware	100	75
Accommodation	100	68
Cuisine	100	63
Service	100	65
Miscellaneous	100	71

OVERALL SCORE
342 points out of 500

TUI Queen
★★★★

This stunning rivership provides the ultimate in creature comforts.

Manager/operator......................................TUI Travel
Entered service...2007
Registry ....Malta
Identification number ....ENI 04806540
Length (m/yds)...135.0

Number of decks (excluding sun deck) 3
Cabins (total) 52
Balcony cabins .... Yes (French and full)
Lift (elevator) .... Yes
Rivers sailed ....Various European rivers

This is a beautifully designed and built vessel that exudes elegance and style. The three suite categories (two have beds with river views) are really spacious, light and nicely outfitted, and have either full or French balconies. Bathrooms have heated floors and large showers; four have bathtubs. Good food and service. Overall, it's excellent! TUI will operate this rivership until the end of summer 2014 only.

Berlitz's Ratings		
	Possible	Achieved
Hardware	100	85
Accommodation	100	85
Cuisine	100	65
Service	100	67
Miscellaneous	100	78
OVERALL SCORE		
380 points out of 500		

TUI Sonata
★★★+

This rivership should provide you with a really fine cruise experience.

Manager/operator......................................TUI Travel
Entered service...2010
Registry ....Germany
Identification number ....ENI 65000001
Length (m/yds)...135.0

Number of decks (excluding sun deck) 3
Cabins (total) 89
Balcony cabins .... Yes (French)
Lift (elevator) ....No
Rivers sailed ....Various European rivers

With the propulsion machinery separated from the passenger accommodation, this twin cruiser's stylish cabins (many of which have French balconies) are quiet, although small with fixed beds (one converts to a sofa by day). Large glass windows allow great views from the lounge and restaurant. The food is adequate, although uninspiring and lacking in variety. TUI will operate this rivership until the end of summer 2014 only.

Berlitz's Ratings		
	Possible	Achieved
Hardware	100	75
Accommodation	100	68
Cuisine	100	63
Service	100	65
Miscellaneous	100	71
OVERALL SCORE		
342 points out of 500		

Ukraina
★★+

A rivership passable for anyone on a tight budget – just.

Manager/operator	Nicko Tours
Entered service	1979
Registry	Ukraine
Identification number	ENI 42000001
Length (m/yds)	115.7

Number of decks (excluding sun deck)	2
Cabins (total)	79
Balcony cabins	No
Lift (elevator)	No
Rivers sailed	Danube

The interior decor of this older-style rivership is tired and sombre. The cabins are small and utilitarian, with windows or portholes and either fixed or pull-down beds; some cabins have lower and upper berths. The (tiny) bathrooms have curtained-off showers only. The galley is small, and the food is basic. A budget option.

Berlitz's Ratings

	Possible	Achieved
Hardware	100	48
Accommodation	100	44
Cuisine	100	43
Service	100	44
Miscellaneous	100	48

OVERALL SCORE
227 points out of 500

Van Gogh
★★★

A standard older vessel good for French ambience and food.

Manager/operator	CroisiEurope
Entered service	1999
Registry	France
Identification number	ENI 02205451
Length (m/yds)	110.0

Number of decks (excluding sun deck)	2
Cabins (total)	76
Balcony cabins	No
Lift (elevator)	No
Rivers sailed	French rivers

If you like unpretentious French cuisine and wine and are happy with a comfortable but small cabin with slim beds, no balcony and a tiny bathroom with a limited storage space, then *Van Gogh* may appeal to you. Go for the comfortable ambience and for the itinerary and destinations. Note that shore excursions cost extra.

Berlitz's Ratings

	Possible	Achieved
Hardware	100	59
Accommodation	100	57
Cuisine	100	60
Service	100	56
Miscellaneous	100	58

OVERALL SCORE
290 points out of 500

Vasco da Gama
★★★

This standard rivership without balconies provides comfortable transport.

Manager/operator................................CroisiEurope
Entered service.................................2002
Registry ....Portugal
Identification number ....MMSI 263022000
Length (m/yds).................................110.0

Number of decks (excluding sun deck) 2
Cabins (total) 71
Balcony cabins ....No
Lift (elevator) .... Yes
Rivers sailed .... Douro

The rather average-looking *Vasco da Gama* delivers a decent middle-of-the road cruise experience, although the cabins are quite small, as are the bathrooms, and storage space is very limited. The French food is unfussy but lacks creativity due to the vessel's small galley, and the wine glasses are small.

Berlitz's Ratings		
	Possible	Achieved
Hardware	100	60
Accommodation	100	57
Cuisine	100	60
Service	100	56
Miscellaneous	100	60
OVERALL SCORE		
293 points out of 500		

Victor Hugo
★★★

A consistent and standard river cruise that is nothing special.

Manager/operator................................CroisiEurope
Entered service.................................2000
Registry .... France
Identification number ....ENI 01823025
Length (m/yds).................................82.5

Number of decks (excluding sun deck) 2
Cabins (total) 49
Balcony cabins ....No
Lift (elevator) ....No
Rivers sailed ....Danube, Rhein

Victor Hugo has dated interior decor, small cabins without balconies, slim, short beds (most of which cannot be moved together) and tiny bathrooms with minimal storage space. But if you like unpretentious French food, wine and ambience, it may suit. Choose it mainly for the itinerary and destinations. Note that shore excursions cost extra.

Berlitz's Ratings		
	Possible	Achieved
Hardware	100	60
Accommodation	100	58
Cuisine	100	62
Service	100	58
Miscellaneous	100	60
OVERALL SCORE		
298 points out of 500		

Vienna I
★★★★

Contemporary and casual, this rivership provides a good-value experience.

Manager/operator............... Various tour operators
Entered service..................................2006
Registry ....Malta
Identification number ....ENI 09948012
Length (m/yds)..................................135.0

Number of decks (excluding sun deck) 3
Cabins (total) 84
Balcony cabins .... Yes (French)
Lift (elevator) ....No
Rivers sailed ....Danube

With the propulsion machinery separated from the passenger accommodation, all this twin cruiser's stylish cabins (many with French balconies) are quiet, although small. Beds are fixed (one converts to a sofa). Large glass windows allow great views in the lounge and restaurant. The food is nothing special, but there is a decent variety.

Berlitz's Ratings		
	Possible	Achieved
Hardware	100	77
Accommodation	100	76
Cuisine	100	75
Service	100	74
Miscellaneous	100	73
OVERALL SCORE		
375 points out of 500		

Viking Aegir
★★★★

Choose this rivership for a well-organised, high-quality cruise experience.

Manager/operator...................Viking River Cruises
Entered service..................................2012
Registry ....Switzerland
Identification number ....ENI 07001957
Length (m/yds)..................................135.0

Number of decks (excluding sun deck) 3
Cabins (total) 104
Balcony cabins .... Yes (French and full)
Lift (elevator) .... Yes
Rivers sailed ....Danube, Rhein

The well-designed *Viking Aegir* has a functional minimalist, although not luxurious, interior. The innovative, practical layout of the cabins includes French balconies, good living space and bathrooms with large (glazed) shower enclosures. Most of the food is pretty varied and tasty, although the main dinner courses are underwhelming. The excursion programme is excellent.

Berlitz's Ratings		
	Possible	Achieved
Hardware	100	84
Accommodation	100	84
Cuisine	100	76
Service	100	75
Miscellaneous	100	76
OVERALL SCORE		
395 points out of 500		

Viking Alsvin
Not Yet Rated

This stylish, spacious vessel will offer a well-organised cruise.

Manager/operator .... Viking River Cruises
Entered service 2014
Registry .... Switzerland
Identification number .... n/a
Length (m/yds) 135.0

Number of decks (excluding sun deck) 3
Cabins (total) 95
Balcony cabins .... Yes (French and full)
Lift (elevator) .... Yes
Rivers sailed .... Danube, Rhein

With its light Scandinavian-style interior, *Viking Alsvin* will have a spacious, airy feeling. Well-designed double-sized suites and roomy cabins should have good soundproofing, French balconies, ample storage space and really comfortable generously sized beds. There will be a tastefully decorated restaurant, and an alternative 'Aquavit Terrace' for breakfast and lunch, offering good, unfussy food.

Berlitz's Ratings		
	Possible	Achieved
Hardware	100	NYR
Accommodation	100	NYR
Cuisine	100	NYR
Service	100	NYR
Miscellaneous	100	NYR
OVERALL SCORE		
NYR points out of 500		

Viking Atla
★★★★

A good choice for a stylish, first-rate river cruise.

Manager/operator .... Viking River Cruises
Entered service 2013
Registry .... Switzerland
Identification number .... ENI 07001968
Length (m/yds) 135.0

Number of decks (excluding sun deck) 3
Cabins (total) 95
Balcony cabins .... Yes (French and full)
Lift (elevator) .... Yes
Rivers sailed .... Various European rivers

With a Scandinavian minimalist interior decor, characterised by light colours, *Viking Atla* is a very comfortable rivership. All cabins have full or French balconies (some have both), a really practical layout and good bathrooms with large glazed shower enclosures. The suites are extremely spacious. The straightforward cuisine is tasty, and there's a good variety.

Berlitz's Ratings		
	Possible	Achieved
Hardware	100	84
Accommodation	100	84
Cuisine	100	76
Service	100	76
Miscellaneous	100	76
OVERALL SCORE		
396 points out of 500		

Viking Baldur
★★★★

A good choice for a well-programmed, stylish, first-rate river cruise.

Manager/operator.................... Viking River Cruises
Entered service...2014
Registry .... Switzerland
Identification number ....n/a
Length (m/yds)..135.0

Number of decks (excluding sun deck) 3
Cabins (total) 104
Balcony cabins .... Yes (French and full)
Lift (elevator) .... Yes
Rivers sailed .... Danube, Rhein

Viking Baldur is well designed, with a Scandinavian minimalist but functional interior. An innovative, practical layout includes decent storage space, very comfortable beds, French balconies and generously sized bathrooms with large shower enclosures. The cuisine is nicely varied, with decent ingredients, but the small-portion main dinner courses are underwhelming.

Berlitz's Ratings		
	Possible	Achieved
Hardware	100	84
Accommodation	100	84
Cuisine	100	76
Service	100	76
Miscellaneous	100	76
OVERALL SCORE		
396 points out of 500		

Viking Bestia
Not Yet Rated

This stylish vessel is set to be great for a well-organised cruise.

Manager/operator.................... Viking River Cruises
Entered service...2014
Registry .... Switzerland
Identification number ....n/a
Length (m/yds)..135.0

Number of decks (excluding sun deck) 3
Cabins (total) 104
Balcony cabins .... Yes (French)
Lift (elevator) .... Yes
Rivers sailed .... Danube, Rhein

With a light Scandinavian-style interior, *Viking Bestia* will have a spacious, airy feeling. The well-designed, functional double-sized suites and roomy cabins should have French balconies and extremely comfortable, generously sized beds. There will be a tastefully decorated restaurant, and an alternative 'Aquavit Terrace' for breakfast and lunch, offering good, unfussy food.

Berlitz's Ratings		
	Possible	Achieved
Hardware	100	NYR
Accommodation	100	NYR
Cuisine	100	NYR
Service	100	NYR
Miscellaneous	100	NYR
OVERALL SCORE		
NYR points out of 500		

Viking Bragi
★★★★

A stylish choice for a well-programmed, first-rate river cruise.

Manager/operator................... Viking River Cruises
Entered service... 2012
Registry .... Switzerland
Identification number ....ENI 07001961
Length (m/yds)..135.0

Number of decks (excluding sun deck) 3
Cabins (total) 95
Balcony cabins .... Yes (French and full)
Lift (elevator) .... Yes
Rivers sailed .... Various European rivers

With its Scandinavian minimalist interior decor, characterised by light colours, *Viking Bragi* is airy and very comfortable. All cabins have full or French balconies (some have both) and are really practical, with attractive bathrooms that have large glazed showers. The suites are extremely spacious. The unfussy cuisine is tasty, and there's a good variety of dishes.

Berlitz's Ratings		
	Possible	Achieved
Hardware	100	84
Accommodation	100	84
Cuisine	100	76
Service	100	76
Miscellaneous	100	76
OVERALL SCORE		
396 points out of 500		

Viking Buri
Not Yet Rated

This stylish vessel should be great for a well-organised cruise.

Manager/operator................... Viking River Cruises
Entered service... 2014
Registry .... Switzerland
Identification number .... n/a
Length (m/yds)..135.0

Number of decks (excluding sun deck) 3
Cabins (total) 95
Balcony cabins .... Yes (French)
Lift (elevator) .... Yes
Rivers sailed .... French rivers

With a light Scandinavian interior, *Viking Buri* will feel lovely and spacious. Functional, well-designed double-sized suites and roomy cabins will have good soundproofing, French balconies and generously sized beds that are extremely comfortable. The tastefully decorated restaurant and the alternative 'Aquavit Terrace' (the latter for breakfast and lunch only) should offer good, fuss-free food.

Berlitz's Ratings		
	Possible	Achieved
Hardware	100	NYR
Accommodation	100	NYR
Cuisine	100	NYR
Service	100	NYR
Miscellaneous	100	NYR
OVERALL SCORE		
NYR points out of 500		

Viking Delling
Not Yet Rated

Should be a good choice for a first-rate river cruise on a stylish vessel.

Manager/operator .... Viking River Cruises
Entered service 2014
Registry .... Switzerland
Identification number .... n/a
Length (m/yds) 135.0

Number of decks (excluding sun deck) 3
Cabins (total) 95
Balcony cabins .... Yes (French and full)
Lift (elevator) .... Yes
Rivers sailed .... Various European rivers

There will be natural light everywhere aboard *Viking Delling*, with its stylish Scandinavian interior. Whether you choose a suite for more space, or a regular cabin, you'll find a practical design that is extremely comfortable, with good storage. All rooms will have full or French balconies. The restaurant is likely to offer decent food, although lacking 'wow' factor.

Berlitz's Ratings

	Possible	Achieved
Hardware	100	NYR
Accommodation	100	NYR
Cuisine	100	NYR
Service	100	NYR
Miscellaneous	100	NYR

OVERALL SCORE
NYR points out of 500

Viking Douro
★★★★

Choose this stylish rivership for a good-quality Douro river cruise.

Manager/operator .... Viking River Cruises
Entered service 2011
Registry .... Switzerland
Identification number .... n/a
Length (m/yds) 79.5

Number of decks (excluding sun deck) 3
Cabins (total) 62
Balcony cabins .... Yes (French)
Lift (elevator) .... Yes
Rivers sailed .... Douro

The compact *Viking Douro* is a comfortable vessel, with minimalist Scandinavian-style interior decor. All cabins have French balconies, a good array of facilities and nice bathrooms, although storage space is limited. The restaurant is attractive, although seating is tight. The cuisine includes international and regional dishes. It's tasty, but unfussy, with a decent variety.

Berlitz's Ratings

	Possible	Achieved
Hardware	100	77
Accommodation	100	73
Cuisine	100	73
Service	100	73
Miscellaneous	100	75

OVERALL SCORE
371 points out of 500

Viking Eistla
Not Yet Rated

A stylish, contemporary rivership for a really well-organised cruise.

Manager/operator...................Viking River Cruises
Entered service...2014
Registry ....Switzerland
Identification number ....n/a
Length (m/yds)...135.0

Number of decks (excluding sun deck) 3
Cabins (total) 95
Balcony cabins .... Yes (French and full)
Lift (elevator) .... Yes
Rivers sailed ....Various European rivers

Viking Eistla will have an extremely comfortable Scandinavian blonde-wood interior, flooded with natural light. Well-designed and appointed suites and cabins (all with full or French balconies) will be both comfortable and practical, with bathrooms that have large, glazed shower enclosures. The tastefully decorated restaurant and alternative 'Aquavit Terrace' (the latter for breakfast and lunch) will offer good, unfussy food.

Berlitz's Ratings

	Possible	Achieved
Hardware	100	NYR
Accommodation	100	NYR
Cuisine	100	NYR
Service	100	NYR
Miscellaneous	100	NYR

OVERALL SCORE
NYR points out of 500

Viking Embla
★★★★

This stylish vessel is excellent for a well-organised cruise.

Manager/operator...................Viking River Cruises
Entered service...2012
Registry ....Switzerland
Identification number ....ENI 07001957
Length (m/yds)...135.0

Number of decks (excluding sun deck) 3
Cabins (total) 95
Balcony cabins .... Yes (French and full)
Lift (elevator) .... Yes
Rivers sailed ....Danube, Rhein

With Scandinavian minimalist interior decor, *Viking Embla* is airy and very comfortable. All cabins have full or French balconies (some have both) and are really practical, with good bathrooms with large glazed shower enclosures. The suites are extremely spacious. The food is tasty, and there's a variety of dishes – unfussy, simple fare rather than fancy cuisine.

Berlitz's Ratings

	Possible	Achieved
Hardware	100	84
Accommodation	100	84
Cuisine	100	76
Service	100	75
Miscellaneous	100	77

OVERALL SCORE
396 points out of 500

Viking Europe
★★★★

This rivership is a good choice for a good-quality river cruise experience.

Manager/operator .... Viking River Cruises
Entered service 2001
Registry .... Switzerland
Identification number .... ENI 04800250
Length (m/yds) 114.3

Number of decks (excluding sun deck) 3
Cabins (total) 75
Balcony cabins .... No
Lift (elevator) .... Yes
Rivers sailed .... French rivers

Nicely outfitted, *Viking Europe* has interior decor that is Scandinavian and minimalist and really very comfortable. The cabins (all of which are located forward of the restaurant and are quiet) have comfortable beds and (upper deck only) windows that open. The cuisine is good, with ample choice and variety, but there's really no 'wow' factor.

Berlitz's Ratings		
	Possible	Achieved
Hardware	100	73
Accommodation	100	67
Cuisine	100	74
Service	100	75
Miscellaneous	100	73
OVERALL SCORE		
362 points out of 500		

Viking Forseti
★★★★

This rivership has state-of-the-art features and good food and service.

Manager/operator .... Viking River Cruises
Entered service 2013
Registry .... Switzerland
Identification number .... ENI 07001965
Length (m/yds) 135.0

Number of decks (excluding sun deck) 3
Cabins (total) 95
Balcony cabins .... Yes (French and full)
Lift (elevator) .... Yes
Rivers sailed .... Various European rivers

Viking Forseti has a minimalist interior flooded with natural light. The well-designed, nicely appointed suites and cabins (all with full or French balconies) are comfortable and practical. The bathrooms have large, glazed shower enclosures. The tastefully decorated restaurant and alternative 'Aquavit Terrace' (the latter for breakfast and lunch) both offer good, unfussy food to match.

Berlitz's Ratings		
	Possible	Achieved
Hardware	100	84
Accommodation	100	84
Cuisine	100	76
Service	100	76
Miscellaneous	100	76
OVERALL SCORE		
396 points out of 500		

Viking Freya
★★★★

This high-tech, stylish vessel offers a well-organised cruise.

Manager/operator	Viking River Cruises	Number of decks (excluding sun deck)	3
Entered service	2012	Cabins (total)	95
Registry	Switzerland	Balcony cabins	Yes (French)
Identification number	ENI 07001954	Lift (elevator)	Yes
Length (m/yds)	135.0	Rivers sailed	Danube, Rhein

The well-designed *Viking Freya* features minimalist Scandinavian decor. A practical, innovative layout has created reasonably spacious cabins with French balconies and a decent amount of storage space, and bathrooms with heated flooring and high-tech shower walls that convert from clear to frosted. The restaurant is attractive and offers a good variety, using quality ingredients.

Berlitz's Ratings

	Possible	Achieved
Hardware	100	85
Accommodation	100	84
Cuisine	100	76
Service	100	76
Miscellaneous	100	77

OVERALL SCORE
398 points out of 500

Viking Gullveig
Not Yet Rated

Choose this stylish contemporary rivership for a well-organised cruise.

Manager/operator	Viking River Cruises	Number of decks (excluding sun deck)	3
Entered service	2014	Cabins (total)	95
Registry	Switzerland	Balcony cabins	Yes (French)
Identification number	n/a	Lift (elevator)	Yes
Length (m/yds)	135.0	Rivers sailed	Danube, Rhein

Viking Gullveig will have an extremely comfortable Scandinavian blonde-wood interior flooded with natural light. Well-designed, nicely appointed suites and cabins (all with French balconies) should be both comfortable and practical, with bathrooms that have large, glazed shower enclosures. The tastefully decorated restaurant and alternative 'Aquavit Terrace' (the latter for breakfast and lunch) will offer good, unfussy food.

Berlitz's Ratings

	Possible	Achieved
Hardware	100	NYR
Accommodation	100	NYR
Cuisine	100	NYR
Service	100	NYR
Miscellaneous	100	NYR

OVERALL SCORE
NYR points out of 500

Viking Heimdal
★★★★

This airy, spacious vessel offers a stylish, well-organised cruise experience.

Manager/operator .... Viking River Cruises
Entered service 2014
Registry .... Switzerland
Identification number .... n/a
Length (m/yds) 135.0

Number of decks (excluding sun deck) 3
Cabins (total) 95
Balcony cabins .... Yes (French and full)
Lift (elevator) .... Yes
Rivers sailed .... French rivers

With its pale wood Scandinavian interior, *Viking Heimdal* has a spacious, airy feel. The double-sized suites and spacious cabins have good soundproofing, are well designed and functional, and all have full or French balconies. The generously sized beds are comfortable. The tastefully decorated restaurant and alternative 'Aquavit Terrace' (breakfast and lunch) offer good, unfussy food.

Berlitz's Ratings		
	Possible	Achieved
Hardware	100	84
Accommodation	100	84
Cuisine	100	76
Service	100	76
Miscellaneous	100	77
OVERALL SCORE		
397 points out of 500		

Viking Helvetia
★★★★

An excellent choice for a high-quality river cruise.

Manager/operator .... Viking River Cruises
Entered service 2006
Registry .... Germany
Identification number .... ENI 04804700
Length (m/yds) 131.8

Number of decks (excluding sun deck) 3
Cabins (total) 99
Balcony cabins .... Yes (French)
Lift (elevator) .... Yes
Rivers sailed .... Rhein

Nicely outfitted, *Viking Helvetia* has an airy, very comfortable, Scandinavian minimalist design scheme. The cabins – all of which are located forward of the restaurant – have high ceilings, good soundproofing, comfortable beds and, on the upper deck only, windows that open. The cuisine is good and varied, but the 'wow' factor is missing.

Berlitz's Ratings		
	Possible	Achieved
Hardware	100	74
Accommodation	100	67
Cuisine	100	74
Service	100	75
Miscellaneous	100	73
OVERALL SCORE		
363 points out of 500		

Viking Hemming
Not Yet Rated

A stylish, contemporary rivership for a really well-organised cruise.

Manager/operator...................Viking River Cruises
Entered service...2014
Registry ....Switzerland
Identification number ....n/a
Length (m/yds)..135.0

Number of decks (excluding sun deck) 3
Cabins (total) 53
Balcony cabins .... Yes (French)
Lift (elevator) .... Yes
Rivers sailed .... Douro

With a blonde-wood Scandinavian interior, *Viking Hemming* will have a spacious, airy feeling. A practical, innovative layout will create reasonably spacious cabins with French balconies, a decent amount of storage space, very comfortable beds and bathrooms with large shower enclosures. The tastefully decorated restaurant and alternative 'Aquavit Terrace' (breakfast and lunch) should offer good, unfussy food.

Berlitz's Ratings

	Possible	Achieved
Hardware	100	NYR
Accommodation	100	NYR
Cuisine	100	NYR
Service	100	NYR
Miscellaneous	100	NYR
OVERALL SCORE		
NYR points out of 500		

Viking Hermod
Not Yet Rated

Choose this stylish, contemporary rivership for a really well-organised cruise.

Manager/operator...................Viking River Cruises
Entered service...2014
Registry ....Switzerland
Identification number ....n/a
Length (m/yds)..135.0

Number of decks (excluding sun deck) 3
Cabins (total) 95
Balcony cabins .... Yes (French and full)
Lift (elevator) .... Yes
Rivers sailed ....French rivers

With its Scandinavian interior, *Viking Hermod* will have a spacious, light-filled feel. The double-sized suites and roomy cabins should have good soundproofing, be well designed and functional, and all have full or French balconies. The large beds should be extremely comfortable. The tastefully decorated restaurant and 'Aquavit Terrace' (the latter for breakfast and lunch) will offer good, unfussy food.

Berlitz's Ratings

	Possible	Achieved
Hardware	100	NYR
Accommodation	100	NYR
Cuisine	100	NYR
Service	100	NYR
Miscellaneous	100	NYR
OVERALL SCORE		
NYR points out of 500		

Viking Idi
Not Yet Rated

Choose this stylish contemporary rivership for a very well-rounded cruise.

Manager/operator .... Viking River Cruises
Entered service 2014
Registry .... Switzerland
Identification number .... n/a
Length (m/yds) 135.0

Number of decks (excluding sun deck) 3
Cabins (total) 95
Balcony cabins .... Yes (French and full)
Lift (elevator) .... Yes
Rivers sailed .... Danube, Rhein

Viking Idi will be light and airy with a minimalist blonde-wood interior and a two-deck-high atrium lobby. The practical, well-designed cabins (all with full or French balconies) will be very comfortable, with ample storage. The suites should be especially spacious. Bathrooms will have large glazed showers. The restaurant (and 'Aquavit Terrace' for breakfast and lunch) will offer good, unfussy food.

Berlitz's Ratings		
	Possible	Achieved
Hardware	100	NYR
Accommodation	100	NYR
Cuisine	100	NYR
Service	100	NYR
Miscellaneous	100	NYR
OVERALL SCORE		
NYR points out of 500		

Viking Idun
★★★★

This stylish vessel is great for a well-organised cruise.

Manager/operator .... Viking River Cruises
Entered service 2012
Registry .... Switzerland
Identification number .... ENI 07001951
Length (m/yds) 135.0

Number of decks (excluding sun deck) 3
Cabins (total) 104
Balcony cabins .... Yes (French and full)
Lift (elevator) .... Yes
Rivers sailed .... Danube, Rhein

With its Scandinavian minimalist interior, characterised by light colours, *Viking Idun* is airy and very comfortable. All cabins have full or French balconies (some have both) and are really practical, with attractive bathrooms that have large glazed showers. The double-sized suites are extremely spacious. The unfussy cuisine is tasty, and there's a good variety of dishes.

Berlitz's Ratings		
	Possible	Achieved
Hardware	100	84
Accommodation	100	84
Cuisine	100	76
Service	100	76
Miscellaneous	100	77
OVERALL SCORE		
397 points out of 500		

Viking Ingvi
Not Yet Rated

This stylish rivership will launch you on a well-organised cruise.

Manager/operator.................... Viking River Cruises
Entered service..2014
Registry .... Switzerland
Identification number ....n/a
Length (m/yds)..135.0

Number of decks (excluding sun deck) 3
Cabins (total) 104
Balcony cabins .... Yes (French)
Lift (elevator) .... Yes
Rivers sailed ....Rhein

Viking Ingvi will have a minimalist yet comfortable Scandinavian interior, flooded with natural light. The well-designed, nicely appointed suites and cabins (all with French balconies) should be both comfortable and practical, with bathrooms that have large, glazed shower enclosures. The tastefully decorated restaurant and alternative 'Aquavit Terrace' (the latter for breakfast and lunch) should offer good, unfussy food.

Berlitz's Ratings		
	Possible	Achieved
Hardware	100	NYR
Accommodation	100	NYR
Cuisine	100	NYR
Service	100	NYR
Miscellaneous	100	NYR
OVERALL SCORE		
NYR points out of 500		

Viking Jarl
★★★★

Good choice for a well-programmed first-rate river cruise on a stylish vessel.

Manager/operator.................... Viking River Cruises
Entered service..2013
Registry .... Switzerland
Identification number ....ENI 07001970
Length (m/yds)..135.0

Number of decks (excluding sun deck) 3
Cabins (total) 95
Balcony cabins .... Yes (French and full)
Lift (elevator) .... Yes
Rivers sailed .... Various European rivers

With wood-rich Scandinavian interior decor *Viking Jarl* has a spacious, light-filled feeling. The double-sized suites and reasonably spacious cabins have good soundproofing, are well designed and very functional, and all have full or French balconies. The generously sized beds are really comfortable. The tastefully decorated restaurant (and alternative 'Aquavit Terrace' for breakfast and lunch) offers good, unfussy food to match.

Berlitz's Ratings		
	Possible	Achieved
Hardware	100	84
Accommodation	100	84
Cuisine	100	76
Service	100	76
Miscellaneous	100	77
OVERALL SCORE		
397 points out of 500		

Viking Kvasir
Not Yet Rated

This superbly designed, comfortable, contemporary ship will be a winner.

Manager/operator .... Viking River Cruises
Entered service 2014
Registry .... Switzerland
Identification number .... n/a
Length (m/yds) 135.0

Number of decks (excluding sun deck) 3
Cabins (total) 95
Balcony cabins .... Yes (French)
Lift (elevator) .... Yes
Rivers sailed .... Various European rivers

Viking Kvasir will be well designed, with a Scandinavian minimalist interior. An innovative, practical layout will include decent storage space, French balconies and bathrooms with heated flooring and high-tech shower walls that change from clear to frosted. The cuisine should be nicely varied, with decent ingredients, but the small-portion main dinner courses are likely to be slightly underwhelming.

Berlitz's Ratings

	Possible	Achieved
Hardware	100	NYR
Accommodation	100	NYR
Cuisine	100	NYR
Service	100	NYR
Miscellaneous	100	NYR

OVERALL SCORE
NYR points out of 500

Viking Legend
★★★★

This rivership is an excellent choice for a good-quality river cruise.

Manager/operator .... Viking River Cruises
Entered service 2009
Registry .... Switzerland
Identification number .... ENI 07001911
Length (m/yds) 135.0

Number of decks (excluding sun deck) 3
Cabins (total) 95
Balcony cabins .... Yes (French)
Lift (elevator) .... Yes
Rivers sailed .... Danube

The nicely appointed *Viking Legend* has a very comfortable Scandinavian minimalist interior. The cabins (all of which are located forward of the restaurant and are quiet) have comfortable beds; those on the upper deck have windows that open. The cuisine is good, with ample choice and variety, but there's really no 'wow' factor.

Berlitz's Ratings

	Possible	Achieved
Hardware	100	75
Accommodation	100	68
Cuisine	100	74
Service	100	74
Miscellaneous	100	74

OVERALL SCORE
365 points out of 500

Viking Lif
★★★★

Choose this stylish contemporary rivership for an excellently organised cruise.

Manager/operator .... Viking River Cruises
Entered service 2013
Registry .... Switzerland
Identification number .... n/a
Length (m/yds) 135.0

Number of decks (excluding sun deck) 3
Cabins (total) 95
Balcony cabins .... Yes (French)
Lift (elevator) .... Yes
Rivers sailed .... Various European rivers

With its wood-rich Scandinavian interior, *Viking Lif* has a spacious, light-filled feeling. A practical, innovative design incorporates French balconies, decent storage space, extremely comfortable beds and bathrooms with large shower enclosures. The tastefully decorated restaurant and alternative 'Aquavit Terrace' (the latter for breakfast and lunch only) offer good, unfussy food to match.

Berlitz's Ratings		
	Possible	Achieved
Hardware	100	84
Accommodation	100	84
Cuisine	100	76
Service	100	76
Miscellaneous	100	77
OVERALL SCORE		
397 points out of 500		

Viking Magni
★★★★

This is a great choice for a stylish, contemporary cruise.

Manager/operator .... Viking River Cruises
Entered service 2013
Registry .... Switzerland
Identification number .... n/a
Length (m/yds) 135.0

Number of decks (excluding sun deck) 3
Cabins (total) 104
Balcony cabins .... Yes (French and full)
Lift (elevator) .... Yes
Rivers sailed .... Various European rivers

With its Scandinavian minimalist interior, characterised by pale colours and blonde wood, this fine rivership is light and airy. All cabins have full or French balconies (some have both) and are practical, with attractive bathrooms with large glazed showers. The suites are spacious. The unfussy cuisine is tasty, and there's a good variety of dishes.

Berlitz's Ratings		
	Possible	Achieved
Hardware	100	84
Accommodation	100	84
Cuisine	100	76
Service	100	76
Miscellaneous	100	77
OVERALL SCORE		
397 points out of 500		

Viking Neptune
★★★★

This rivership is an excellent choice for a good-quality cruise.

Manager/operator .... Viking River Cruises
Entered service 2001
Registry .... Germany
Identification number .... ENI 04800510
Length (m/yds) 114.3

Number of decks (excluding sun deck) 3
Cabins (total) 75
Balcony cabins .... No
Lift (elevator) .... No
Rivers sailed .... French rivers

The nicely appointed *Viking Neptune* has a very comfortable Scandinavian minimalist interior. The cabins (all of which are located forward of the restaurant and are quiet) have comfortable beds; those on the upper deck have windows that open. The cuisine is good, with ample choice and variety, but there's really no 'wow' factor.

Berlitz's Ratings		
	Possible	Achieved
Hardware	100	72
Accommodation	100	66
Cuisine	100	74
Service	100	75
Miscellaneous	100	73
OVERALL SCORE		
360 points out of 500		

Viking Njord
★★★★

This stylish vessel is a good choice for a well-organised cruise experience.

Manager/operator .... Viking River Cruises
Entered service 2012
Registry .... Switzerland
Identification number .... ENI 07001955
Length (m/yds) 135.0

Number of decks (excluding sun deck) 3
Cabins (total) 104
Balcony cabins .... Yes (French)
Lift (elevator) .... Yes
Rivers sailed .... Danube, Rhein

Viking Njord is well designed, with a functional Scandinavian minimalist interior. An innovative, practical layout has created reasonably spacious, well-appointed cabins with French balconies, decent storage space and bathrooms with heated flooring and high-tech shower walls that change from clear to frosted. The restaurant has attractive table settings and serves a good variety of food using quality ingredients.

Berlitz's Ratings		
	Possible	Achieved
Hardware	100	85
Accommodation	100	84
Cuisine	100	76
Service	100	76
Miscellaneous	100	77
OVERALL SCORE		
398 points out of 500		

Viking Odin
★★★★

A stylish choice for a well-programmed, first-rate river cruise.

Manager/operator...................Viking River Cruises
Entered service...2012
Registry ....Switzerland
Identification number ....ENI 07001950
Length (m/yds)...135.0

Number of decks (excluding sun deck) 3
Cabins (total) 104
Balcony cabins ....Yes (French and full)
Lift (elevator) ....Yes
Rivers sailed ....Danube, Rhein

With its Scandinavian minimalist interior decor, characterised by light colours, *Viking Odin* is airy and very comfortable. All cabins have full or French balconies (some have both) and are really practical, with attractive bathrooms with large glazed showers. The double-sized suites are extremely spacious. The unfussy cuisine is tasty, and there's a good variety of dishes.

Berlitz's Ratings	Possible	Achieved
Hardware	100	84
Accommodation	100	84
Cuisine	100	76
Service	100	75
Miscellaneous	100	77

OVERALL SCORE
396 points out of 500

Viking Prestige
★★★★

Choose this rivership for a fine-quality, well-organised cruise experience.

Manager/operator...................Viking River Cruises
Entered service...2011
Registry ....Switzerland
Identification number ....ENI 07001942
Length (m/yds)...135.0

Number of decks (excluding sun deck) 3
Cabins (total) 97
Balcony cabins ....Yes (French)
Lift (elevator) ....Yes
Rivers sailed ....Danube, Rhein

With Scandinavian minimalist decor, *Viking Prestige* is a delightfully comfortable contemporary rivership. The cabins (including six for single occupancy) have very really comfortable beds, and many have French balconies. The well-designed bathrooms include good-sized showers, while two suites also have bathtubs. The cuisine is good, with decent choice and variety, but it just lacks the 'wow' factor.

Berlitz's Ratings	Possible	Achieved
Hardware	100	76
Accommodation	100	66
Cuisine	100	74
Service	100	75
Miscellaneous	100	73

OVERALL SCORE
364 points out of 500

Viking Pride
★★★★

This rivership is an excellent choice for a good-quality river cruise.

Manager/operator....................Viking River Cruises
Entered service...2001
Registry ....Switzerland
Identification number ....ENI 04800210
Length (m/yds)...114.3

Number of decks (excluding sun deck) 3
Cabins (total) 75
Balcony cabins ....No
Lift (elevator) ....No
Rivers sailed ....French rivers

The nicely appointed *Viking Pride* has Scandinavian minimalist interior decor and is really very comfortable. The cabins (all of which are located forward of the restaurant and are quiet) have comfortable beds; those on the upper deck have windows that open. The cuisine is decent, with ample choice and variety, but there's no 'wow' factor.

Berlitz's Ratings

	Possible	Achieved
Hardware	100	71
Accommodation	100	66
Cuisine	100	74
Service	100	75
Miscellaneous	100	73

OVERALL SCORE
359 points out of 500

Viking Rinda
★★★★

Choose this stylish, contemporary rivership for a well-programmed cruise.

Manager/operator....................Viking River Cruises
Entered service...2013
Registry ....Switzerland
Identification number ....ENI 07001966
Length (m/yds)...135.0

Number of decks (excluding sun deck) 3
Cabins (total) 95
Balcony cabins ....Yes (French and full)
Lift (elevator) ....Yes
Rivers sailed ....Various European rivers

Viking Rinda is another example of a rivership with minimalist (but warm) Scandinavian interior decor. All cabins have full or French balconies (some have both) and are really practical, with ample storage space and good bathrooms with large glazed shower enclosures. The suites are extremely spacious. The unpretentious cuisine is tasty and nicely varied.

Berlitz's Ratings

	Possible	Achieved
Hardware	100	84
Accommodation	100	84
Cuisine	100	76
Service	100	76
Miscellaneous	100	77

OVERALL SCORE
397 points out of 500

Viking Skadi
★★★★

This stylish vessel provides a comfortable, well-organised cruise.

Manager/operator.................. Viking River Cruises
Entered service................................2013
Registry ....Switzerland
Identification number ....ENI 07001960
Length (m/yds)..135.0

Number of decks (excluding sun deck) 3
Cabins (total) 95
Balcony cabins .... Yes (French and full)
Lift (elevator) .... Yes
Rivers sailed ....Various European rivers

With its Scandinavian minimalist interior decor, characterised by light colours, *Viking Skadi* is airy and very comfortable. All cabins have full or French balconies (some have both) and are really practical, with attractive bathrooms with large glazed showers. The doubled-sized suites are extremely spacious. The unfussy cuisine is tasty, and there's a good variety of dishes.

Berlitz's Ratings		
	Possible	Achieved
Hardware	100	84
Accommodation	100	84
Cuisine	100	76
Service	100	77
Miscellaneous	100	77
OVERALL SCORE		
398 points out of 500		

Viking Spirit
★★★★

A very good choice for a high-standard river cruise.

Manager/operator.................. Viking River Cruises
Entered service................................2001
Registry ....Germany
Identification number ....ENI 04800380
Length (m/yds)..114.3

Number of decks (excluding sun deck) 3
Cabins (total) 75
Balcony cabins ....No
Lift (elevator) ....No
Rivers sailed ....French rivers

The nicely appointed *Viking Spirit* has Scandinavian minimalist interior decor and is very comfortable. The cabins (all of which are located forward of the restaurant and are quiet) have comfortable beds; those on the upper deck have windows that open. The cuisine is good, with ample choice and variety, but there's just no 'wow' factor.

Berlitz's Ratings		
	Possible	Achieved
Hardware	100	72
Accommodation	100	66
Cuisine	100	74
Service	100	75
Miscellaneous	100	73
OVERALL SCORE		
360 points out of 500		

Viking Tor
★★★★

A superbly designed, very comfortable contemporary ship for great cruising.

Manager/operator....................Viking River Cruises
Entered service...2013
Registry ....Switzerland
Identification number ....ENI 07001962
Length (m/yds)...135.0

Number of decks (excluding sun deck).................3
Cabins (total) 95
Balcony cabins ....Yes (French)
Lift (elevator) ....Yes
Rivers sailed ....Danube, Rhein

Viking Tor is well designed, with a Scandinavian minimalist interior. An innovative, practical layout has created cabins with French balconies, decent storage space, very comfortable beds and generously sized bathrooms with large shower enclosures. The food is decent, varied and uses quality ingredients. The small-portion mains at dinner are good, although not outstanding.

Berlitz's Ratings		
	Possible	Achieved
Hardware	100	84
Accommodation	100	84
Cuisine	100	76
Service	100	76
Miscellaneous	100	77
OVERALL SCORE		
397 points out of 500		

Viking Torgil
Not Yet Rated

This stylish rivership will launch you on a well-rounded cruise.

Manager/operator....................Viking River Cruises
Entered service...2014
Registry ....Switzerland
Identification number ....n/a
Length (m/yds)...135.0

Number of decks (excluding sun deck).................3
Cabins (total) 53
Balcony cabins ....Yes (French and full)
Lift (elevator) ....Yes
Rivers sailed ....Douro

Viking Torgil will have a minimalist Scandinavian interior flooded with natural light. The well-designed, nicely appointed suites and cabins (all with full or French balconies) will be both comfortable and practical, with good storage space. A cheerfully decorated restaurant will offer decent food, although lacking the 'wow' factor.

Berlitz's Ratings		
	Possible	Achieved
Hardware	100	NYR
Accommodation	100	NYR
Cuisine	100	NYR
Service	100	NYR
Miscellaneous	100	NYR
OVERALL SCORE		
NYR points out of 500		

Viking Var
★★★★

This stylish vessel is a good choice for a well-organised cruise.

Manager/operator................... Viking River Cruises
Entered service..2013
Registry ....Switzerland
Identification number ....ENI 07001963
Length (m/yds)...135.0

Number of decks (excluding sun deck) 3
Cabins (total) 95
Balcony cabins .... Yes (French and full)
Lift (elevator) .... Yes
Rivers sailed ....Danube, Rhein

With a Scandinavian-style interior, *Viking Var* has a spacious, airy feeling. The double-sized suites and spacious cabins have good soundproofing, are well designed and functional, and all have full or French balconies. The large beds are really comfortable. The tastefully decorated restaurant and 'Aquavit Terrace' (the latter for breakfast and lunch) offer good, unfussy food.

Berlitz's Ratings		
	Possible	Achieved
Hardware	100	84
Accommodation	100	84
Cuisine	100	76
Service	100	76
Miscellaneous	100	77
OVERALL SCORE		
397 points out of 500		

Viktoria
★★★+

A well-designed vessel with some attractive features.

Manager/operator............... Various tour operators
Entered service..2004
Registry ....Germany
Identification number ....ENI 09948008
Length (m/yds)...126.7

Number of decks (excluding sun deck) 3
Cabins (total) 76
Balcony cabins .... Yes (French)
Lift (elevator) ....No
Rivers sailed .... Danube, Main, Rhein

Viktoria has tasteful decor and a pleasant wellness area with sauna. The nicely decorated cabins, many with French balconies, are quite spacious with twin side-by-side beds that can be separated if desired. The restaurant has a warm wood interior, and the cuisine is reasonably sound, although the variety is limited for dinner (good at breakfast).

Berlitz's Ratings		
	Possible	Achieved
Hardware	100	73
Accommodation	100	74
Cuisine	100	61
Service	100	61
Miscellaneous	100	71
OVERALL SCORE		
340 points out of 500		

Virginia
★★+

This older, very small rivership delivers a basic, low-cost cruise.

Manager/operator............... Various tour operators
Entered service...1965
Registry ....Netherlands
Identification number ....ENI 6000051
Length (m/yds)..67.5

Number of decks (excluding sun deck) 3
Cabins (total) 53
Balcony cabins ....No
Lift (elevator) ....No
Rivers sailed ....Various European rivers

Virginia has just two public rooms: a lounge/bar and restaurant, both set low down. The cabins are refurbished but don't have balconies. The bathrooms are tiny. Foodwise, there's little choice due to the small galley, and the self-service buffets are poor. This is no-frills river cruising, so go only for the destinations or the price.

Berlitz's Ratings

	Possible	Achieved
Hardware	100	40
Accommodation	100	38
Cuisine	100	45
Service	100	47
Miscellaneous	100	47

OVERALL SCORE
217 points out of 500

Vista Explorer
★★★+

Expect good value for money from this modern, high-density rivership,

Manager/operator............................ 1AVista Reisen
Entered service...2001
Registry ....Malta
Identification number ....ENI 04804640
Length (m/yds)..125.5

Number of decks (excluding sun deck) 3
Cabins (total) 84
Balcony cabins ....No (1 suite w/balcony)
Lift (elevator) ....Yes
Rivers sailed ....Various European rivers

Vista Explorer is colourfully decorated in both the public areas and the cabins. The cabins are quite spacious, and many feature twin beds that convert to queen-sized beds. Only one suite has a French balcony; all the others have windows. The bathrooms are quite decent. The open-seating aft-located restaurant provides reasonable food, but young wines.

Berlitz's Ratings

	Possible	Achieved
Hardware	100	67
Accommodation	100	68
Cuisine	100	64
Service	100	62
Miscellaneous	100	68

OVERALL SCORE
329 points out of 500

Vista Prima
★★★+

This smart, comfortable rivership provides good-value river cruising.

Manager/operator............................ 1AVista Reisen
Entered service.................................2010
Registry ....Switzerland
Identification number ....ENI 07001923
Length (m/yds)....................................110.0

Number of decks (excluding sun deck) 3
Cabins (total) 76
Balcony cabins .... Yes (French)
Lift (elevator) .... Yes
Rivers sailed .... Rhein, Mosel

Vista Prima is a nicely designed contemporary rivership with restrained interior decor. The cabins are a decent size and well laid-out, and many have French balconies. The bathrooms are reasonably spacious and nicely equipped. The restaurant is pleasant, but cramped, and serves decent, although not sparkling, meals. A good budget choice.

Berlitz's Ratings		
	Possible	Achieved
Hardware	100	73
Accommodation	100	73
Cuisine	100	64
Service	100	63
Miscellaneous	100	70

OVERALL SCORE
343 points out of 500

Vivaldi
★★★

This standard, French-style rivership offers a good-value cruise.

Manager/operator...............................CroisiEurope
Entered service.................................2009
Registry ....France
Identification number ....ENI 01823464
Length (m/yds)....................................110.0

Number of decks (excluding sun deck) 3
Cabins (total) 88
Balcony cabins ....No
Lift (elevator) .... Yes
Rivers sailed ....Danube, Rhein

If you are happy with average (although unpretentious) French food and wine and don't mind a small (no balcony) cabin, slim beds and a tiny bathroom with limited storage space, *Vivaldi* may well suit. Go for the French ambience, the itinerary and destinations, and the price point. Note that shore excursions cost extra.

Berlitz's Ratings		
	Possible	Achieved
Hardware	100	63
Accommodation	100	58
Cuisine	100	60
Service	100	57
Miscellaneous	100	60

OVERALL SCORE
298 points out of 500

Volga
★★+

This older rivership is passable for anyone on a very tight budget.

Manager/operator .... Nicko Tours
Entered service 1970
Registry .... Ukraine
Identification number .... ENI 42000003
Length (m/yds) 116.0

Number of decks (excluding sun deck) 3
Cabins (total) 79
Balcony cabins .... No
Lift (elevator) .... No
Rivers sailed .... Danube

Most people take a river cruise primarily for the itinerary and destinations. If you fit into this category, then this rivership, with its small cabins, tiny bathrooms and limited storage, may be acceptable. There's a cramped, but homely restaurant, but the food isn't great, because the galley is tiny and limited in terms of output.

Berlitz's Ratings	Possible	Achieved
Hardware	100	44
Accommodation	100	44
Cuisine	100	46
Service	100	47
Miscellaneous	100	51
OVERALL SCORE		
232 points out of 500		

Credits

Photo Credits

123RF 55
A-Rosa Tours 32
Alamy 29, 100, 103, 104, 106/107
Avalon Waterways 22, 26, 33, 36, 46/47
Bigstock 58, 68, 70, 73, 74, 76, 81, 85, 86
CroisiEurope 56, 95, 96, 98, 99
Douglas Ward 5, 12, 14, 27, 31, 38, 39, 40, 41, 42
Dreamstime 2/3, 4/5, 30, 59, 65, 75, 77, 88, 91, 93, 101, 102
Fotolia 67

Glyn Genin/Apa Publications 92
iStock 15
Lydia Evans/Apa Publications 97
Nicko Tours 19
Robert Harding 52
Sea Cloud Cruises 1, 8, 13, 20, 24, 50, 108
Transocean 35
Uniworld Cruises 6, 7B, 7T, 11, 16, 21, 23, 25, 28, 51, 84, 87, 90, 109, 110
Viking River Cruises 10, 45, 61, 63, 64, 69, 78, 82

Cover Credits

Front cover: Danube River Cruiser and Tari Grad, *AWL Images*. **Back cover top to bottom:** Alemannia Sundeck, *Nicko Tours*; Queen Isabel Stateroom - Category 1, *Uniworld Cruises*; River Royale, Rhone, Burgundy & Provence Cruise, *Uniworld Cruises*; Queen Isabel al Fresco Dining, *Uniworld Cruises*.

Insight Guide Credits

Distribution

UK
Dorling Kindersley Ltd
A Penguin Group company
80 The Strand, London, WC2R 0RL
sales@uk.dk.com

United States
Ingram Publisher Services
1 Ingram Boulevard, PO Box 3006
La Vergne, TN 37086-1986
ips@ingramcontent.com

Australia and New Zealand
Woodslane
14 Apollo St, Warriewood
NSW 2102 Australia
info@woodslane.com.au

Worldwide
Apa Publications GmbH & Co.
Verlag KG (Singapore branch)
7030 Ang Mo Kio Avenue 5
08-65 Northstar @ AMK
Singapore 569880
apasin@singnet.com.sg

© 2014 Apa Publications (UK) Ltd
All Rights Reserved

Printed by CTPS-China

Berlitz Trademark Reg. U.S. Patent Office and other countries. Marca Registrada. Used under licence from the Berlitz Investment Corporation

First Edition 2014
Reprinted 2015

NO part of this book may be reproduced, stored in a retrieval system or transmitted in any form or means electronic, mechanical, photocopying, recording, or otherwise, without prior written permission of Apa Publications. Brief text quotations with use of photographs are exempted for book review purposes only. Information has been obtained from sources believed to be reliable, but its accuracy and completeness, and the opinions based thereon, are not guaranteed.

www.berlitzpublishing.com

Written by
Douglas Ward

Edited by
Tom Stainer and Clare Peel

Picture research by
Jo Mercer

Map Production
Apa Cartography Department
Maps © 2014 Apa Publications (UK) Ltd

Tell Us Your Thoughts

Dear River Cruiser,

I hope you have found this first edition of Berlitz River Cruising in Europe book both enjoyable and useful. If you have any comments or queries, or experiences of river cruising that you would like to pass on, or perhaps some ideas for subjects that could be included in the future, I would be delighted to read them. With your help, I can improve and expand the guide in future editions.

The world of river cruising is evolving fast and certain facts and figures may have changed since this guide went to print, so if you have found any outdated information in these pages, please do let me know and I will make sure it is corrected as soon as possible.

You can write to me by email at:
berlitz@apaguide.co.uk

Or by post to:
Berlitz Publishing
PO Box 7910
London SE1 1WE
United Kingdom

Thank you,

Douglas Ward

Index

BERLITZ CRUISING & CRUISE SHIPS

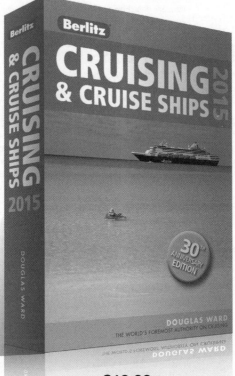

£18.99
704 pages, ISBN: 9781780047546

Douglas Ward, author of the best-selling *Berlitz Cruising & Cruise Ships,* tells you everyth
you need to know to choose the right cruise for you, giving you a complete rundown of t
different cruise lines and their facilities, food, atmosphere and service.
The reviews are completely independent and based on personal experience: Douglas Wa
has spent more than 5,900 days at sea, participating in over 1,000 cruises, meticulousl
noting and evaluating every facet of life aboard a cruise ship.

- DETAILED AND FRANK REVIEWS OF OVER 280 SHIPS
- FULL-COLOUR PHOTOGRAPHY AND MAPPING
- MONEY-SAVING ADVICE
- APP AND E-BOOK ALSO AVAILABLE